The
Roller-
Coaster
Years

The Roller-Coaster Years

Raising Your Child Through the Maddening Yet Magical Middle School Years

Charlene C. Giannetti and Margaret Sagarese

Broadway Books New York

BROADWAY

THE ROLLER-COASTER YEARS. Copyright © 1997 by Charlene C. Giannetti and Margaret Sagarese. All rights reserved. Printed in the United States of America. No part of this book may be reproduced or transmitted in any form or by any means, electronic or mechanical, including photocopying, recording, or by any information storage and retrieval system, without written permission from the publisher. For information, address Broadway Books, a division of Bantam Doubleday Dell Publishing Group, Inc., 1540 Broadway, New York, New York 10036.

Broadway Books titles may be purchased for business or promotional use or for special sales. For information, please write to: Special Markets Department, Bantam Doubleday Dell Publishing Group, Inc., 1540 Broadway, New York, NY 10036.

BROADWAY BOOKS and its logo, a letter B bisected on the diagonal, are trademarks of Broadway Books, a division of Bantam Doubleday Dell Publishing Group, Inc.

Library of Congress Cataloging-in-Publication Data
Giannetti, Charlene C.
    The roller-coaster years : raising your child through the
maddening yet magical middle school years / Charlene C. Giannetti
and Margaret Sagarese. — 1st ed.
      p. cm.
    Includes bibliographical references.
    ISBN 0-553-06684-6 (pbk.)
    1. Child rearing. 2. Preteens—Psychology. 3. Preteens—Family
relationships. I. Sagarese, Margaret. II. Title.
HQ768.G53   1997
649′.124—dc21   96-53468
                                          CIP

Designed by Bonni Leon-Berman

   06 20 19 18 17 16 15

To our middlers, Joseph, Theresa, and Skyler
Rose, whose growing up inspired us to grow
as parents and cultivate new parenting skills.
We love you.

Contents

Acknowledgments

The idea for this book was not hatched overnight. It took years—ten to be exact. The two of us had worked together on a business newsletter and were eager to coauthor a book. Nothing surfaced that was compelling enough to sustain our interest. When our talks focused more on what was happening in the lives of our middle schoolers rather than in the world of business, we knew we had found the topic for our book. We both believe that writers write best when they are passionate about their subject matter. And what topic was more near and dear to our hearts than our children and helping them survive and thrive during these important years?

Our initial investigation into the subject matter led us to the National Middle School Association, a fortuitous discovery. NMSA, with its breadth and depth of knowledge and experience, proved to be instrumental during the research phase of our book. Our heartfelt thanks to John Lounsbury, head of NMSA's publications division, whose enthusiasm for our project never wavered. Despite his demanding schedule, he always found time to talk with us. He provided invaluable assistance with our survey by supplying us with the names of principals in middle schools in each of the fifty states and six Canadian provinces. He guided us to numerous experts and resources inside NMSA's vast educational network. His encouragement and wisdom were most welcomed.

Ross Burkhardt, who was NMSA's president during the time we worked on the book, was generous with his time, knowledge, and resources, as he helped to sketch for us an accurate portrait of the middle school student he knows so well. We could easily see why Ross is so popular with his students at the A. G. Prodell Middle School in Shoreham, New York. His classroom, with its groupings of stuffed chairs and pillows, was warm and welcoming. The assignments that Ross fashions for his children—having them do video recaps of the 1960s, for example—were another example of his creativity and involvement as a teacher. His students are lucky to have him, and we were lucky to share him for a time.

In addition to its numerous publications, NMSA hosts many conferences each year. As we began the research for our book, we attended one held by the New England League of Middle Schools in Providence, Rhode Island. NELMS's Executive Director Robert C. Spear was most gracious in providing us with access to the many talks and exhibits at this exposition. We thank him and his staff.

Our gratitude to all the parents, teachers, and students who took the time to complete and return our lengthy questionnaire. The response was overwhelming, not only in terms of those surveys that were returned, but also because of how much was written on many of the forms. So many times, it was apparent that our questions had touched a nerve. We could almost hear the anguish in these voices. Teachers expressed their frustration trying to teach young people who are distracted in class because their home lives are in disarray. Parents lamented the electronic media's hold over their children's lives and worried about the future. And the students themselves came across as the walking paradoxes that we know to be the middle schooler. The same child could fill out a questionnaire and seem childlike and innocent on one page and streetwise and cynical on the next. We are grateful to all of them for taking the time to express their feelings to us.

We are indebted to the many other experts who gave so willingly of their time and knowledge. The list is too lengthy to detail here, but you will see their names sprinkled throughout the book.

Our agent, Denise Marcil, was steadfast in her support of our project. We would also like to thank her assistant, Jeff Rutherford, for all of his help.

We were most fortunate to have as our editor Janet Goldstein, every author's dream. From the beginning, Janet believed in us and our idea. Her instincts, both as an editor and as a parent, helped us to home in on many of the issues discussed in this book. Our gratitude to Betsy Thorpe, Janet's assistant, for her meticulous attention to all the details throughout the book's progress.

To all our relatives, friends, and fellow parents, for your love, patience, insight, and help while we labored these many months. We could not have done it without you.

Most of all, to our children, Charlene's Joseph and Theresa, and Margaret's Skyler Rose, without whom this book could not have been written.

Introduction

Getting a View from the Ferris Wheel

"The biggest challenge in dealing with this age group is their roller-coaster emotions."

(Middle school teacher from Washington)

"She's driving me crazy!" the mother of a thirteen-year-old girl confessed to a friend over the phone. "Her math teacher called to tell me she hasn't handed in any homework for three days. You should see her room! I expect the board of health will soon condemn it. And the way she dresses! The other day she sprayed blue streaks in her hair and painted her fingernails to match."

She sighed. "But you know, she can be such fun! The other night she challenged me to a game of cards, Go Fish, like we used to play when she was younger. We played for almost two hours and talked about everything—school, music, her French club, several books she's read, our last summer vacation. And I was reminded what a great kid she is—smart, funny, warm, caring.

"Of course, it was just a lull in the storm," she said, sadness in her voice. "By the next morning, we were at each other's throats again. I just can't wait until these years are over!"

Parenting a child from ages ten through fifteen is truly challenging. Like the view from a Ferris Wheel, the highs are exhilarating; but looking down can be flip-flop stomach scary. It is the best of times and the worst of times.

"How can this be?" parents ask themselves and each other. How could a child, who yesterday was so happy, cooperative, and sharing have metamorphosed into such a moody, angry, and selfish individual? Parents lose patience and heart, particularly when they are on the receiving end of so much hostility:

"Why can't I stay out until midnight? I'm old enough."

"I hate you! You never let me do anything!"

"It's my room and I like it messy!"

"I won't change my dress! It's not too tight!"

"Why can't you be like David's dad? He never yells."

"I don't care if the whole family's going to the museum. It's boring. I'd rather hang out with my friends."

"This dinner sucks! Why couldn't we go out for pizza?"

"What do you mean I've been on the phone for over an hour? I just got on!"

"You're ruining my life!"

Soon it seems like all your close encounters—with an alien being who bears just a passing resemblance to your son or daughter—are of the angry kind. Two-way communication stops. You feel your offspring spinning out of control, out of your orbit. You, of course, want your child to be independent, to explore new worlds. Yet how will you be able to exert any control once he has left your atmosphere? Will the gravitational pull of your love and concern be strong enough to help him steer clear of all the destructive forces that he will encounter?

"My son always depended upon me for help and advice," remarked the father of a thirteen-year-old. "Now he credits me with as much intelligence as a sow bug."

"My daughter is a total enigma to me," confided another mother. "I have no idea what makes her tick and it scares me to death."

As mothers of children in this age group, we, too, have had moments when we felt ill-prepared for the challenges of parenting. On more than one occasion we have faced problems—cliques, setting limits, school issues—that have sent us scrambling for advice and guidance. Again and again we found it difficult to come up with the authoritative information we needed to help us make sound parenting decisions. While there are many books to help parents through other stages of their children's development—infancy, toddlers, preschool, grade school, and teens—we found surprisingly little written to help parents cope with the overwhelming physical, intellectual, and emotional changes experienced by the ten- to fifteen-year-old.

In fact, this age group is one that has somehow fallen between the cracks. As parents, and as a society, we are now playing catch-up. *Great Transitions: Preparing Adolescents for a New Century*, a 1995 report from the Carnegie Council on Adolescent Development focusing on ten- to fourteen-year-olds observed: "A social consensus holds that knowledge about infant and child development is critical to a child's future. No such consensus yet exists in defining the knowledge parents should have about the adolescent years or about their roles during that critical period."

Perhaps one reason a consensus on parenting ten- to fifteen-year-olds has been slow to develop is that there is no one foolproof way to parent them. In contrast to early childhood, children in this age group mature at wildly different rates. As a result, children younger than ten and older than fifteen may exhibit many of the same characteristics we'll be describing.

Just look around your son or daughter's class. Some children are tall and mature looking; others small and childlike. And the differences are more than skin deep. While one twelve-year-old may fight for later curfews and more freedoms, another may withdraw, shunning family and friends. These two reactions are typical and normal ones for a child going through puberty. Yet each child manages to worry a parent.

The Life of a Ten- to Fifteen-Year-Old

The old saying goes: "Don't judge someone until you have walked a mile in his shoes." So, for a moment, imagine what your life would be like if you encountered some of the same difficulties in your own life as those being endured by your young adolescent:

Congratulations! You've been promoted, moved up another step on the ladder. Initially, you're euphoric, expecting you can now operate with more freedom. It doesn't take long, however, for you to see that there are many negatives and few positives resulting from your new position. Your workload has doubled. Your added responsibilities now require you to toil at home an hour or more every evening on projects you regard as little more than busywork. And your boss doesn't seem to trust you. He is constantly second-guessing you, listening in on your phone calls, going through your papers when you're not looking. Nothing seems to please him. Yesterday he reprimanded you because your desk was untidy!

Your coworkers aren't much help. There is an in-group and you are decidedly on the outs. No matter what you wear or how you comb your hair, someone manages to make a snide remark. Would it be paranoid to say that they are out to get you? The other day, one of them criticized your proposal in a meeting, embarrassing you in front of the client. Work is difficult enough without having to worry about being sabotaged by your peers.

On top of everything else, you feel lousy these days. Maybe it's the flu that's making you so tired. You can't seem to get out of bed in the morning. And your appearance! Your face has broken out and nothing seems to help. You've put on maybe ten pounds since the holidays, all in the wrong places. You looked in the mirror this morning and couldn't believe what you saw. Too many sweets, no doubt. Nothing in your closet fits. Time to diet again.

Doesn't sound like much fun, does it? Welcome to your child's world! These young people are living life in a pressure cooker. Is it any wonder they occasionally explode? Here are just a few of the frustrations they must contend with:

They yearn for independence when they are still being told what to do by their parents, teachers, and older siblings.

They are the target of many advertising campaigns, yet have little disposable income of their own.

They worry about their appearance while nature is wreaking havoc with their bodies.

They long for peer acceptance while some of those same peers make life miserable for them.

They worry about doing well in school while their workload and responsibilities increase.

They are on the brink of adulthood, yet have trouble controlling childlike impulses.

They are eager to voice their opinions, but they still have difficulty formulating coherent arguments.

They maintain a hectic schedule—between school, sports, social events, and extracurricular activities—at a time when their physical development demands they sleep more.

These years have never been easy for children or their parents. In 400 B.C. Socrates observed: "Young people nowadays love luxury; they have bad manners and contempt for authority. They show disrespect for old people and love silly talk in place of exercise. They no longer stand up when older people enter the room; they contradict their parents, talk constantly in front of company, gobble their food and tyrannize their teachers."

"Adolescence hasn't changed," observed Dr. Ralph I. Lopez, a Manhattan specialist in adolescent medicine. "We didn't invent it."

Of course many things have changed since the days of Socrates. The world has become a more dangerous and stressful place for young people. When today's parents were this age, their lives were fairly stable and uncomplicated. The vast majority of children lived in two-parent families. Schools were safe, uncrowded, and close to home. The only people in the neighborhood who carried guns were policemen.

Contrast that lifestyle to the one now experienced by a young person. More than half of all American children will spend at least part of their childhood or adolescence in a single-parent family, according to the Carnegie Commission. Violence for many is an accepted part of their lives. Children ages twelve and up are the most common victims of crime and two-thirds of their victimizers are other children. Many have witnessed a violent crime. Alcohol and drug abuse is prevalent. (Thirteen percent of young adolescents have used marijuana.) The number of children having children is staggering. (Forty percent of ninth graders have had sexual intercourse and 20 percent of high schoolers say they have had at least four partners.)

There is scientific data to prove that these children, because of better nutrition, are reaching puberty at an earlier age. (The average age of menstruation is now twelve, compared to thirteen back in 1960.) But in many ways, the intellectual and emotional maturity of these children has not caught up. Some are forced into adult situations before they are able to cope. They are bombarded with TV shows, movies, videos, and music that contain violence and explicit language and images.

Peer pressure has always been an issue with this age group, but these days a parent has genuine cause to worry. A lapse in judgment may have serious, irreversible consequences. A fifteen-year-old who has unprotected sexual intercourse, for example, risks not only an unplanned pregnancy but also AIDS. (Every month, the number of teens who test positive for the HIV virus doubles.)

No wonder parents are anxious! Saving a young adolescent from danger is more complicated than catching a toddler who is about to fall off the monkey bars. We can't hover over our ten- to fifteen-year-olds, arms outstretched, in the event of an accident. For the most part, they're on their own, traveling to and from school, spending the afternoon at the mall, or going to the movies. Sometimes we have to let our children suffer the consequences. We hope for two things: That those consequences won't be too severe and that they will learn something valuable from the experience.

Losing control is never a pleasant feeling, and losing control over someone you love, someone you know still needs your guidance, is downright chilling.

Some parents react by withdrawing. "Grit your teeth and get through it," the parent of an older teen advised. "It will be over in a few years."

Other parents recede into the background assuming it's appropriate. They believe the following statements:

Young children need parents more than older children do.

Young adolescents need to be left alone in order to become independent.

My child has a personal life now and it doesn't include me.

Ten- to fifteen-year-olds care more about what their peers think than what their parents think.

For the record, all these perceptions are wrong! Young adolescents need more, not less, from parents. Children in this age group care what parents think, far and above what anyone else thinks.

These young people are walking contradictions and the greatest inconsistency involves their parents. "Young adolescents are a dichotomy," admits Ross Burkhardt, past president of the National Middle School Association (NMSA), veteran middle school teacher, and parent. "Mom and Dad are extremely important even though they don't want to admit it. This can be very confusing for parents."

Parents who believe that their children really mean it when they say, "Leave me alone," need to take another look. What a child may be saying is, "I want more privacy than you are giving me now. But don't go too far. I might need you later."

The parenting job is not less important as a child grows beyond ten. The fact is that hands-on parenting makes or breaks the future of young adolescents. The Carnegie Council points out, "Studies show that although young adolescents crave—and require—adult support and guidance as they struggle toward independence, it is during the period ages ten through fourteen when these essential requirements are least likely to be met. If the nation continues to neglect this age group, millions of young adolescents will become 'lifelong casualties' of drug and alcohol abuse, teen pregnancy, AIDS, suicide, violence, and inadequate education."

Parents who misread their middlers will miss a golden opportunity—perhaps their last chance for many years—to play an active role in their children's lives.

Why the Term "Middlers"?

Prepubescent. Preteen. Preadolescent. The very terms used to describe this period suggest these years are merely a prelude to something else and not worthy of focusing on for too long. Yet this phase of life entails changes as dramatic and significant as the toddler years, and presents opportunities (or lost chances) for your child's success in school, relationships, and life.

We have introduced the word "middler" to emphasize the unique and far-reaching developmental tasks and situations that emerge during these years. When parents comprehend what their children are feeling and struggling with developmentally, they have a different (and wiser) perspective to evaluate behavior, attitudes, and shortcomings. They can stop worrying, "Is my child bad?" and focus on dilemmas and solutions rather than labels. Moreover, sharing this information about what's normal with a middler is reassuring, even empowering.

The word "middler" reflects the influence of the middle school, an institution that has become, after parents, the most important influence in the lives of these children. Begun in the early 1960s, the middle school movement, advocating a five-to-eight- or six-to-eight-grade configuration, was a response by educators to develop a curriculum that would best serve the distinctive qualities and learning style of the ten- to fifteen-year-old. Team teaching and integrative curriculum are just a few of the changes that middle schools brought about to nurture young adolescents not ready emotionally for the impersonal atmosphere of high school. Middle school educators, led by the National Middle School Association (NMSA), are constantly reevaluating teaching techniques, exploring new ways in which the ten- to fifteen-year-old can best be taught, and broadcasting what they learn to the parent community.

This book is a step toward giving parents the information they need during these critical years. Within these pages you will find many facts, an abundance of anecdotes (comfort that you are not alone), expertise culled from interviews with leading experts brought together for the first time, and advice, sometimes plain and simple and other times presented in exercises designed to enhance your parenting skills.

Each of us brings to the job of mother and father our own unique style of parenting, the result of many factors—our upbringing, current family makeup, community, religion, economic situation, set of values. You will be asked to give some thought to your own parenting posture. Are you rigid or too friendly? How you parent significantly affects your actions, and equally compelling, your young adolescent's reactions. (In Chapter Nine on drugs, for example, you'll see how your answers influence your child's decision-making.)

We will share with you the results of a survey we conducted with the assistance of the NMSA. We mailed questionnaires to all fifty states and six Canadian provinces, soliciting opinions from parents, teachers, and the middlers themselves. You will hear the voices of these children and adults throughout these pages. Our findings will enlighten, surprise, alarm, and ultimately reassure you as you devise your own parenting plan for these six important years.

And don't forget: what works for one family may not work for yours. You need to know your own child, educate yourself, trust your instincts, and be flexible enough to admit when you go wrong.

Once you appreciate what your child is going through (and examine your responses as well), it will be much easier for you to stay solidly in his or her corner. You are your child's advocate, the person who knows your child best. If you've allowed your middler to push you away, now is the time to get close again. We hope this comprehensive guide will help. We want to inform, not alarm, educate not aggravate, middler parents. We want you to acquire the skills you need to parent, but we also want you to enjoy your experiences with these bright, entertaining, and energetic human beings.

Strategies: Discover Your Past As Middlers

Have you forgotten what it's like to be a middler? Take time to remember. Here are some ways to manage that:

1. Locate an old photo of yourself, one when you were the same age your child is now. Look at your expression. Can you recall what you were thinking that day? How about your appearance? It all comes flooding back, right? How you hated that shirt your mother made you wear for your picture. Or how that haircut made you look like a geek. And great timing on that pimple on your nose!
2. Call your mother, father, sister, brother. Talk about what you were like at ten, eleven, fourteen. Chances are your memories and theirs will be quite different. Were you really as helpful around the house as you tell your children you were? (Your parents may disagree!) Did you spend hours on the phone? Play loud music? Watch too much TV? What did you and your siblings fight about? Perhaps you weren't as "perfect" as you recall.
3. Call an old school friend. Did you really work as hard in school as you tell your child you did? (Locate an old report card to uncover the true story!) What does your friend remember? What did you obsess about? Did you get into trouble? Doing what? What you learn may surprise you.
4. Talk to your spouse. Encourage your husband or wife to take a walk into the past. Share what you have learned.
5. Play some music, songs that were popular when you were your middler's age. Close your eyes and try to remember where you were, what you were doing, and how you felt as you listened. What long-forgotten feelings are resurfacing? Lust? Fear of not being accepted by the group? Longing for more freedom?

Going through these exercises will give you a deeper appreciation of what it is like to be your child's age. Try to hold on to those memories as you parent. Your life wasn't uncomplicated as a middler. Neither is your child's. A little empathy will go a long way.

Are You Spending Enough Time with Your Middler?

According to a 1995 *New York Times* poll, children spend on average three hours a day with parents, which is 40 percent less time spent than in 1960. How much of that time is spent in meaningful communication? The University of Michigan polled 1,500 households, concluding mothers spend less than thirty minutes a day in conversation (not criticizing or delivering commands), while fathers on weekdays tallied up eight minutes on average.

We wondered if parents agree they are spending less time with their children. So we asked. In our survey, 51 percent of parents said they spent less time with their young adolescent than they did five years ago.

Middlers love their families and need time and attention from parents. Let us count a few statistical ways:

- Ninety-three percent of nine- to eleven-year-olds consider being part of a loving family to be much more important than owning material things, according to a survey done by Nickelodeon TV. A surprising response from our material girls and boys.
- Eighty-eight percent credit family as their greatest source of self-esteem. (Nickelodeon survey)
- Among students ranging in age from ten to thirteen, 72 percent wanted to talk to their parents *more* about schoolwork according to the National Commission on Children. Forty percent of parents in another study confessed they are not devoting enough time to their children's education.

"Children do suffer from a lack of emotional contact with their parents," says Dr. Robert Motta, director of the doctoral program in school-community psychology at Hofstra University. "The child who feels he is not the parent's primary focus suffers damage to self-esteem, but gets by. The danger lies in the contingent fact that parents then stop serving as the child's guide in terms of discipline and emotional support."

If you don't put in the hours, you cannot be your child's most prized possession, her source of positive self-image, his tutor, and guiding light.

The
Roller-
Coaster
Years

One

Playing Mind Reader

Understanding Your Middler's
Developing Intellect

"These kids really make me laugh!"

(Seventh-grade teacher from California)

Every age of a child has its joys but the years from ten to fifteen are truly exceptional. Being with your middler—whether you are playing ball, shopping, visiting a museum, or just talking—can be a lot of fun. You can actually carry on a conversation, a meaningful conversation, with your child. "Did you see this story in the morning newspaper about . . . ?" What follows can be a lively exchange where you will no doubt marvel at all your offspring knows. There is serious brain activity going on here as your middler develops the ability to think in a more abstract way.

Middlers are funny. These are the years when children acquire a more sophisticated sense of humor, finally moving away from all those bathroom jokes. "Imagine a profession where you actually get paid for having fun!" enthused one teacher. "That's what teaching middle level is all about . . . FUN. The students are spontaneous, yet honest. Corny jokes and uncontrolled laughter roll from their mouths."

We can almost hear parents reading this statement ask incredulously: "Fun? My son or daughter fun? Are we talking about the same child?"

Well, yes—and no. Dr. Ralph I. Lopez, specialist in adolescent medicine, points out that each child is actually three children:

1. The kid you know who behaves as your son or daughter.
2. The kid who may tell another adult, like a teacher, things he or she won't tell parents.
3. The kid who hangs out with other kids.

So that same child who may delight a teacher will come home and anger a parent. Part of it has to do with who your child is; the other part has to do with how your child feels he should be around you. Society in general and parents in particular can be overly critical and harsh with middlers. "The delinquent minority gets all the news," observed a seventh-grade teacher from New Mexico. "The majority of today's youth are super good kids who want to be successful and happy."

"There is a preponderance of dismal statistics, which the media always picks up," admitted Michael Conn, a member of the Children's Environments Research Group within the Environmental Psychology Department of CUNY Graduate Center. "This negativity has to do with funding patterns. If adolescent pregnancy is a problem, funding results, and so negatives are reported. Ditto with drug abuse."

Yet reading the daily headlines may cause a parent to quake. All this bad news perpetuates stereotypes of this age group. You expect the worst and you get it. Pretty soon the bad times outnumber the good and you have forgotten that your child can be fun, generous, and responsible.

That fact was brought home to us one night as we checked into one of the many parenting bulletin boards online that dealt specifically with the ten- to fifteen-year-old. Every single item posted was a cry for help.

"My twelve-year-old won't do his homework! What can I do?"

"My daughter is turning thirteen soon and is acting like someone I don't even know. Lying, stealing, answering back. Help!"

The entries continued in this negative way until the mother of a three-year-old joined in the electronic conversation to exclaim: "Oh, wow! I am the mom of a three-year-old boy and I read this area to see what we are in store for. Sounds a little intimidating. Also makes me grateful for the sweetness and light I've got right now."

But there are many moments of "sweetness and light" with middlers. "My daughter pretended to be the tooth fairy when I recently had a wisdom tooth extracted," said the mother of an eleven-year-old.

"She left a very funny note under my pillow along with a certificate for a free frozen yogurt of my choice."

Educators and other professionals who have studied middlers as a group also believe there is much good news. "New knowledge about adolescence has begun to illuminate the positive and adaptive qualities of this transitional stage in development as well as the problems," according to *Great Transitions: Preparing Adolescents for a New Century.* "Although young adolescents are often stereotyped as moody, rebellious, self-indulgent, and incapable of learning anything serious, research indicates that this portrait is greatly overdrawn."

Based on the results of our survey, middler parents do delight in the fun side of their children. Even though they complained about moodiness, messy rooms, and lost homework papers, they also boasted about their children, eager to point to their accomplishments and happy times they have shared. "No day is the same," said the Idaho parent of two middlers. "They are humorous and love life. I enjoy their energy level and being able to do things together."

Budding Intellects

Middlers are changing every day on many different fronts. Those chameleon-like qualities can keep us on our toes. As parents, it's vital that we maintain a positive and optimistic view of our children and their future potential. What follows is an overview of the major intellectual developments that are changing the way our children see and respond to the world around them. We hope you will see similarities with your own child that will help you to appreciate his or her very special qualities.

SKILLMASTERS
*Middlers begin to appreciate—and exploit—
their unique abilities.*

By the time they are ten, children have been exposed to a wide range of activities and interests, inside and outside of school. With few exceptions, these pursuits have been parent or teacher-driven. Certain pastimes are required coursework at school—team sports and art, for example. Others are avocations that parents deem important for their children—piano, ballet, tennis, skiing. During the middle school years, children begin to express their own preferences in somewhat forceful terms. They are no longer complacent about being dragged from one location to the next. Requiring them to practice a musical instrument they loathe will be an exercise in frustration.

Most middlers are not trying to be rebellious. They are merely coming into their own. They are growing physically and their new bodies—stronger, taller, and more coordinated—allow them to succeed at endeavors that were out of their reach before. They are learning about themselves and that learning curve involves discovering what they enjoy and do well. "I dance," enthused a seventh-grader from Idaho. "I enjoy it and I'm good at it." Because of their intellectual development, many young people are able to articulate exactly why they pursue various activities. "I play volleyball because you work as a team with one goal—bump, set, spike," said a fifteen-year-old female from Saskatchewan, Canada. "I get a sense of satisfaction and accomplishment out of playing it well." Similarly, an eighth-grader from Louisiana said: "I like to play football for the strategy involved."

This coming together of determination and skill means that there will be many opportunities for you to relish your child's accomplishments, whether in the classroom, in the concert hall, or on the playing fields. "My son loves soccer and has really worked at improving his game," said one father. "He plays defense and because he is not credited with scoring the goals, his contributions may often be overlooked by others. But I know how hard he works and the phenomenal job he does. And he knows I know. It has been a terrific experience for both of us to watch his progress."

In the classroom, middlers may begin to focus on particular classes that interest them, sometimes to the detriment of other subjects. A fascination with space may precipitate studying the planets, visiting a planetarium, and spending time with a telescope. If the interest wanes, the telescope may end up in the junk heap. But if it continues and grows, the child may become a serious student of astronomy. Watching your child become so enamored will be exciting for you, as well as an opportunity to learn about something that you may have overlooked. Nothing pleases a middler more than turning the tables on an adult, becoming instructor rather than student.

This journey of self-discovery has a downside. Your middler's preoccupation with self may begin to resemble arrogance, indifference, and anger if his efforts fall short.

"My daughter woke up three months ago a changed person when she turned eleven," said one mother. "All of sudden my bubbling, open little girl turned into a moody and private person. It was hard for me to take! So much happens to girls this age. She summed it up one day, 'I just wish I was Peter Pan.' She wants so much to grow up but it can be hard."

You look at your child as having her whole future ahead of her. Yet what she sees is that she is leaving her childhood behind to move into another part of her life that doesn't seem as safe or secure.

Have you ever had a career change? If so, you might have some idea of what your middler is experiencing. It probably took you a while to sort things out. Chances are once you did, you discovered talents and abilities you never knew you possessed.

Eventually, most children sort it all out, too, emerging in late adolescence as the self-assured, confident people we always knew they would be. Remarked a clairvoyant seventh-grader from Vermont: "I am someone who is going to get somewhere."

GREAT THINKERS
Middlers begin to develop sophisticated reasoning powers.

Your middler's way of reasoning is vastly different from the way he thought as a child. A young child tends to think in concrete terms: A person who is crying is sad, while a person who is smiling is happy. A middler is able to look for deeper meaning. A person's tears may be ones of happiness, or a person's smile may be a mask to hide sadness.

We saw evidence of this abstract thinking in our surveys. In describing themselves, only 15 percent wrote down a straightforward physical account ("I have blue eyes, blond hair"), something a young child is most likely to do. The overwhelming majority used words that went beyond surface appearances to provide a philosophical and psychological portrait of themselves. For example:

"I see a kid who is searching for answers to the deep questions of life and just starting to get them." (Thirteen-year-old boy from New Jersey)

"I see a big nose and big curls. I also see a future pediatrician." (Thirteen-year-old girl from California)

"I see a black kid who tries hard at everything he does and wants to make something of himself." (Thirteen-year-old boy from Louisiana)

"I see pride and confidence." (Thirteen-year-old from Idaho)

"I see a girl wondering what the future holds for her generation." (Fourteen-year-old from California)

"I see a girl who is worried about the little things—how I look, am I popular, do I make the right choices?" (Twelve-year-old from Maine)

"I see someone who has the ability to do whatever I want if I take the right roads." (Twelve-year-old boy from Vermont)

Soon your middler will be applying his intellectual prowess to problem-solving. Keep in mind, however, that your son's brain power is still developing. It will be many years before he is able to think and reason like an adult. During this transition period, he may need some assistance in formulating his arguments. Providing such assistance doesn't mean making a decision for him. A light touch is called for. The Vermont mother of a twelve-year-old performed that feat.

Mom: "What an unpredictable set of events! Whoever thought the district music festival would conflict with your GS (giant slalom) race. I know you feel GS is your better event . . ."

Child: "I really want to be in the festival, but want to qualify for the state ski races."

"Long before our car ride ended," the mother said, "he came up with an appropriate plan of action with a little guidance but mostly empathetic 'Hmms,' etc."

Moments such as these can be satisfying. Other times, however, your budding intellectual may test your nerves and patience. Arguing with your middler can often be as demanding as a presidential debate. He no longer will yield to your point of view without a good fight. He's not trying to be difficult. But his developing mind will no longer accept the simple explanations that may have placated him in the past. Let's take one example. It's Saturday afternoon and your son has agreed to accompany you to the grocery store to help with the shopping. While you are pleased he is coming, you are not pleased with the way he has decided to dress—in torn jeans, a dirty T-shirt, and a baseball hat worn backward.

Here's the discussion that follows:

"Jed, I would prefer that you wore another pair of pants and a clean shirt."

"These are fine. Why should I change?"

"Because I would like you to."

"Well, I don't want to. Why do I have to get dressed to go shopping?"

"Because I might see some of my friends and I would like you to look presentable."

"I am presentable. And they're your friends, not mine. Why should I care what they think of my clothing?"

It's frustrating to have a child who refuses to yield without a good reason. And, let's face it, there are many occasions when we want things done just because. It's hard to justify such a request.

"Pick up your room."

"Why?"

"Because you won't be able to find anything."

"I can find whatever I need."

"How can you be comfortable with all this junk around?"

"I'm perfectly comfortable."

"What if company comes?"

"I'll close the door."

"Suppose it's one of your friends?"

"My friends' rooms are even worse."

"AAAARRRGGGGHHH!"

Of course, these two examples deal with the superficial—sloppy clothes, messy rooms. These are hardly infractions that start someone on the road to ruin. But they will suffice as a good warm-up for the discussions that really count. You know what we mean, those dealing with drugs, alcohol, tobacco, sex. Be forewarned that you will need to be armed with more than "because I said so's," when you discuss any of these topics. (We will help prepare you for these discussions in later chapters.) The positive side of all this is that once your child has played devil's advocate with you, he will be well prepared to resist pressure from his peers.

ANTHROPOLOGISTS
Middlers are fascinated with the outside world and how it affects them.

These children are eager to learn about their world. Even the child who finds science textbooks boring is apt to be concerned about the environment. More than 35,000 middlers belong to the environmental group Greenpeace. "I have many students with strong convictions about religious and society's morals and values," said a middle school teacher from Saskatchewan. "Most are honest and concerned with the environment and other people's lives."

When the Sunday newspapers arrive, your child may no longer be content with the funnies. She will scan the headlines, eager to understand what is happening at home as well as abroad. Soon your middler begins to make connections between what she is learning at school and the real world. "In math we learned about sales tax," said a seventh-grader from California. "I need to know that to figure out how much something costs."

Certain coursework is apt to bore middlers because they see no way to immediately use the information they are studying. These children live in the here and now. The concept of learning facts because they might be able to use them in the future eludes them. Why learn if they can't use that knowledge right away?

But for those subjects that are relevant, middlers will attack them with enthusiasm. "We always see violence around us," said an eighth-grader from California. "We were born with it. In history class we are taught about how we declared war. How can we as a nation and individuals look beyond that or are we too scared about what we might find?" Chances are this student will not rest until she has received some answers to her questions.

ATTENTION-SEEKERS
Middlers still need and seek out approval of parents and other adults.

Because middlers are seeking to establish their own identities many parents feel they are being pushed away. The truth is just the opposite. "These children are so hungry for positive attention," said a seventh-grade teacher from New Mexico. "They are still willing to be molded by your wisdom and the experiences you offer to them."

Teachers notice this every day in their classrooms. "The kids get very sensitive," said one teacher. "They are so worried that they aren't liked, that everyone's watching them." Students will constantly ask, "How did you like my project?" or "Did you enjoy my composition?"

"Was my poem any good?" They are desperately seeking sustenance in the form of a compliment, a smile, a kind word.

Attentive teachers experience the boomerang effect: former students return to once again bask in the attention. "I have several students from years ago who come in after school to see me," said Lisa Garcia, a teacher in Tucson, Arizona. "Others call me on the phone, to see how I'm doing and to ask me math questions. One girl remembered a game I have, a logic problem. She called me up to see if she could borrow it."

The simple fact is that these young people still need and want parents and other adults in their lives. They need their love, their guidance, their hugs, their encouragement, their wisdom. "You can't straighten their hair in public, but they still want you to love them," said Judith Baenen, president of St. Mary's Academy in Englewood, Colorado. "You can do the hugging at home."

ACTIVISTS
Middlers believe they can make a difference.

As middlers become more aware of the larger world that exists outside their own, they begin to focus on the problems and injustices they see. "My students worry about their future in our world and about the welfare of others," said one seventh- and eighth-grade teacher from Nevada. "They want the world to be a better place."

True to form, they will want to make changes and make them fast. When that's not possible—and ninety-nine times out of a 100, it probably won't be—they will be angry and frustrated.

Middlers resemble the freshman congresspeople who come storming into Washington in January following an election. Most often, these newly elected representatives are young, idealistic, full of enthusiasm, and still euphoric over being voted into office. They have ideas and no one—in some cases, not even the President—is going to tell them something is impossible. In two years, after running up against the Washington bureaucracy, some will despair, yet others will have learned how to cut through red tape.

One mother gave this example: "My son loves guinea pigs and he was appalled when he visited a local pet store and found that these animals were being kept in cages that were crowded, unclean, and without adequate food and water supplies. He complained to the store manager but was shrugged off. I guess the manager felt he was just a kid. So my son came home and called the ASPCA. At first they refused to take his complaint seriously, but they finally sent out an investigator to look into the matter."

The middler complaint voiced most often is, "It's not fair!" "Kids this age have a very strong sense of justice," said Joe Kelly, managing editor of *New Moon,* a magazine written for girls by girls. "Fairness and justice are the same thing." Because adults make the rules, middlers often find themselves chafing under the bit of grown-up authority.

But if the circumstances are right, these children can move beyond criticism and accomplish a great deal. "One large common denominator is that these things (girls putting out a magazine such as *New Moon,* for example) happen when an adult respects the children," Kelly said. "I see that every day with our magazine. The kids are running the magazine. We have created an environment where they can use their inherent power and then we can follow them. Because our society is the way it is, they seldom get to use that power."

IDEALISTS
Middlers begin to develop their own set of personal values.

A father lectures his son about staying away from drugs and then pours himself a tumbler of Scotch.

A mother complains to her daughter about the lyrics of a rock song, then swears at a cab driver.

A teacher requires his students to hand in homework on time but is always late returning tests.

Gotcha!

Any one of the above examples is liable to illicit a strong reaction when witnessed by a middler. As we get older, we begin to reconcile the contrary nature of everyday life. Even if you are against swearing, it's hard not to blurt out a four-letter word when a passing car hits a puddle and drenches your new suit with mud. Middlers, with their developing sense of values, will zero in on these discrepancies. So you may start out reprimanding your son for smoking and wind up defending your drinking. Chances are it will keep you on your toes. "Most ten- to fifteen-year-olds are genuine and real," said a seventh- and eighth-grade teacher from California. "No phony cover-ups or mind games. They tell you straight up how it is."

Young children generally espouse the views of their parents. "I enjoy watching the values I've been teaching them become their own," said the California mother of two middlers. But the ten- to fifteen-year-old will start to scrutinize those values more carefully.

"We had a mini course in debating and the kids decided they wanted to focus on welfare," said Susan Berrington, a seventh-grade social studies teacher at Mount View Middle School in Marriottsville, Maryland. One boy, who was from a very conservative right-wing family, signed up for the debate to argue against welfare. Berrington explained, however, that he had to do research, pro and con, before he chose a side. After looking into the subject, he changed his opinion.

"He came to the conclusion that some compassion was necessary and that some people might need welfare payments," she said. "He didn't come through with his stereotypical line."

SOCIAL WORKERS
Middlers are sympathetic and, with guidance, begin to see and meet other people's needs.

These children have a sweet, giving nature that comes out often in most unexpected ways. One teacher in a tough, inner-city school told about an autistic boy in her class who was gifted but frequently disrupted the classroom. On one occasion he threw a chair at another boy in the class who happened to be a gang member, an incident that might have triggered retaliation after school. But the gang left the autistic boy alone. "They understood that throwing things was the only way he could deal with a situation," said the teacher.

The concern the children showed toward this autistic child, however, lasted throughout the entire school year. Whenever the autistic boy ran out of the classroom, other students, boys as well as girls, would go after him, to make sure he was okay.

Our surveys were filled with accounts from parents and teachers of the good deeds their children have done, whether for a stranger in a faraway country or a good friend at home. "Kids care about the homeless and lost ones of our society and they can make a tremendous difference in the lives of displaced people," said a fifth-grade teacher from Vermont.

"There is a lot of good in these children," said Judith Baenen. "People who have worked with the middle schoolers love them. They sit and talk. Whatever the project is, they do it. They're always friendly, never complaining."

INNOCENTS
Middlers can still look at the world with wide-eyed wonder.

On the threshold of adulthood, middlers have not lost their innocence. "She's young enough to be very happy to play as a child, but also exploring adulthood," said a mother from Vermont. "I love to watch."

One teacher noted that her students are still pleased with stickers and prizes that the high school kids might think are not cool. "These students," she noted, "are a wonderful blend of näiveté and budding sophistication."

Caught between childhood and adulthood, your daughter may have a hard time "acting her age." If she behaves like a child, you are apt to criticize her for childish behavior, yet when she attempts to act grown up, she may wind up embarrassing herself. In their book, *Young Adolescent Development and School Practices: Promoting Harmony,* John Van Hoose and David Strahan noted that middlers often use mature words in the wrong context. They related the story of one young girl who said her mother was trying to lose weight by seeing a ventriloquist. Another student said she was absent from school because she had an "appendage" on her tonsil. A boy said he was taking "rheumatism," rather than Robitussin for his cold, while another actually said his ovaries were bothering him. In our survey, one boy described himself as being "too big for his bridges."

Van Hoose and Strahan also observed that middlers try to make sophisticated arguments but often get the basic facts wrong. For example, a bright eighth-grader, hoping to get across the seriousness of the AIDS epidemic said that 95 percent of the American population would contract the disease by the year 2000. "It is so common for students to half listen and misinterpret because their minds skitter rapidly from one thought to another, with many of these thoughts being unrelated," said the authors.

How adults react to these lapses in behavior will greatly affect a middler's self-esteem and willingness to take chances. Experts advise that adults not correct a child in front of others. Van Hoose and Strahan observed, for example, that even though the statistic on AIDS was incorrect, a teacher could have used the opportunity to discuss the disease and its rapid spread.

COMEDIANS
Middlers begin to develop a sophisticated sense of humor.

While bathroom humor is still popular among some middlers, most have begun to move on to more sophisticated humor. They are likely to appreciate jokes that are filled with puns and wordplay, the better to show off their rapidly increasing vocabulary. Jokes that poke fun at contemporary figures such as politicians and celebrities will get them laughing. They are eager to jump in with their own contributions, many fancying themselves as stand-up comedians, or, at least, the head writer behind the jokester.

For the parent in the audience, middlers provide many opportunities to laugh. And many of these occasions occur spontaneously without any prelude. "We were walking down the main street of town and were passing a museum," said one mother. "Several ladders were laid against the side of the building and there was a flurry of activity, with workmen on the ladder, on the ground, and in the windows. 'I wonder what's going on?' I asked my son. Without missing a beat he said in his best newscaster's voice, 'Statue threatens to jump from museum window! Details at eleven!' It was priceless!"

A father gave this account of his two middler twin daughters: "A car commercial came on TV that described a vehicle as being 'like a rock.' " The conversation continued:

First daughter: Why are they talking about a car, comparing it to a rock?

Second daughter: Well, it's dependable . . .

Father: It's sturdy . . .

First daughter (without missing a beat): It doesn't move."

Needless to say, a hearty laugh was had by all. Middler humor will often zero in on the inconsistencies or hypocrisy in the adult world.

There are times, however, when middler humor goes awry. Remember that these children are still figuring out the difference between sarcasm and satire. Their jokes can sometimes be biting and cruel. "They are not intending to be rude, but they can be blunt," said one teacher. She cited two examples from her own experiences. One student told her: "You blow your nose just like my mother." Another told one of her colleagues: "You certainly have a full figure."

Adults would be wise to follow the example of this teacher and not overreact when they are on the receiving end of young adolescent humor. Chances are the comment was not meant maliciously. The best advice anyone can heed is to relax, enjoy, and laugh a lot.

Going Round with Your Middler

Your middler is changing day-by-day. It stands to reason that you need to make some adjustments, too. Here are some suggestions:

Leave your middler in charge. Satisfy your son's desire to be the authority by giving him responsibility. Are you going out for an hour? Leave your middler in charge to take phone messages, start dinner, or baby-sit a school-age sibling. Make sure to compliment him on a job well done.

Over time your middler will gain a new perspective on what is involved in taking over. It's not as easy as it looks. Younger siblings may complain, "That's not fair!" and he will have to justify his decisions. Eventually, your middler will grow more self-confident as he comes to realize that there are many jobs you do trust him to perform well.

Encourage your middler's enthusiasm. Does your daughter rant and rave about adults who pollute? Don't turn a deaf ear to her complaints. Tell her you understand her feelings and volunteer to help her channel her anger into action. Does she want to complain? Suggest she write a letter to the editor of the local newspaper. Is she looking for a wider audience? Perhaps a newsletter or web page is what she is looking to do. Offer your expertise or find another parent who is knowledgeable.

Find ways for your child to help others. Your child may have opportunities at school and church to get involved in community projects. If not, create those situations. The holidays are always a time of need for some in your town or city. Taking your child with you to serve the homeless at a shelter or to help out at a children's Christmas party will allow him to see firsthand how his involvement can make a difference.

Feed her intellectual growth. Look for ways to discuss important issues with your daughter. Discuss ethical questions. Propose hypothetical problems. State how you feel, then ask, "What's your opinion?" Make it clear you don't expect her to agree with you. Help her to avoid, however, reaching snap judgments without looking at the facts and assessing the consequences.

Build a bridge between school and the world. Reading the daily newspaper over breakfast will produce many opportunities for your son to relate what he is learning in school to what is happening in the world. Talk about a country in the headlines. Does this country have geographical features your son has studied? The business pages may provide the opportunity to use math skills. You can study the writing in various stories to talk about sentence structure and grammar. Just reading the weather forecast can launch you into a scientific discussion.

Ease the transition from childhood to adulthood. Young adolescents sometimes believe that growing up means leaving behind childlike interests and activities. Where possible, show her that even though she is getting older, she can still enjoy many of the same things she enjoyed as a child. Prove it to her by joining in.

Teach correct social behavior. How should the telephone be answered? Cover the mechanics of introducing an adult to one of his friends. When is it proper to begin eating when dining with others in a restaurant? Also provide some guidance with regard to personal hygiene, dress, and makeup. Be gentle, be helpful, and be ready to answer questions.

Your child's growth during the middle years can be mind-boggling. While you can actually see the physical changes, the intellectual ones are less obvious. Once you know how your child's thinking is developing, however, you will become more adept at mind reading, not to mention coping with middler mind games.

Strategies: Develop the Art of Adolescent Affection

Try to find a moment each day when you can show your middler how much you care about him. You already do? Think again. You may be conveying good thoughts to your child less regularly than you think. *YM* and *Family Circle* magazines conducted a joint survey and asked how often mothers told their daughters "I love you." Nearly 75 percent of the mothers said "frequently," while only half of the daughters reported hearing those three words on a regular basis.

What you say and how you deliver those sentiments will, of course, depend on your own personal style and that of your child, but here are some suggestions:

• *Write a note.* Do you pack your daughter's lunch? Then along with her tuna sandwich pack a note praising something she did. Or just say, "I love you."

• *Leave a voice mail.* If he will arrive home from school before you do, call ahead of time and leave a message telling him you miss him and can't wait to see him.

• *Tell him in person.* Don't save your face-to-face meetings just for angry confrontations. Sit him down and tell him how much you care about him.

• *Give a hug.* Hugs and kisses are still important for these children. Look for other ways to offer physical affection. Try brushing your daughter's hair or giving her a manicure. One mother reports that her son routinely asks her to put on his acne cream.

• *Follow-up a punishment.* Probably the most important time to let your child know how much you care is right after you have punished him. That may be the hardest time for you to say it and the hardest time for him to hear it.

Two

House of Mirrors

Coping with Growing Bodies and Distorted Images

"I don't own any mirrors. My looks aren't right; my feelings aren't right. Nothing's right."

(Fourteen-year-old Washington girl)

When ten- to fifteen-year-olds look at themselves, they see a brigade of distorted images. The experience may be only slightly less horrifying than peering into a fun house mirror. Whether the reflection they see resembles Dumbo, the fat lady of circus fame, or a teenage werewolf, middlers are not happy about the way they look.

"Self-consciousness has always been a part of his character to a small degree," confesses the mother of a ten-year-old boy, "But we notice that lately he acts as if people are looking at him through a magnifying glass."

Most, if not all, middlers are supersensitive about their bodies. Why? They are in the throes of a growth spurt unlike any other. In fact, only one in five youngsters will feel actual growing pains. These can include aches in the shins, calves, and thighs of both legs or in the heels of the feet. The growing pains usually occur during the night, poorly timed preadolescent wake-up calls from nature. Luckily, most are passing sensations and short-lived, disappearing in a few minutes or, at most, lasting up to a half hour.

Moreover, nearly every member of this age group feels the psychic pain of growing up. The goal of this chapter is to familiarize you with the details of your child's physical development and the debut of puberty. Myths and well-meaning mistakes will be illuminated and replaced with insights to enhance your child's coping skills. Preoccupation with body image and a predisposition toward distorted self-images is leading too many young people toward eating disorders. We will sound an alert and educate you to steer your child away from thin-thinking and toward a healthy and fit lifestyle. Fortunately, parents can learn the skills required to nurture middlers through a time of monsterish hallucinations, defusing distorted images along the way.

The Mega-morphosis

Many parents are well aware of a young child's awkward milestones, like losing a front tooth. Few are as well-informed about exactly what our ten- to fifteen-year-olds are experiencing. To understand how young adolescents feel, you need to look at the unprecedented growth spurt that is transforming them. It goes beyond the term metamorphosis, to proportions best described by the term *mega-morphosis.*

Chances are you have recognized active growing periods before. Your toddler loses that baby look or your second-grader shoots up. Yet, for the most part, growth during these early years is slow and steady. For ten- to fifteen-year-olds, growing up and out is rapid. Spurts lasting less than a year—adding three to five inches—are common. During the total span of early adolescence, the average young person gains twelve inches in height. That's a 20 percent jump for girls.

Weight increases twenty to thirty pounds, approximately ten pounds a year. It's not unusual for a ten-year-old girl to weigh in at seventy-five pounds and, by the time she reaches sixteen, tip the scale at 125 pounds. Girls add inches to their hips as well as their frame. Boys eventually outpace girls in height and muscle. For both genders gaining weight is normal; failing to is not.

In a youth culture where sleek fashion models have starring roles, girls can mistake filling out for becoming the worst thing imaginable: fat. (More about this miscalculation made by both girls and boys later.)

Mr. Rogers's song *Everything Grows Together* scored many a middler's early childhood, but now an unsettling dilemma occurs. Only one part of the body—the feet or the nose—grows.

On a frosty day in December at a northeastern middle school bus stop, the mother of a sixth-grader chastised a shivering eighth-grader for braving the frigid temperatures and deep snowfall without his hat, gloves, or boots. The boy defended himself with exasperation, she recalls.

"Nothing fits me!" the boy wailed. "All of a sudden my feet grew from a size seven to nine so I can't get my boots on. My hands outgrew the gloves I had." It wasn't the protests that struck this mom as much as the desperation in the boy's voice. His body seemed beyond his control.

All parts of the body do not grow at the same time or rate. Hands and feet outpace arms and legs. The backbone grows more slowly than other bones giving these children their typical gangly, Gumby look. Angles and planes in the face change unevenly. Ten- to fifteen-year-olds look out of proportion because sometimes they are—temporarily. They don't realize this fact unless you tell them they are a work in progress.

Both genders could be called "growthletes" because of their outstanding strides in development, but the label wouldn't fit both at the same point in time. Girls begin on average two years earlier than boys, anywhere from the age of eight to thirteen. Sixth-grade girls regrettably will always tower over their male peers. Once the male spurt begins, though, boys grow faster (four to five inches a year) and for a longer time. By fifteen, the boys are taller, heavier, and stronger because they acquire more muscle in their chest, shoulders, and arms.

Within each gender, an individual and unique schedule exists. There are ranges, but this is why a seventh-grade class has some boys who look like children and others who look like strapping young men. Girls, too, run the gamut from shapeless to downright curvy and sexy.

Think of what this can do to a pair of best friends. One remains a child while the other comes under the sway of raging hormones. Suddenly their physical abilities, interests, and emotions are pulling them apart.

Every growthlete grapples with feeling as if he has been invaded by some new breed of body snatchers. Whether it is on his lips or not, the "Am I normal?" quandary is uppermost on his mind and his angst meter. One survey of sixth-graders found that 60 percent of the girls and 40 percent of the boys worried a lot about their looks. There really is no *normal*.

At this stage in social development, children are bent on fitting in. Middlers adhere to dress codes, protocols, even vocabularies that are governed by peer approval. When it comes to growing in sync, they are dreaming the impossible dream.

What middle schoolers hate the most is being different from everyone else; yet that's exactly what early adolescence deals out to them, according to Judith Baenan, president of Saint Mary's Academy. When one wants to be just like everyone else, being different is more than just worrisome, it is a real burden.

Puberty—Hers

As the hormones kick in, girls show the first signs of puberty with the appearance of pubic and underarm hair, and swelling around the nipples as breasts "bud." Over the next few years, breasts go from fleshy and shapeless to firm and full. Girls retain more body fat than boys as female hips, thighs, and buttocks round out. Ovaries, fallopian tubes, and the uterus have been growing all along internally and invisibly. The milestone is menstruation.

Unlike the last generation, many mothers today have gone out of their way to prepare their daughters for menstruation, to defuse some of the anxieties they remember. Despite this enlightened approach, many are surprised when girls seem just as uncomfortable as ever.

The mother of an almost twelve-year-old testified her daughter was downright indignant about the onset of her first period. "What's this!" the child exclaimed with irritation. Then despair took over as she nixed swimming plans and attending a sleep-over party. Her reaction climaxed with, "I don't want to grow up. I wish I could be like that child vampire in *Interview with the Vampire.*"

Her mother confided, "I had prepared my daughter for this, so why was she so unprepared emotionally? I didn't want her menstrual memories to be like mine, mired in confusion and shame. What I recall is the Kotex arriving in huge cardboard boxes, whisked away like contraband, hidden in a closet. The coming-of-age milestone was a secret, a nuisance, a curse. I wanted my daughter to celebrate becoming a woman."

As this mother learned much to her dismay, putting a positive spin on menstruation is not an easy assignment. Despite the fact that the details of the feminine cycle have been explained patiently and precisely by parents, and reiterated in health-class curriculum, many girls are still plagued with a range of responses from uneasiness to downright disgust.

Parents of girls need to distinguish between what they can and cannot do to ease this transition into womanhood. A can-do strategy: provide hygiene guidelines. Reduce the inconvenience and insecurity with premenstrual planning. Here are a few ways to do this:

Avoid surprise accidents. Teach your daughter to chart her periods. At first, this task is difficult. Adolescent medical specialists point out that many girls (exactly how many is not known) experience irregular episodes the first year or two. In time a pattern will develop.

Rehearse a "be-prepared" scenario. Store an extra pad or tampon in her backpack or locker. Ask her to check school bathrooms for vending machines that offer supplies. Remind her that the school nurse is always there in a pinch.

Address concerns. Although charting and being prepared is sound advice for a majority, some girls are destined for a lifetime of irregular menstrual cycles. Others will worry because periods never start. Explain the wide range in the onset of menstruation—from ten to sixteen. What's abnormal is if menstruation starts and becomes sporadic due to extreme exercise or grueling regimens associated with track, dance, or gymnastics. Should this occur, consult your doctor.

Give her the option of using a tampon. If using pads is not satisfactory, let her practice the use of tampons. A young girl who hasn't had intercourse can use a tampon because the hymen usually has a natural opening large enough to accommodate one.

Instruct her about toxic shock syndrome. Toxic shock syndrome is a bacterial infection triggered by infrequently changed tampons. Changing tampons five times a day is the rule of thumb. Avoid overnight use. Use panty liners during the times of very light flow.

Debunk the "everyone-will-know" fear. With the blood flow, countless girls are afraid everyone will be able to tell they are menstruating by the way they smell. Don't discount the impact of all those feminine hygiene deodorant commercials. Assure your daughter that basic attention to changing pads or tampons and frequent baths or showers will guarantee an unnoticeable passage through menstruation.

Smoothing over the psychological turmoil of puberty is clearly less science and more art. The most important piece of advice: be sensitive. Even though you as a modern mother want to banish negative thoughts about becoming a woman, you simply can't. Transforming from girl to woman is a complex, mammoth undertaking. How your daughter handles her blooming is frankly her call, not yours. Observe. Listen. If she expresses negative reactions such as regret, sadness, anger, or loss, let her vent them. Avoid the mistake the next mother made.

"I was so wrapped up in trying to get my daughter to celebrate her coming of age, I was like a steamroller. When she cried about losing her childhood and insisted she didn't want any part of becoming a woman, I was oblivious. It wasn't until later, when my periods began to go irregular, that I fully comprehended the sadness of leaving behind an era. I didn't understand that my daughter was mourning the loss of childhood until I found myself mourning the loss of my childbearing years. You can't argue away loss no matter how hard you try, or how well-meaning you are."

Although you cannot unequivocally banish negative reactions to menstruation, you may be able to change the focus. One reason this time is so unsettling, is because young girls don't know what to expect. The next exercise will give your daughter a sense of control.

What's Your Menstrual Makeover?

If Cher, the ultra-hip maven of *Clueless* was giving advice on (as she coined menstruation) "surfing the crimson tide" it would be a menstrual makeover. Have your daughter learn to recognize her menstrual personality by monitoring herself. In the process she will acquire a sense of ownership over this monthly cycle and an intimate understanding of her body's nuances.

Every female has a highly personal experience with menses. Some have physical symptoms such as cramps or energy bursts. Others have emotional sensations, ranging from the blues to creative surges and concentration highs.

Have your daughter chart her period on a calendar. Examine the week prior and week of her active cycle. Check off any of the following characteristics:

more energy_____   or more tired_____
moody_____   How so? grumpy_____   nervous_____
depressed_____   cry at the drop of a hat_____
a sense of well-being_____
more hungry_____   craving chocolate_____   sweets_____
more thirsty_____
headaches_____   stomach cramps_____   nausea_____
bloated tummy_____   swollen ankles_____   sore breasts_____
backache_____   runny nose_____   mouth sores_____
better concentration_____   rush of new ideas_____
skin changes_____   blemishes_____   a rosy glow_____

This process enables your daughter to observe what happens to her body. In so doing, she moves beyond the fears, mysteries, and mystiques that plagued yesteryear's young girls.

Most pubescent girls get little help in navigating the girl-to-woman territory. Mainstream culture lacks the clear-cut rites of passage practiced by some ethnic groups. Jewish girls have a bas mitzvah at thirteen, (boys have a bar mitzvah), a synagogue service of memorized and recited prayer, followed by a celebration, marking their passage. Native American Navajos have *Kinaalda,* an endurance run of physical tests for girls designed to shape the body and spirit for adulthood. Cuban Americans mark their daughter's turning fifteen with an elaborate party, called a *quince.* The "sweet fifteen bash," which has evolved from the Hispanic *quinceanera,* is a Latino debutante ball, complete with feasting and a choreography of mambo and conga dancing.

If your heritage has no rite or ritual that demarcates puberty and reinforces it positively, try to invent one. Ask your daughter for suggestions. Here's how one mother improvised:

"My husband and I wanted our daughter to remember her first period. Our brainstorm: to dress in red. We fished bright red T-shirts, shorts, and socks out of drawers and set out on a day's activity of bike-riding. Tongue-in-cheek I suggested we call our celebration Happy Egg Drop Day, to honor the first egg. We could drink Bloody Marys (of course our daughter would have a Virgin Mary-please), eat egg drop soup or egg foo yong. Our daughter, who hadn't cracked a smile all day, laughed in spite of herself. It was then that I realized we had accomplished, if only for a moment, our goal. Our child would always remember this day, her first as a woman. She would never forget the three of us, bicycling along, like one long bright red flag, waving in the gusty breeze on which her womanhood was launched."

Puberty—His

Puberty is marked in boys with the growth and drop of testicles and the darkening of the sac, the scrotum, which holds them. The penis grows, probably in inverse proportion to locker room anxiety. Hair appears on the upper lip and in the pubic area. The voice begins to break.

Any and all of these werewolf-esque variations can be very upsetting for young men. Still it is less acceptable for boys to "act out" in comparison to girls who are notorious.

"I have a twelve-year-old daughter. After watching the mood swings and hormonal explosions, I have come to the conclusion the ozone layer is not being depleted by aerosol sprays—the true cause is the effects of all those exhaling sighs that come from preadolescent girls."

Amusing? While humor is often a useful strategy, the comical imaginings of this parent mask a stereotype that is damaging to girls and inhibiting to boys. The dramatic and emotional flare of pubescent girls is sexistly burlesqued time and again. Boys, on the other hand, don't have any legendary caricature to don to release feelings of stress. Does it follow that boys have fewer problems with puberty? No. Parents need to be aware of the following misconceptions.

Myth # 1 Boys are luckier because they don't have periods.

While it is true that boys don't have to cope with the monthly nuisance of periods, they have their own particular pubescent scourge—ejaculation. Testosterone development produces sperm whose buildup gives way to nocturnal emissions.

According to Dr. Laurence Steinberg, professor of psychology at

Temple University, a substantial minority of boys, one in five, are frightened the first time they ejaculate or have a wet dream. A boy frightfully wonders, "Has my body sprung a leak?" or "Have I caught a venereal disease?"

Boys are plagued more often with oily skin problems. Higher perspiration levels curse them with sweaty palms, and (don't laugh) smellier feet! They don't feel lucky, which leads into the next myth.

Myth #2 Boys are not as upset by changes in their bodies as girls are.

Many ten- to fifteen-year-olds experience deep embarrassment. For example, some worry about growing breasts. "Am I turning into some kind of freak?" Swelling under the nipples does happen to some boys in the early stages of puberty. It disappears within a year.

While girls dread the occasional menstrual accident, boys have to bear the ever-present, humiliating risk of spontaneous erection. It's not something your son is going to describe in response to your "Did anything interesting happen at school today?" probe, yet you can bet all boys have faced the bulging battle at one time or another. Standing on line in the cafeteria, getting up to answer in class, wherever or whenever, it's always upsetting.

Cracking voices render many voluntarily speechless. Or silent as this mother explains:

"My son sang in his school choir every year. He especially enjoyed the Christmas concert. In sixth grade, he begged me to let him drop out. When pressed to explain why, he said he just never knew what sound was going to come out of his mouth. I didn't realize how deep his embarrassment was until that moment."

Add these emotionally corrosive labels—"shrimp," "skinny," "puny" to a boy's life. Because muscle doesn't build up until the later years of puberty, many boys must often endure a few years of excruciating image battery.

Myth #3 These days all children are better informed about puberty.

Daughters are better educated by mothers in matters of menstruation and pregnancy than the last generation. And sex education exposes both young adolescent girls and boys to the facts of life earlier and more thoroughly than in years past. Does that mean boys and girls get equal access to puberty information? No.

Parents remain less willing to dwell on puberty details with their sons. Why? You cannot discuss the ABCs of *his* puberty, namely erection and ejaculation, without veering into issues such as masturbation, sexual fantasies, and erotic dreams. Menstruation just doesn't lead a parent down the same linguistic path. Parents may be graduates of the libertine 1960s or liberal 1970s, but many still get uncomfortably tongue-tied with sexual discussions bordering on such sensitive areas.

Many parents try valiantly to broach these subjects. For those who are sexually squeamish, look for help. (Chapter Ten is devoted entirely to the issue of sexuality and how best to deal with your child's.) Here are some suggestions:

• An adolescent pediatrician can be the perfect person to answer questions or concerns your son may have. Locate a specialist in adolescent medicine by contacting The Society for Adolescent Medicine, 1916 NW Copper Oaks Circle, Blue Springs, Missouri 64015

• Get books and leave them around for your child. For a comprehensive, yet lighthearted adolescent-friendly guide, try *It's Perfectly Normal—A Book About Changing Bodies, Growing Up, Sex and Sexual Health* by Robie S. Harris, published by Candlewick Press, Cambridge, Massachusetts.

• Ask your son to show you notes, text, or hand-out materials about puberty from health class. Offer to review these with him. Go over them yourself and quiz him informally.

A final word of advice comes from a parent, who says it as well as anyone, professional or otherwise, "Remember, there is only one person who is more uncomfortable about all this puberty stuff than you are, and that is your child!"

Tuning Into Body Rhythms

Let's take a detour for a moment, from the emotional strains of developing, and focus on one side effect, the physical toll. Growing up for middlers is a roller coaster of physical jolts. It is both energizing and exhausting. One moment your son seems restless with tapping feet, drumming fingers, flitting from room to room like a fly. Without warning, he descends into a lifeless lethargy, slumped over the sofa. With uncanny accuracy, exhaustion always seems to coincide with your request to take out the garbage or help with the yard work!

One mother articulated typical annoyance, "When she gets home from school, my thirteen-year-old daughter dives full speed into some project like sorting 300 hockey playing cards, or creating a scrapbook with scissors flying. An hour later when I ask her to help with dinner, set the table, she insists that she's too beat to help!"

Parents naturally assume this "I'm too tired" refrain is downright laziness or deliberate lack of cooperation. The truth of the matter is that middlers are not lying, evading responsibility, or playing dead. They are a breed at the mercy of growth cycles and hormonal changes. Ten- to fifteen-year-olds are besieged with periods of intense energy, and alternately with stretches of equally compelling fatigue. Energy swings are beyond their control.

By knowing middlers are quick-change artists and not con artists, parents can rest assured that their children have legitimate reasons for behavior that can resemble whirling dervishes or zombies from hour to hour. This is not to say your son can cop out anywhere, anytime you want him to do something.

The best way to handle energy drains and drives is to work with them. Is there a way to synchronize your expectations with your middler's energy meter? Yes. Learn to discern your own child's body rhythms.

The science of chronobiology is the study of the body's biological rhythms. There are daily, monthly, seasonal, and yearly cycles. Scientists have watched daily rhythms to pinpoint the body's peak times, when the body is most—and least—physically capable, intuitive, creative, or sensual. For example, the senses of smell, sight, and touch are most acute in late afternoon. One's mood is best in the *a.m.,* which means irritability is at its zenith in the late afternoon. Watching the body's clock can help anyone approach learning tasks, physical feats, or creative challenges with better odds for success.

A bit of chronobiology is useful in parenting this age group. Conduct an experiment to identify your child's body rhythms. Take note of his vitality levels for a few days. Include weekdays and weekends. If your schedule makes it difficult to monitor your child, ask your child-care provider or a sibling to help. By answering the following questions, you will be able to clock your young adolescent's energy ups and downs.

- What time of the day is he a bundle of activity?
- Is there a zombie hour? A regular time when she is rolled up in a fetal pretzel on the rug in front of the television or in the bedroom?
- Does your child require an unwind hour? Watch for a period of inactivity after school, after dinner.
- Is he a morning person? A night bird?
- Is there a social peak somewhere in the day's schedule, when she telephones friends or he schedules "meets"?
- Is a weekly cycle at work? Does he start school projects on weekends or on a Monday?
- Does she prefer getting a jump on assignments ahead of time, or the adrenaline rush of last-minute deadlines?
- Does he have a preferred homework hour? A music hour when CDs are played, instruments practiced?

Human beings are creatures of habit. Children are, too. You will be surprised how predictable the cycles are. Once you know your child's activity patterns, you can dovetail your expectations to take advantage of energy fevers or curtail them to coincide with energy lapses. Tuning into the rhythms of your particular child can make his life, and yours, less rife with conflict.

The Weight of Appearance Anxiety

Mirror, mirror on the wall, who's the fairest of them all? In our survey, we asked, "When you look in the mirror, what do you see?" One response, "Me? Weird hair."

A thirteen-year-old Floridian lamented, "I see myself as completely out of proportion. Nothing seems to look right or be in the correct position."

"My daughter," offered a bewildered parent, "can look in the mirror at 8:30 and be pleased with what she sees. Two hours later she will look again, focus in on all her imperfections and be miserable."

At no other stage of development are human beings so insecure about their looks. Body image at this age is a collage of uncertainties, fears, and self-critical beliefs. "What am I going to look like next month, next year? Will I always be this short? So tall? Do I look normal?" Silently and secretly, these are what our middlers are asking the looking glass. Most, if not all, have a chronic case of appearance anxiety.

In a context of terror and horror surrounding bodily images, no other issue looms larger than the issue of weight, to be more precise— fat. Insecure to begin with, young girls and boys are faced with enormous pressure to be thin. This skinny imperative comes from within, from their circle of peers and the culture. The sculpted, beautiful bodies of supermodels (including males), the merger of music and fashion on MTV and VH1, the exercise video, action movies, teen magazines—these cultural bombshells bombard girls and boys with flawless body images that few will ever achieve.

White and Asian middlers feel the most pressure. In the past African-American, Latino, and Native-American young adolescents have had more leeway on body size because in their culture larger bodies suggest power and prosperity. There are now indications that this, too, is changing. According to Allison Abner, coauthor of *Finding Our Way: The Teen Girl's Survival Guide,* "Because black supermodels don't reflect larger African-American body types, and are little more than black faces on white body types, it's an impossible stretch for young people of color, too." That's a long way from the pressure of 1960s cover girl Twiggy, who influenced basically white females.

Puberty transforms the female body into a more rounded version, away from the popular ideal of thinness. Almost half of young girls worry about their weight, according to early adolescent specialist, Dr. Andrea Marks. "Instead of worrying about being fat, we wore girdles," she observed. "Our children are growing up in a different era, at age three to four reacting negatively to silhouettes that are too fat. Eleven- and twelve-year-olds are becoming anorexic and bulimic."

Girls Incorporated, a national youth organization, conducted a nationwide survey designed by Louis Harris and Associates, Inc. called "Recasting TV: Girls Views." In the feedback from 2,000 girls and boys (grades three through twelve), model and athlete worship influenced by television watching was clear. When asked to create TV shows, one-third of both boys and girls wrote a scenario in which the twelve-year-old girl grows up to be a celebrity—defined as a model for 19 percent of girls and 16 percent of boys.

The career choice for the character of a twelve-year-old boy? Both girls (28 percent) and boys (27 percent) chose a celebrity, namely a professional athlete in 12 percent of all responses for both genders.

This brings us to an interesting point about boys. They are hardly immune from significant pressure to mirror impossible physical standards. The professional athlete is the male equivalent of the female fashion model, an equal nightmare in terms of measuring up.

Here you have a group with acute anxiety about their looks. Model and athlete envy fan those flames of insecurity. What do they do? Obsess. Diet. You can't escape unnerving statistics about sixth-grade dieters or seventh-grade longings to be thinner. Parents must digest how threatening the issue is to the well-being of this age group.

There has been a dramatic rise in eating disorders in the past twenty-five years. Anorexia nervosa, bulimia, and binge eating all begin during early adolescence, between the ages of twelve and fifteen.

The American Anorexia/Bulimia Association (AABA) warns: 1 percent of teenage girls will develop anorexia. (Ten percent of those will diet themselves to death.) Five percent of college-age women are bulimic, bingeing and purging their bodies. New York Hospital-Cornell Medical Center's Westchester Division's treatment program noted a rise from 4 to 13 percent in male patients from 1983 to 1995. Alana Kaufman, AABA Outreach Director adds, "Statistics can be misleading. They describe only those who fit the exact criteria of eating disorders—specific weight loss or derailed menstruation, and not the many young people with anorexic mentalities heading for trouble."

Eating disorder victims are prone to mood swings, bouts of depression, and low self-esteem. Doesn't that describe your typical preadolescent at least some of the time? Is your daughter watching her weight or ignoring her nutritional needs? Are dieting impulses nothing to be alarmed by or reason to act? Getting a handle on thin thinking versus weight obsession can be confusing. If you suspect your child may be flirting with trouble, watch for the signs listed on the next page.

Danger Signs of an Eating Disorder

Behaviors. Key words here are *obsessions* and *compulsions*. Look for excessive weight loss. Anorexics have an intense fear of being fat and/or gaining weight. Note eating rituals. Moving food around, slicing, even hiding it, red flag victims. Monitor bingeing, fasting, and excessive exercise patterns.

"My sixteen-year-old gymnast daughter has just been diagnosed with the beginnings of anorexia," said one mother. "She was concerned with everything she ate, only eating two bagels a day, going to the gym and working out for hours and then coming home and exercising even longer. She complained of fatigue and was very depressed. When she asked me how someone can make herself throw up, I sought professional help."

Participation in at-risk activities. Certain activities, gymnastics, ballet, or wrestling, are surrounded by an ethos where stringent weight standards, perfectionism, and high achievement prevail. This combination can steer a child over the edge toward an eating disorder.

Family history of illness. If obesity, depression, or substance abuse runs in the family, your child can have a propensity toward eating disorders.

Chronic illness. New evidence suggests chronic illnesses, such as diabetes, asthma, attention deficit disorder, and seizure disorder, make young people more likely than their peers to develop eating disorders. University of Minnesota School of Public Health researchers believe such difficulties damage young people's self-images, making them more vulnerable.

Vegetarian connection. Vegetarian eating is gaining popularity among young people. One in four teens describes being vegetarian as "in," according to Teenage Research Unlimited, a Northbrook, Illinois, trend-tracking company. Even those who wholeheartedly endorse vegetarian diets as healthy warn they can be used by some to disguise an eating disorder.

Eating disorder victims, known for being fixated on the issue of control, are drawn to the structure and rules vegetarian eating offers. It appeals to their rigid, obsessive nature. If your son or daughter stops eating meat, is this a New Age experiment? Or is it a smoke screen obscuring an eating pathology in the making? How do you decide?

Two questions, posed by experts, can help parents distinguish between unhealthy versus healthy motives for embracing this popular, alternative lifestyle.

1. "Is the person willing to eat vegetarian foods that contain fat such as tofu and avocados, or do they rigidly avoid such things?" poses Director Jean Rubel, of Oregon's Anorexia Nervosa and Related Eating Disorders Inc. (ANRED). *Fat* and *rigidly* are the key words here. Vegetarians are not fat-phobic. They don't find substituting meat with substantial choices stressful.
2. "Is the person's diet rigid and socially isolating?" asks Judy Krizmanic, author of *A Teen's Guide to Going Vegetarian*. Watch to see if your eater uses vegetarianism to withdraw from dining situations. Vegetarians are flexible in social situations. They either find veggie fare or make choices. What they don't do is bow out of company or eating.

If you have lingering doubts, don't dismiss them. One junior high school teacher pleads for parental vigilance and warns against dismissing questionable signs.

"I had to send a young girl to the hospital after she had taken an overdose of diet pills," she said. "She admitted to skipping meals and making herself vomit. She had the perception of being too fat (she was by no means fat!) After this, I contacted another mother because I was concerned about several statements her daughter made. She was a tall, thin girl who seemed very upset when she had to be weighed during a routine physical. When I mentioned my findings and questioned her eating habits at home, her mother seemed rather nonchalant and stated, 'She wants to be a model and idolizes Kate Moss.' I repeated my concerns and advised her to keep a watch on the situation."

What Parents Should (and Should Not) Do

If you see the signs of an eating disorder, all experts recommend reaching out to a professional. This is not the kind of problem a parent can fix. Commenting on your child's thinness can be misconstrued as a compliment (encouraging more dieting) or taken as a criticism (wounding an already damaged self-image). Neither threats, bribes, nor begging a child to eat will turn things around. Harping on eating habits or calories consumed only intensifies a power struggle. You as a parent cannot force your child to eat properly or stop her from bingeing or purging.

Instead, discuss your fears with your family doctor, school counselor, or nurse, or call your local mental health center. They can provide you with referrals for treatment options, which usually involve therapy in a variety of settings from groups to inpatient or outpatient care, under the supervision of a specialist in eating disorders.

Sometimes the overweight issue is not a middler's problem, but a parent's wanting a thinner child. Parents are being influenced by a society that is aiming a fat-phobic telescope at children. You can't pick up a magazine without seeing articles titled "How to Fat-Proof Your Youngsters," or "Keeping Your Child Off the Fat Track." Childhood obesity is a national epidemic scream the headlines. One in four American children is fat!

Parents of middlers are told to pay special attention. A 54 percent increase in obesity occurred among six- to eleven-year-olds; 39 percent among twelve- to seventeen-year-olds. (Obesity is defined as a child weighing 20 percent above ideal weight for age, sex, and height.)

The underlying coercion is explained by Michelle Stacey, author of *Consumed,* a history of American attitudes toward food, a magazine columnist and mother of two. In a *New York Times Magazine* piece she wrote, "Aerobicized, high-achieving adults don't want to display fat children. These days fat more than ever suggests sloth, improper eating habits, and a lack of education. Obesity carries a powerful message about social class." But Ms. Stacey continues, "I am more afraid of my daughter's developing an eating disorder than I am of her being fat."

This remark suggests the double bind swirling around weight questions. It seems parents are damned if they watch how much their children eat and damned if they fail to watch! However, if you are worried about your middler being overweight, what course of action is appropriate?

A groundswell of nutritionists, psychologists, adolescent specialists, and doctors are trying to get across a new message. Stop counting calories and start counting push-ups. Diets don't work for adults or children. Dieting mothers and fathers only beget dieting children. Here is a guide for parents of ten- to fifteen-year-olds.

Lifestyle Watching, Not Weight Watching

Check with your medical adolescent specialist first. Weight is a slippery commodity during the middler years. Do you think your son is too chunky? Your daughter too thin? Keep in mind bodies are in the midst of an upward and outward transformation. Get a second opinion.

Be sympathetic. The world in which your middler lives is rigged with risks and temptations. Gone are the 1950s when young people got exercise easily by riding bikes across town to school, or roaming the woods without fear. Our children are kept inside or chauffeured for their own protection. Youngsters of yesteryear snacked simply on potato chips or popcorn. Now endless choices summon: whether to eat Doritos—nacho cheese flavored or cool ranch or taco supreme! Gourmet popcorn varieties are endless. It takes an entire supermarket aisle to stock the snack foods.

Launch a campaign in your household emphasizing what food can do FOR you not TO you. Teach your children about the relationship between food and energy, between food and mood. Middlers are preoccupied with their bodies and very receptive to anything relating to them. Information about how certain foods can diminish symptoms like premenstrual syndrome or fatigue is readily available. Experts say brazil nuts or a glass of grapefruit juice dispel that exhausted feeling. Fruit salad with oranges fights irritability. A tuna salad sandwich combats that feeling-drained sensation. Have your children test out such findings.

Promote healthy eating. Start with breakfast. (Experts say that eating patterns are being established up to approximately age twelve.) Children who skip breakfast, 51 percent, according to a Gallop poll, miss out on nutrients that promote better concentration. Check into school lunch quality. Is your school cafeteria serving fatty burgers or healthy alternatives? Ask the PTA to nutritionally evaluate the menu.

Have dinner together. Ritual family meals may be hard to coordinate for pressed parents and overscheduled middlers, but worth the effort. Mealtime eating discourages grazing, which can evolve into bingeing. Dining together feeds your child's hunger for connection and sustenance, emotional nutrition that is very important to young adolescents who tend to feel lonely and alienated.

Limit fast food. Considering both parents are in the workplace, it's not surprising that America's food dollar is too often spent on fast foods. After a hard day's work, McDonald's seems like a great idea, affording relaxation and a welcome break from cooking. Mom or Dad sharing quality time (if not a quality meal). McDonald's made a great commercial spot out of that fantasy. Does it beat scurrying around the kitchen while the family chants, "When is dinner going to be ready?" Yes! Fast-food excursions are okay, just be selective when you eat out. Opt for healthy broiled items or salads.

Guide, don't police, weight loss. If your child is advised to follow a weight-loss program, don't become the diet police. Dr. Kelly Brown proved too much parental involvement undermines youngsters' efforts. Adolescents *gained* weight if their mothers accompanied them to programs featuring behavior modification focused on learning about nutrition and exercise. They *lost* weight if they attended without their mothers, or when they and their mothers attended separately.

Increase physical activity. Middlers spend too much time in a sedentary state. Television is the Number One culprit. The average adolescent tunes into twenty-two hours of television per week, according to the Carnegie Council. TV-watching peaks at age twelve. Add listening to CDs, playing video games, or punching personal computers. (A complete media survey is coming up in Chapter Eight.) Schedule activity into your child's day. This entails reviewing your family lifestyle. Replace ritual family TV-watching with evening walks or bike rides.

Encourage sports. You say your daughter is simply uninterested or your son is too uncoordinated to play? According to Kenneth H. Cooper, M.D., M.P.H., a nationally recognized leader in fitness and health issues, author of *Kid Fitness: A Complete Shape-Up Program from Birth Through High School,* "Almost every child, even those who may initially appear uncoordinated or unathletic, can become a competent athlete and develop the skills and fitness needed to enjoy a variety of sports." Don't overlook alternatives to competitive and team sports—karate, cross-country skiing, in-line skating.

Sports Smarts for Parents

In the quest to find the right physical activity, what about injury? Sports and sports-mindedness are touted as the greatest lesson a parent can foster in sons and, even more importantly, daughters. Self-esteem, power, equality, teamwork, fitness, and discipline are a few of the assets participating in sports can bequeath. But what about the risks?

Parents want to know: Will heading that soccer ball clear across the field lower my son's IQ? Does my daughter's petite size compared to her larger teammates or gargantuan opponents spell trouble? Is my son being trained too hard? Are growing bones accidents waiting to happen? Does being out of proportion physically put middlers at greater risk?

Concern is legitimate. Each year, 775,000 children under the age of fifteen are treated in hospital emergency rooms in the United States for sports injuries, according to the National Electronic Injury Surveillance System of the U.S. Consumer Product Safety Commission.

Are middlers especially vulnerable? Yes and no. Apparently around the ages of twelve to fourteen, young adolescents do enter a zenith of growing called "peak height velocity," according to Albert Hergenroeder, M.D., chief of Adolescent and Sports Medicine at Texas Children's Hospital and also a board member of the Society of Adolescent Medicine. This is a vulnerable time for injury because growth plates, which are the areas of developing cartilage where bone growth occurs, are weaker. Knees, lower legs, and hips are common areas of complaints. Until growth plates close and growing stops, risk exists.

The good news—growthletes are not vulnerable because they are temporarily out of proportion. Injury rates rise because older children play more complex and competitive games. And for mothers who are leery of their daughters' sports performances, Dr. Hergenroeder notes, "Girls get hurt as often as boys, no more and no less."

Safe Sports Action Strategies for Parents

Susceptibility to injury is no reason to stay away from athletics. To offset liabilities, follow these guidelines:

Teach your daughter sports readiness. Instruct her to be well-rested, well-informed about rules, well-protected with appropriate equipment, clothing, protective guards, and sunscreen, and well-hydrated before and during play.

Select well-matched teams. Teams are traditionally grouped by chronological age. Since middlers grow so unevenly, same-age players can be incompatible teammates, miles apart in skill level, ability, size, and physical maturity. It makes better sense to group athletes by physiological age, height, and weight measures, pre- or post-puberty development and maturity. If your son looks mismatched on a team, look for another one.

Evaluate coaches. Dr. Michael Goldberg, New England Medical Center orthopedics chairman pointed out, "Classroom education is successful because teachers are thoroughly trained in the developmental stages of students. Coaches in community sports programs do not receive the same training. We don't require of coaches what we require of teachers." It's up to parents to oversee coaching regimens. Are coaches grouping teams appropriately? Teaching young athletes conditioning skills such as warming up and stretching? Encouraging playing by rules that are ethical, safe, and positive? Using common sense in matters such as heading the soccer ball (not repeatedly in practice sessions)? If not, speak up.

Listen to physical complaints. Don't pressure a child to play through pain or allow her to continue if injured. The young tend to think they are invincible.

There are no magic words or wands to ease the anxieties and angst that ten- to fifteen-year-olds experience. Young girls and boys have to live through a time of bodily distortions. They have to face down distorted images that appear from outside and inside themselves. You can help them shatter the fun house mirror brigade without giving a thought to years of bad luck. Eventually your child will see a better, healthier reflection in the mirror. It won't happen overnight, but it will happen.

Strategies: Dos and Don'ts for Positive Image Building

- *Don't comment on looks.*
- *Do compliment performance.* A "You're beautiful" will only trigger disbelief. A "Great goal!" or "Well done!" is specific. Such kudos middlers can believe.
- *Don't tease.*
- *Do be sensitive to blossoming bodies.* Joking may ease a parent's discomfort, but at a child's expense.
- *Don't underestimate the power of your weight-phobic example.*
- *Do model physical activity and fit consciousness.*
- *Don't disregard specific appearance issues such as skin breakouts.*
- *Do consult a dermatologist.* Parents who think blemishes and blotches are part of growing up, or a result of not enough face-washing, are living in the Dark Ages. Increased oil production under the skin causes pimples or acne. Treatments ranging from Retin-A to antibiotics can cure problem skin. Middlers of color are prone to keloids, dark blotches caused by overhealing. Avoid over-the-counter bleaching remedies. Opt instead for the dermatologist to prevent permanent scarring. When the American Medical Association polled 1,000 adolescents twelve to eighteen years old, 40 percent were self-conscious, yet only 16 percent sought help.
- *Don't let media images of thinness and beauty go unchallenged.*
- *Do broaden beauty's definition to embrace all sizes, races, and ethnic features.*
- *Don't dodge questions about sexuality or refer them to the other parent.*

- *Do remember boys need information about women; girls about men.*
- *Don't overlook your daughter's negative expressions about herself.*

Do become another kind of mirror into which your child can look without fear. Reflect back visions of love, reassurance, and promise. Since love is blind, perhaps you can blind your middler to the distorted images that go along with growing bodies.

Three

Haunted House

The Emotions and Tensions Your Middler Feels

"I worry about a bad hair day." (Twelve-year-old boy)
"I worry about my mom in heaven."
(Eleven-year-old boy)
(Both worrying in Tennessee)

During young adolescence every child dwells in a haunted house at least some of the time. Worrying about what lies around the bend is part of the experience. Even though their friends are close by, they tiptoe around flanked by paranoia. As middlers walk away from the Mother Country and venture into their New World, the unknown commodity of adulthood is scary. Driven to explore who they are and who they will become, they can't shake the tensions that accompany change and changing. Young adolescents are eager to grow up and apprehensive about the future simultaneously. Being torn between the two worlds of childhood and adulthood is unnerving. Many feel as if they are stumbling around in the dark much of the time. Fending off insecurities can be a full-time job.

In this chapter, we will delve into the psyche of young adolescents and see what kinds of worries swirl around inside their heads. Being a middler isn't easy. How much anxiety, depression, and anger go along with the territory? How does a parent distinguish between normal childhood stress and serious psychological distress? Is there any way to help middlers minimize the fears that haunt them? There are remedies that can be applied to distill young adolescent blues and fortify wounded self-esteem. We all want to help our children cope with the middler ages. Coping—it's a major challenge we and our middlers have in common.

Manic Maniacs

Recently, two psychology professors, David G. Myers of Hope College in Michigan and Ed Diener from the University of Illinois, reviewed two decades worth of happiness studies. These life satisfaction polls were conducted by assorted researchers, ranging from the Gallop Organization to the National Opinion Research Center at the University of Chicago, from *Forbes* magazine to the National Institute on Aging. Despite the differences in the caliber of the research, Myers and Diener discovered some interesting correlations. Neither money nor education, gender, or age gave anyone an edge in attaining contentment. Rich folks, smart ones, young ones, and white males all had the same odds for being satisfied (or dissatisfied) as their poorer, older, less intelligent, and minority contemporaries.

What did surface were four basic traits that happy people typically possess. First, by and large, happy people like themselves. Second, they feel a sense of personal control over their lives. Third, they are optimistic; and finally, fourth, most are extroverts. These findings have profound resonance where young adolescents are concerned. When you gauge these characteristics against standard young adolescent culture, it's not surprising that the middler years are not record-breaking in terms of life satisfaction.

Most young adolescent boys and girls don't like themselves much of the time. With little control over their lives, feelings of powerlessness are the status quo. That's already two strikes against them. Although these middlers could be stereotyped accurately as budding extroverts, their friendships are hardly restorative and emotionally rewarding on a regular basis. The only good news here is that many middlers are optimistic, but that upbeat mentality has a tendency to bottom out with roller-coaster regularity.

Does this mean that all young adolescents are destined to drag their feet through a bleak world until the later teen years? No, not necessarily *all* young adolescents and certainly *not all of the time.* But it is perfectly normal for young boys and girls to spend considerable time sulking in their rooms or grouching through the week.

The truth is that middlers are like manic-depressives en masse, Supermiddler one minute and a basket case the next. They alternate between periods of excitement, even euphoria and periods of worry.

Think about their collective experience. Young adolescence is an era of high points. There's that "home alone" freedom, the first kiss, the first love. Your son rides the crest of scoring the winning goal, this time all the more sweet because of peer adulation. Your daughter experiences the altruistic glow that comes from helping others during her Feed the Hungry drive. He wins the election for class president. She aces a perfect score with her clarinet in the music competition. Creativity, idealism, romance, leadership—middlers are entering a thrilling time.

At the other end of the development spectrum, there are huge disappointments that cut to the quick. Young adolescents disappoint themselves and each other. Girls and boys realize they are not as beautiful physically as they'd like to be. Betrayals by best friends are devastating. As are romantic rejections, which break the hearts of both genders.

Middlers have higher powers of analysis and as they comprehend the world and the people in it, what they see can be depressing. Problems that have no simple solutions, and flaws with no easy fixes. For the first time it hits home that the world is a complicated, hurtful, and dangerous place as well as one pregnant with possibility. Chances are your sons and daughters will feel elation and despair and get to know each intimately.

Both faces were evident in our survey. The remarks we received sketched the "schizophrenic" nature of this population, exhibiting extremes of emotion and self-image. Their bright side was **Invincible.** "The best part of being my age is I am in the prime of my youth," crowed a thirteen-year-old boy from Iowa. **Optimistic.** "When I look in the mirror I see a content, independent young woman with bright hope and brighter dreams," mused a fourteen-year-old Washingtonian. **Confident.** "I see big blue eyes and a winner!" A winning persona was attested to by countless kids from Iowa clear across to the Hawaiian Islands. **Happy,** despite the odds. "When I look in the mirror, I see a happy person," claimed a New Mexico eighth-grader.

Their dark side was **Despondent.** "I see someone who is very depressed, someone who is very self-conscious," revealed a Minnesota fourteen-year-old girl. **Angry.** "If I could do one thing I'm not allowed to do it would be to kill somebody," growled a Midwestern thirteen-year-old. **Hopeless.** "If I could change one thing in my life, I would never go home," swore a fourteen-year-old stepchild.

Can children be divided into "the haves and the have nots" in terms of sound, staid mental health? Of course there are some young adolescents who definitely have severe problems. (We'll get to them in a few moments.) However, it's normal for most middlers to vascillate and this means many spend time fretting, mooning, fuming, or licking wounds.

Oftentimes the reactions of rage, impatience, humiliation are out of proportion to the event that triggered the emotion. For example, your daughter storms in muttering, "This has been the worst day of my life!" Why? She found out she can't take French next year, her favorite NHL hockey team lost the play-offs, and to top things off her nose looks like the Rocky Mountains! This may be tough, but hardly as serious as she makes it out to be. But then again you're not a middler. Your son may be in a deep funk locked in his room. Over what? He won't tell you, but next morning the sunny side of his disposition has returned. He's all psyched up because tryouts for the basketball team are scheduled for today, and he's a sure thing.

Natural Worrywarts

What's behind the emotional exaggerations and mood swings? The dark side of the psychic pendulum reflects worry. Obsessing is a middler pastime. Pennsylvania State University researchers chronologically pinpointed the onset of worrying. After reading stories to youngsters and asking them to postulate about the worries of the fictional characters, they noticed that around the age of eight, children began spinning elaborate tales of worry. Apparently this birth of fretting coincides with two developments: children's awareness of a world around them and a lessening of the egocentrism of early childhood.

Once a child is capable of calculating anxieties, how much worrying occurs? A landmark study of seven- to twelve-year-olds revealed that children had, on average, eight items on their worry agenda. The concerns of these otherwise psychologically healthy youngsters were so redundant and commonplace that the psychologists concluded fretting was perfectly normal.

The faces of worry look different as a child grows. Being afraid of the dark is typical of three-year-olds. Ghosts, witches, and supernatural beings scare the living daylights out of six-year-olds. Middlers have their own particular host of worries, ranging from the ridiculous to the sublime.

"Having a bad hair day," the dread quoted at the start of this chapter may seem superfluous, unless you happen to be fourteen and fixated on your appearance. Losing a parent, however, which no doubt prompted the concern about "Mom in heaven" illustrates the other, serious end of the distress meter. Middlers have both kinds of fears, mundane as well as profound.

You may not hear them spoken aloud. A New Jersey mother expounds, "I would have to say that my children (aged ten and fourteen) don't express their fear outright. I think children feel they are invincible at the beginning of adolescence and that nothing can happen to them. As they mature, their fears materialize. I think they express their apprehension in different ways, such as not wanting to do an activity because it's *boring* when in reality they are afraid of failing."

To familiarize you with the Richter scale of anxieties lurking inside your middler, we've assembled this list of classic worries culled from research and surveys done on this age group.

1. *Social anxiety.* "I worry about everybody hating me." (Fourteen-year-old girl from Minnesota)

   Peers are central to your young adolescent. Because feeling the crowd's approval is so important to a middler's sense of self, most worry endlessly about what others think of them. Experts even have a name for this syndrome: social anxiety. The majority of teachers (71 percent) we polled agreed students spend most of their time worrying about their peers and being popular.

   At the root of this "what-others-think" phobia is, oddly enough, the emergence of conscience. Until a child reaches the age of ten, conscience is not completely formed. Once the struggle to decipher right and wrong is fine-tuned, the ability to judge comes to the forefront. As middlers learn to judge, the process, in a sense, backfires and ricochets. They worry about being judged by others. And they judge themselves rather harshly, too. The fear of ridicule, standing out, embarrassment, and being shunned are just a few variations on social anxiety.

To escape these horrid fates, many young adolescents try desperately to look and act like one another. They avoid doing anything that will draw attention to themselves. Walking on eggshells, being tentative about each and every step, is the middler gait.

2. *A parent dying.* "I worry about my parents getting killed or sick; about there being a fire in the house or a burglar." (Thirteen-year-old girl from Oregon)

In a survey of 8,000 young adolescents, a whopping 47 percent confessed to this worry, which was reported in *The Quicksilver Years—The Hopes and Fears of Early Adolescence,* by Peter Benson, Dorothy Williams, and Arthur Johnson.

A parent dying is the Number 1 most traumatic life experience, according to the Adolescent Life-Change Event Scale. The scale measures the stress attributed to happenings in the life of adolescents. For example, a brother or sister dying is Number 2 in terms of emotional reverberations, while having someone new (such as a grandparent or an adopted brother or sister) move into your family registers a comparative Number 26.

As young adolescents start venturing into hypothetical thinking, it's their destiny to fantasize their worst nightmare: losing a parent. A middler's life is still very much dominated by parents. When every day at school resembles a gauntlet of cruelty and derision, young adolescents need parents as the ultimate sanctuary. It is that unconditional love upon which young adolescents rely (even if it's not always obvious). Just the thought of losing it is terrifying.

3. *Divorce.* "I'm afraid my parents might get a divorce." (Twelve-year-old girl from Tennessee)

Surely you've run into this: You and your spouse have had a tiff or a loud argument. Later your middler sheepishly inquires: "Are you and Daddy going to get a divorce?" Reassure your child. Explain that all adults get into arguments occasionally but no, it doesn't signal that a divorce is imminent. If divorce is a possibility, now is the time to face the music. Confess that your marriage is not as stable as it once was, but point out that it is a problem between spouses and your child is not responsible for the tension.

You have to look at the world from the vantage point of a middler. All around them they see divorce. Families are here today, gone tomorrow. Half of all first marriages and 65 percent of second marriages fail. Every middler knows at least one child of divorce and they all know it's no picnic. Their paranoia is not unreasonable given the society in which we live. When we were their age, "homeless" and "single parent" weren't in the vernacular. In the heat or aftermath of parental squabbles, it's inevitable that a middler considers: "If it happens to all those other kids, it could happen to me!"

4. *School.* "I worry about not being able to pass computer technology. I worry am I cool enough, am I going to get beat up. Will I get good grades?" (Twelve-year-old boy from South Carolina)

Tests in school, academic performance, and too much homework—these are the immediate traumas with which most middlers grapple. School is their life. When we discuss in detail how to help your middler succeed later, you will be equipped to turn down that worry meter.

5. *Bodily injury.* "I worry about being mugged or jumped." (Seventh-grade boy from Iowa) "The advice I would give to a close friend about sex is have sex with virgins. You do not have to worry about diseases and stuff." (Fifteen-year-old boy from Kentucky) "I worry about waking up dead." (Fourteen-year-old boy from Hawaii)

Getting hurt or sick is a major preoccupation with middlers. They are a hypochondriacal lot. This is due to their heightened body consciousness during the growth spurt.

KidsPeace, a children's advocacy group, polled 1,000 ten- to thirteen-year-olds and found 47 percent worried about contracting AIDS, getting kidnapped, being physically or sexually abused, and becoming involved with drugs and alcohol. A contributing factor to this array of fears must be the violence young people see all around them and among them. Headlines replay in their minds when they are holed up in their rooms.

In a world where arrest rates for violent crimes committed by juveniles (ages ten to seventeen) doubled in just five years, it's not a bad idea that today's young are wary. Especially since the majority of these crimes occur between 3:00 P.M. and 6:00 P.M., right after school. And sad to say, too many have to fear being injured at home. Child abuse is our national scandal. Factor in bizarre tragedies such as the explosion of the Challenger space shuttle and the death toll on our nation's highways, terrorist bombings in Oklahoma City and at the World Trade Center. Add weather-related flukes such as hurricanes and tornadoes. This plateful of potential disaster would put fear into anyone.

This age group is known to devour horror stories (R. L. Stine owes his fortune to them) and endlessly watch macabre movies. It's their way of trying to tame all the terror and horror that they have begun to realize exists out there.

6. *The future.* "I worry about what's going to happen later in life." (Twelve-year-old girl from Oklahoma) "I worry about lots of things: Are my grades good enough for college? When I grow up am I gonna get a good job?" (Eighth-grade girl from Michigan)

Even at the young end of adolescence, children worry about finding their place in the world. Our survey mirrored a larger study. When Nickelodeon teamed up with the renowned polling firm Yankelovich and quizzed children ages nine to eleven, 67 percent worried about getting a good job. That's up five percentage points in two years. Who's anxious about the need to make enough money? Sixty-two percent. Afraid of not getting into college? Fifty-nine percent. Childhood stress should be an oxymoron, but it's not. Today's middlers seem to have inherited their parents' job-related insecurities and pessimism.

7. *Gender woes.* "When I look in the mirror I see confusion." (Fourteen-year-old girl from Washington)

During the middler years girls experience a confidence gap. Candid and upbeat eleven-year-olds deteriorate emotionally into doubt-ridden and insecure thirteen- and fourteen-year-olds. Girls enter puberty earlier than boys, and therefore confront (and chafe at) issues of attractiveness and popularity sooner. Several excellent books have recently delved into just why young girls are so susceptible to depression and anxiety, which propel many into eating disorders, self-mutilation, out-and-out rebellion against parents, and therapy.

The reason: they come face-to-face with our culture's discrimination and misogyny. At a Yankees baseball game, a twelve-year-old female athlete seriously wants to know, "Why aren't there any women on pro baseball teams?" Our educational system is only now putting women into the history books. Madam Curie and Florence Nightingale finally have company. Society sends confusing signals to daughters. Be smart but not intimidating. Be sexy but be careful. Be beautiful or else! Diet. Get plastic surgery for a smaller nose and bigger breasts.

Is it any wonder female middlers have a self-esteem complex and crisis? A young adolescent girl is charged with defining herself. The ingredients given to her to work with—inferiority, physical perfection, thinness, compliance—do not help her draw a cheerful picture. In her resonant bestseller, *Reviving Ophelia: Saving the Selves of Adolescent Girls,* Nebraska therapist Mary Pipher, Ph.D. (who has specialized in treating troubled female adolescents) says even healthy girls have only four ways to react to the stultifying "junk" culture: "to conform, withdraw, be depressed, or get angry." Not much of a choice and good reason to be anxious.

Many middler girls are afraid to grow up. They cower before media images. The majority tremble at the thought of not measuring up. They worry they will never be lovable. They break under the pressure, sell themselves short, or sell out their quirky traits or unpopular characteristics. For a few years, being a girl seems to be a no-win situation and it's downright troubling, even devastating.

8. *Racial inequality.* It's heartening to hear that one major survey found that among nine- to thirteen-year-olds, 71 percent said they have close friends of a different race or ethnic origin. But the disheartening truth is that racism is still very much alive, even escalating. Adolescent Skinheads spread resurgent Nazi hate hype. Police investigate vandalism written in racist graffiti. On the streets, playgrounds, and the television set, middlers hear the epithets and see the prejudice.

Middlers of color are growing up and discovering a world that still discriminates against minorities. They (and the adults who cannot protect them) must deal with what Joel Feiner, M.D., author of *Taming Monsters, Slaying Dragons* calls "mini-insults"—being passed over by taxi drivers who favor white passengers, watching people move back when they enter a line. Minorities bear the burden of added, legitimate fears: Will they be mistaken for criminals haphazardly just because of their nonwhite skin? Not only will they be questioned, but will they be beaten by police?

Equality may be in the Constitution and equal opportunity may be the law, but inequality often rules. Given the racist ways of our world, parents of color have a poignant task ahead as they try to reassure their children that they are indeed equal and worthy. Prejudice is equally as dangerous as discrimination to the self-image of young people of color. Dr. Feiner warns, "Racism, like a constant low-grade fever, is a stress intensifier, boosting the effect of other stresses—it makes everything worse." Middlers of color feel this added burden.

When Anxiety Turns Deadly

Certainly there are more scary scenarios besides these, such as a parent losing his job. To major traumas add minor, ordinary hurdles, such as trying out for the basketball team, that send many a middler into quaking. Once children leave behind the simplicity of childhood, they have to face all the demons of impending adulthood. Middlers have no shortage of anxiety-producing possibilities. It almost makes one glad to be middle-aged.

Your role as a parent, first of all, is to assess accurately your middler's psychological health. Make sure that your middler's fears and anxieties are normal as opposed to life-threatening. Once you understand the difference, you can opt for a course of action to help.

What Does Serious Psychological Distress Look Like?

Our survey introduced us to a sad case. At fourteen this young girl described herself as "very depressed." She droned on in her own words, painting a severely unhappy portrait: "My parents and I never have fun times. I never trust them. They nag me about everything. They say I'm stupid and don't know anything. I smoke and I'm a klepto. I was jumped and almost raped. I don't ever really do my homework. I don't tell anyone what happens to me because no one really takes the time to listen to me because they are stuck on themselves. Do I get enough time with my parents? NO."

Despondent, acting out, isolated, lonely, angry—this middler is on the road to personal disaster. She is not in a "funk." She is an example of adolescent depression, a serious mental illness. Experts estimate from three to six million children may suffer from clinical depression. Like their adult counterparts, depressed children are less likely to report depression (compared to other illnesses) and less inclined to go to a doctor and get help.

According to Myrna Weissman, an epidemiologist at New York State Psychiatric Institute in Manhattan, childhood depression is definitely a harbinger of doom. Weissman tracked down 159 of 204 people who were diagnosed with depressive disorders, whom she studied when they were between the ages of ten and thirteen. Nearly 5 percent had taken their own lives during the decade after diagnosis. An additional 30 percent had attempted suicide during that period. Her pioneering findings underscore the severity of adolescent depression and suggest that young people are not getting the treatment that is obviously needed.

Suicides among middlers ages ten to fourteen have skyrocketed, up 120 percent, according to the Federal Centers for Disease Control. And for every completed suicide there are 100 to 200 attempts, estimates the National Committee on Youth Suicide Prevention. It's vital to understand the causes and the symptoms.

Experts believe *both* genetics and environmental factors are likely to contribute. If a parent suffers from extreme melancholy, a child is three times more likely to experience it, too. Situations ranging from dysfunctional families, loss of a parent (whether from death or divorce), physical or sexual abuse, chronic illness, drug and alcohol involvement, and some medications can also play a major causative role.

If you suspect that your child is more than *down,* there are concrete events that can bring on depression. Take a look at your family situation. Have you moved? Are you recently separated, divorced, remarried? Scan the details of her life. Is she starting a new school? Has she recently been heartbroken? Lost a relative or a pet? Consider the traumas with which he might be wrestling. Has your son been ostracized by his friends, cut from the team? Could there be a question of sexual orientation? Homosexual leanings can bring on confusion, guilt, and depression. Gay and lesbian youth account for 30 percent of youth suicides.

After you've scrutinized any events that might lead to his dilemma, look for the following telltale patterns. Specific behaviors are warning signs:

• *An inability to sleep or the other extreme.* All your child does is sleep. She appears chronically listless.

• *No interest in friends, school, activities.* He is downright apathetic across the board and has been for months.

• *Marked changes.* You have thought more than once that *she's not the child she used to be!* Changes can be evident in grades. She is restless and incapable of concentrating. Or in eating habits. She is not eating or is bingeing excessively.

• *Risky behavior business.* You suspect he's experimenting with drugs or alcohol. You worry about sexual promiscuity because she's dressing too provocatively or out late too often with that boyfriend you don't like.

• *Rebellion directed toward parents or teachers.* He may be uncharacteristically aggressive. She may run away (thirteen years of age is the most common for runaways) or be truant repeatedly.

• *Death or suicide themes.* These can surface in writing or in a preoccupation with morose song lyrics or poetry.

If you recognize these, take your middler's emotional temperature. If numbness, feelings of hopelessness and helplessness, indecisiveness, exaggerated hypochondria, and self-destructive inclinations are highly visible, it's time to talk to your middler. If he denies that there's anything wrong with his frame of mind, if she refuses to see anything odd in her actions, these "denials" are added indicators of distress. Consult with your family physician, the school social worker, or a therapist.

If you see any of the next red flag danger signals, DON'T DELAY.

You hear your child make references to suicide. Or someone tells you that your child has been talking like this. Such expressions can be direct as in "I feel like killing myself," or they can be indirect as in "The world would be better off without me." Young adolescents on the verge of self-destruction give tip-offs or "cries for help." For example, they give away prized possessions. Or they romanticize celebrity suicides such as that of Nirvana pop star Kurt Cobain. They suddenly make peace with former antagonists be they friends or family members. Some even pay debts and write wills. And ironically, intentional suicide planners often seem happier just prior to attempting to take their own lives, feeling calmer knowing the end to all this misery is in sight.

If we sound alarming, it is because adolescent depression has been too easily overlooked until it's too late. Every thirty-two seconds a young adolescent attempts suicide, more girls than boys, although the boys have a higher rate of accomplishing the act. A third of suicides happen one hour before school, during school, or one hour after school. The children who made up those skyrocketing statistics were suffering from excruciating psychological pain. The landscape of their inner lives was like a desert, devoid of the survival commodities of intimacy, hope, and security. Each of these young adolescents had a problem or a crisis for which a solution could not be found. Suicide is never random or without a purpose.

Middlers are under the influence of exaggerated emotions. A broken heart, a failed class, being the new student in school—from your adult point of view these certainly don't warrant self-annihilation. These problems are only temporary. But don't forget many middlers are still immature, imprisoned in a "now mentality." Their coping mechanisms are evolving. Sometimes that evolution is not soon enough to quell the turmoil in their psyches or to put their trials and tribulations into proper perspective. Sometimes all the other options are invisible and the long view is out of sight. Sometimes all a middler sees is a nobody going nowhere with only misery for company.

"The best part about being my age? Nothing," confided a Minnesota eighth-grade girl. Would her answers be whispered or snarled? we wondered as we read on. She continued, "When I look in the mirror I see a nobody. I see someone who is going to run away. If I could change one thing, I would not ever go home again. I never tell my parents anything. My parents nag me about everything. Nothing I do is right . . . ever. Do I play sports? No. How much TV do I watch? None. Do I read magazines? No. What's my homework routine? I don't do any. What's been a fun time with my family? Nothing. Do I trust my parents? Hell no!"

This fourteen-year-old is screaming with her apathy and her anger, with her absence of happiness and fantasies of running away.

Your vigilance and instincts can be the saving grace. Eighty percent of suicidal people give clear clues as if they are saying, "Help. Please rescue me!" It's better to jump the gun and investigate depressive tendencies than to rationalize away serious symptoms that can lead (and have in record numbers) to tragic gunfire. Depression is a treatable disease. A combination of medications and psychotherapy cures 80 percent of victims. Never discount your intuition.

Stress-Proofing and Anxiety-Busting Remedies

We can hear your sigh of relief (your middler is not going off the deep end). Your child's overall behavior does not read like a warning label. You know your fear about him being a misfit, a dropout, or a malcontent is just your midnight imagination gone berserk. Your malaise about her being a wallflower, a closet Lolita, or a perennial angry young woman is not grounded in fact. You are just living with the run-of-the-mill occasionally cantankerous, periodically combustible middler.

So how do you deal with that? How do you convince a son that what he is feeling and experiencing is not the end of the world? What can we feed our daughters to supplement the sabotaging diet from the world around them? Are there provisions to make and skills to teach to keep our young adolescents on a more even keel?

The fundamental ingredient to raising a stable young adolescent is your unconditional love. Only your affection can convince your child that he is indeed lovable. It is the most potent antidote to ameliorate your son's worries and your daughters deep self-doubts.

Strong family ties (and these can be effective in single parent, blended, as well as traditional families) are the anchor and the wings that middlers require to help them survive the pitfalls of their youth culture and develop the moral values and work ethic required to become worthwhile and productive adults. As the mother, father, stepparent, or legal guardian of a young adolescent, you must give the sense of security he craves and the essential hopes he needs to feed upon. Without emotional sustenance middlers get lost. The vacuum created by neglect will be filled with drugs or alcohol, delinquency, or promiscuity. On that all the experts and statistics concur.

Aside from your love, middlers benefit from guidance. With the consciousness of those happy people as our guide, here are ways to cultivate those winning dispositions in your child.

Help your middler learn to like himself more. You can begin by engineering a transition from self-conscious to self-confident. All middlers are ultrasensitive worrywarts. Not being comfortable or thrilled with oneself is a middler state of mind. Yet most are capable of feeling better about themselves and acquiring a more complimentary frame of mind.

Too often we erroneously think of self-confidence as a personality trait. In reality, it is a skill and, therefore, can be improved upon. "Think of it like shooting a basketball hoop," say middle school students in a curriculum to which they contributed entitled "Changes" by Henry Vincenzi, Ed.D. With practice, according to these young trainers, a better sense of self can be built with one shot of praise at a time.

You certainly can adapt this middler-to-middler advice. Remind your child of all the things he does well. Encourage her to think well of herself. Make him speak admirably about himself (although do explain when he veers into the obnoxious zone). Emphasize that developing a better self-image is hard in the face of failure or mistakes. It will take an added push occasionally, but feeling good when you look in the mirror is worth the extra effort.

Nurture your daughter toward positive self-determination. Girls' self-esteem goes into a free fall during the middler years. We can't enclose our daughters in a hothouse untainted by the media. We can't burn every fashion magazine or every fashion model at the stake. And we don't know how to circumvent this self-image crisis yet. What we can do is shore up our girls ahead of time.

Charol Shakeshaft, a Hofstra University researcher on adolescent self-esteem, learned that if girls already had positive definitions of womanhood in their psychological repertoire, their self-esteem plummeted less during young adolescence and rebounded faster. Seeing women as powerful, as decision-makers, and not as incidental was the key. Shakeshaft insists, "Earning power had little bearing. A six-figure-salaried lawyer Mom who says, *'Wait till your father gets home'* or *'Don't upset your father tonight'* is still delivering a potent message that men are more important and more worthy of deference." Single mothers, because they exclusively run households, were more likely to engender positive images.

So watch for subtle behaviors within the family that cater to Dad and buckle under to his likes, dislikes, and decisions. If Dad picks out the car you drive, the vacation you take, and if his moods rule the roost, while Mom is left selecting the brand of detergent you buy, no girl in her right mind wouldn't be depressed about joining the ranks of the unimportant, unworthy, and unpowerful.

Although this may seem elementary, talk to your daughter about discrimination. Teach her to ferret out sexism. Let her know that she has the intelligence to recognize antifemale maneuvers and the power to change things just as women have in the last few decades. Then whenever she is made to feel worth *less* than a man and powerless, she will have a well-rehearsed explanation and plan of action, if not an instant redress. She will be less likely to take the diminishing words personally and suffer internal damage to her self-esteem.

Teach your middler how to acquire control over life. Take charge over your personal demons. If you have a personal problem (alcohol, ADD, depression, etc.), get help from a support group or a therapist.

Our children need to realize that failures and weaknesses are human. And they can be reversed. What raises the standard of humanity is facing a problem, asking for support, and overcoming it. Hopefully, your young adolescent will never have to stare down these demons. But just in case, you will have given a blueprint for self-improvement and the message that we are all works-in-progress bent on getting better with age.

Be a stress-busting example. The way you defuse your own stress is one of those lessons middlers are absorbing whether or not you are conscious of it. Do you wind down with a cocktail or by weeding the garden, taking a hot bath or a cup of herbal tea? Take note of the stress-reducing regimens in your home. Explain these rituals to your child. Have your middler develop a relaxation ritual. Emphasize how important recreation and relaxation are in our hectic world.

Steer your middler into rewarding relationships. No parent can insulate a middler from the popularity wars. Your middler's relationship with peers is a rough-and-tumble social initiation. However, you can make those social hurdles less emotionally crushing by directing your natural extrovert into other venues for social companionship.

Choreograph a mentor-protégé coupling around a hobby or a skill your child is excited by or excels in. One mother zeroed in on a marine biology professor at the local college because her daughter has a love affair with sharks dating back to second grade. She encouraged her daughter to solicit help from this "shark expert" for a science project. The collaboration evolved into a pen pal rapport. The sixth-grader was invited subsequently to tour the university science department.

You can assist your middler in contacting local authors if he's literary, home team pro athletes if she's a soccer star, research scientists if he's a science buff, or horticultural experts at a nearby arboretum if she's environmentally oriented. Music lessons can pair your middler with a "talent guide." It depends on what interest your middler shows. Whether it's art, music, hockey, or computers, you can locate a professional who will encourage your middler and serve as a role model of accomplishment.

Such mentor-protégé pairings validate a middler's intellect, athletic ability, or creativity. This kind of socializing builds different parts of a child's identity as an artist or a violinist, sectors separate from the usual definitions by peers, fashion magazines, or other media.

Extracurricular activities provide alternative companions and images of self. Sports remain one of the best choices, especially for girls. Athletes look at their bodies as able, even powerful. This is an invaluable switch from the mirror, which is consulted to decide "Am I pretty enough? Thin enough? Tall enough?" Being part of a team builds self-esteem. The team accepts you for how much effort you contribute, not how you look or how popular you happen to be.

It can be a soccer team, a French club, a yearbook committee that your middler joins. What counts is that he's socializing around an idea, a goal, or an endeavor that is larger than himself. These friendships have a purpose other than crowd approval or best-friends' loyalties. Such motives make them safe, productive, and fun.

Turn your pessimist into an optimist. Middlers hate taking the blame for anything. Who forgot to pick up the bath towel? Write down the phone message? "Not me," says your child. "It's not my fault," is a middler mantra.

So it's paradoxical that middlers are so quick to think the worst about themselves. They figure that the worst things in life are around the corner, from their parents' divorce to flunking Friday's quiz. When something goes awry, young adolescents label themselves "dumb" because they failed a test, "ugly" because their face sprouts blemishes, or "hopeless" because they miss one shot on the basketball court. This pessimism can tattoo stupidity, unattractiveness, or lack of coordination on a middler's psyche, unless a parent steps in to dismiss these unwarranted labels.

Share with your child what you are learning about middler development. For example, how a bad math grade may suggest a learning plateau, how feeling ugly is typical but irrational.

Give them training in optimism, which is a way of looking at life. It entails resilience, not seeing bad things as permanent, and hope, because the future can be controlled. Psychologist Martin Seligman, author of *Learned Optimism* and *The Optimistic Child*, believes parents can guide their children with "optimistic criticism." Point out what's wrong in specific and changeable (fixable) terms as in "You tease your sister too much" not "You're a terrible brother." This gives middlers ways to improve (stop teasing) their behavior.

Pessimism stems from an inability to take the long view. Stuck in "the now," young adolescents are not inclined to think ahead. Mistakes and shortcomings are miscalculated as final judgments. Prod your middler into the realm of next week, or next month, and its possibilities. Teach perseverance. For instance, by setting up a basketball practice routine, you can show your son he can improve his scoring ratio. With regular medication, your daughter can improve complexion problems. Optimism and self-esteem can be achieved by trying, accomplishing (and even failing) over time.

Cushioning the Blow of Divorce

Sometimes the bottom falls out of life and putting all the pieces together is not so simple. Divorce is one such event. Divorce is not the scandal it was in the 1950s. However, because it has become commonplace, don't assume it is not devastating.

Child psychologists tell us that from a child's vantage point divorce can be even more harrowing than death. When someone dies, there is structure in funerals and closure at gravesides. Mourning is appropriate. Relatives gather to bolster one another. Feelings of anger and abandonment are fixed at the time of death and so the healing process can begin.

Contrast these facts with the dissolution of a marriage. Divorce has no structure. The family (as the child has come to know it) is gone, replaced by artificial visitation that often has to be hammered out. During divorce proceedings the extended family is rarely unified and supportive, more likely divided and derogatory. To whom can a child express feelings of mourning? Chances are neither parent is disposed to handle such confessions dispassionately given the turbulent passage each is navigating.

The young adolescent feels plunged into a stew of raw emotions, divided loyalties, and fiscal hardships. It's no stretch of the imagination to see why many children of divorce rise to the surface just plain "pissed off" that this is happening to them!

There is no one single closure for children as there is for the spouse who signs the divorce decree. More than likely, there is a succession of new adjustments: new house, new financial constraints, new school and new friends, new love interests for Mom and Dad, and perhaps a blended family complete with stepparents and stepbrothers and step-sisters. Just the relationship implications of all this can tip the middler Richter scale to earthquake proportions.

"The single greatest challenge in teaching this age group is my wishing I could 'fix' their home situations," said a seventh-grade teacher from Kentucky.

Young adolescents have particular "Achilles' heels," developmentally speaking, which complicate coping with family dissolutions. Psychologically they are in a process of rethinking how they see themselves and trying to define their place in the world. When one's family (one's world) is coming apart at the seams, changing becomes a more harrowing task.

Middlers, looking to family for an oasis from social whirlwinds, find the prospect and aftermath of divorce horrifying. At a time in life when young adolescents desperately value a sense of belonging, having a fractured family is the worst scenario. Charged with learning to comprehend and control their new sexual and aggressive impulses, young adolescents are scared about losing the family structure complete with its checks and balances. When they are at a peak of feeling powerless, watching the family disintegrate exacerbates that out-of-control sensation. Middlers, who often see the world in black and white, have a stark myopic viewpoint that prevents them from understanding the complex motives and culpabilities of each parent in the coming-apart dance. They can easily get caught up in taking sides and become furious at the initiator of the split, according to Judith Waller-stein, divorce expert and author of *Second Chances: Men, Women & Children a Decade After Divorce*. Dr. Wallerstein cautions, nine- to twelve-year-olds can begin to "parent" the needy divorcing spouse, taking on adult tasks of caring, reassuring, and becoming drained emotionally in the role-switching process.

As if one divorce wasn't traumatic enough, many children experience more than one. Approximately 15 percent of children will encounter their parents' serial monogamy—see their divorced parents remarry and redivorce before they reach the age of eighteen. It's a revolving door of stepparents and live-in lovers. Stepsibling attachments are forced on them, adjusted to only to be disrupted again. When researchers compared children of single marital breakups to the multiple variety, they found that more family disruptions equated to higher levels of anxiety and depression, worse academic records, and poorer odds for stable marriages in the future. Why? These players in musical families wrestle with feelings of distrust and betrayal, not to mention all the instability with which they have to contend.

Minimize the stress of divorce with these guidelines. Keep your anger with your ex-spouse out of your child's earshot. When court proceedings pit Mom against Dad, children get caught in emotional crossfire. Arrange your child's life during and after the divorce to ensure access to both parents. Don't use daughters as ammunition, sons as messengers. Amicable rapport is beneficial for adults, too. Studies show remarried partners who felt friendly toward ex-spouses were happier than those who held onto bitterness and hostility.

According to Constance Ahrons, Ph.D., associate director of the Marriage and Family Therapy Program at the University of Southern California, the way society views the institution of divorce and "broken" families smacks of a new prejudice—"divorcism." Dr. Ahrons insists we only hear about the negatives. For example, longitudinal studies by Dr. Judith Wallerstein, which follow divorced families, report: a decade after divorce approximately 41 percent of children still bear the scars. (14 percent had uneven adjustments that defied categorizing). However, we overlook the fact that 45 percent do *not* inherit psychic pathology.

Human beings are resilient. Divorced spouses in surveys long to be on better terms with their exes. All would like relationships that include catch-up chats about old friends and "what's new" rapports.

Ahrons wants to revolutionize how we see and talk about postdivorce families. In her book *The Good Divorce: Keeping Your Family Together When Your Marriage Comes Apart,* she replaces "single parent" family with a new definition: "binuclear," which reflects kinship with both mother and father.

The sense of family is the lubricant that can ameliorate the wounds of divorce for not only middlers, but children of all ages. Whenever possible, maintain the continuity and network of relatives, friends, and neighbors. An alarming 40 percent of high school dropouts were adolescents in families of divorce who moved, and in the process, lost the invaluable ties to friends, teachers, and neighbors.

Single parents (one-half of that new "binuclear" group) are legion, over twelve million families headed by a mother or father, with single fathers now accounting for three million. Look to augment your life with all the help and advice now geared to assist you. (Try reading *Growing Up with a Single Parent: What Hurts, What Helps* by Sara McLanahan, a leading divorce researcher at Princeton University. Raising a family and working full-time, not to mention trying to squeeze in a social life, can be overwhelming. When your time is at a premium, a middler can get lost in the shuffle because a young adolescent is "old enough to take care of himself." Remember your middler is still young enough to need you.

Stepfamilies or blended ones are another chapter of stress as far as many young adolescents are concerned. A fourteen-year-old female Minnesota middler says "Life—i.e., being in a stepfamily is not fair!" In her own words her stepfamily includes, "a bitchy Stepmom, an asshole dad, a queer sister, and an asswipe brother." These stepsiblings make her life more difficult because "they take after their mother!" Similar sentiments are echoed from another boy the same age, also in a stepfamily, who puts "moving out of my house" as the one thing he would most like to do. Many stepfamilies have anger and resentment wallpapering the rooms.

However, family anatomy is not destiny, according to James H. Bray, Texas clinical psychologist and associate professor at Baylor College of Medicine, who has done the first long-term analysis of stepfamilies. There are adjustments and turbulence, but after one to two years he found that most stepfamilies become working, functioning networks with well-adjusted members.

The one snag in this evolution featured middlers. Dr. Bray said,

"There is a reemergence of behavior problems among children from eleven on up, even when they've been in a trouble-free stepfamily situation for five or more years. Both genders are vulnerable." Dealing with identity issues seems to rock their psychic boats. Some wrestle with unresolved questions about why their parents divorced. A good number want more contact with the nonresidential parent.

Dr. Bray advises, "Biological parents, from early on through this period, should take the primary disciplinary role. Stepparents should take a supportive stance, a kind of indirect parenting."

An Alabama seventh-grade teacher lamented that parents—all kinds—are not well-informed about what is happening in their children's lives academically and socially. "I believe that many parents are so concerned about 'having a life' that they are not staying in touch with their own children." All parents should keep her words of warning in mind.

If middlers are destined to "do time" in the Haunted House, in a way it's an apprenticeship for adulthood. Everyone meets up with comedy and tragedy. Facing fears, staring down worry, knowing when to reach for help, these are workouts that will come in handy forever. Understanding one's limits without underestimating one's potential is a fine line. Optimism or pessimism is learned in youth, though its influence is lifelong. Looking past the demons, and the bad moments in life, is the secret knack of survivors.

None of us can guarantee our middlers freedom from stress or disappointment. We can teach them to cope, though. If you as a parent feel you cannot help your middler cope with a specific challenge, problem, or setback, you can steer your child toward a qualified adult who can. The truth about the Haunted House is that it's never really demolished, but walking through it builds character.

Strategies: Help Your Middler Manage Worry

Did you know that 98 percent of worrying is wasted, according to stress management experts?

- Forty percent of worry time focuses on things that never happen!
- Fifteen percent of fretting is wasted on things that turn out better than expected.

- Thirty-five percent is lost on things that can't be changed.
- Eight percent revolves around petty, insignificant items. With these survey results in mind, teach your child to manage troubling issues.

1. *Enlighten your worrywart.* When your child is upset, recount the first two findings. Explain how young adolescence is a period when worrying is commonplace, and often out of proportion to reality. Tell them thoughts can be changed like channels on the TV.

2. *Burst some worry balloons.* Have your child recall an instance when she worried about some event, and, in hindsight, her apprehension looked foolish. Like the time she shuddered when the coach asked to talk to her parents. She was sure she was going to be cut from the soccer team. The coach wanted to recommend she try out for a select, higher-level competition.

3. *Help your child determine whether the worry is* **within** *or* **beyond** *control.* If your son is worried about being invited to a party, show him the guest list is not in his control. On the other hand, if your daughter is worried about an upcoming test, suggest she spend the extra minutes reviewing, rather than fretting, since her performance is within her control.

Since a mere 2 percent of worrying is actually time devoted to disasters that can be averted, teach your children to let a worry be a call to action, or otherwise turned off.

Four

Escape Artist
Your Middler's Battle for Independence

"All adults complain about equality and protecting their rights. What about my rights and freedom! Am I less of a human than an adult?"

(Fifteen-year-old boy from Kentucky)

Middlers may be living in the moment, but they definitely have their eye on the future where the issues of freedom and power are concerned. The boy who once basked in your parental cloak of protectiveness now can't wait to throw it off. Your watchful eye and supervision have become a straightjacket, and your little Houdini is wrestling with breaking free.

Ten- to fifteen-year-olds want control over their schedules and their lives. Yet because of their age, this perfectly logical yearning is fraught with frustration. They want to be accorded the privileges of older teenagers.

"I am eleven years old and that's more than halfway to twenty so stop treating me like a kid."

Living in a chronological limbo between childhood and adulthood, middlers are inevitably struggling to get more—more leeway and privacy, later bedtimes and curfews, fewer parental intrusions into their school and social life. Along the way, many are butting proverbial heads with parents over what is appropriate and what is not allowed.

The issue is control. You, the parent, have got it. Middlers want it. In this chapter, you are going to witness their plight to become independent. Exploring common battle zones, you'll get to see how predictable the escapist middler can be. You will pick up a few maneuvers bound to de-escalate the fray. The goal is to help you make your middler's breaking away easier, less explosive. There is a difference between discipline and control. Mastering the first and gradually relinquishing the latter is a trick that even Houdini would find daunting.

"It's Not Fair!!"

The most familiar battle cry is "That's Not Fair!!!"

"Nobody listens to us," insisted a fourteen-year-old boy from Kentucky. "Adults just assume they know all the facts and they don't. We want more R E S P E C T and freedom."

If you look at life through middlers' eyes, you begin to see their point. Old enough to know what they want to do, middlers are not old enough oftentimes to follow through on their desires. A twelve-year-old wants to come and go freely, but she can't drive a car yet. A thirteen-year-old knows what CD he wants to buy, and where to get the concert tickets, but he can't afford what he wants because he's too young to work. A fourteen-year-old boy, in the grip of urgent sexual awakening, wants to feel what it's like to make love, but is stymied by parental lectures, fears about AIDS, not to mention getting a girl to share his (normal yet inappropriate) desires. In instances like these and many others, the middler feels powerless.

Wish lists aside, even in their everyday lives young adolescents don't have much say. Parents tell them when to rise. "Get, up. You're going to be late for school." And shine. "Make sure you do that math homework so you can pull your grade up." Basketball practice, soccer clinic, music or dance lessons—all are scheduled by the clock. Whose clock? Never the middler's. Parents enforce the rules, the curfews, and order what chores are to do done. "Take out the garbage." "Clean your room." "Change the water in the fish tank." Remember that '50s song "Yakety-Yak"? Well, with two-career families, today's middlers get more reminders from answering machines and refrigerator magnets.

It doesn't fail to register with our kids that almost all parental directives are negative as in *"Don't* stay out past your curfew." "I *don't* want to see any failing grades on that report card." *"Don't* go out until your homework is finished." "Say *no* to drugs, cigarettes, sex." To their ears just about everything is off-limits. *"Don't* you dare get a tattoo on your ankle." "One of those haircuts—please *no.*" *"Don't* get into a car with a boy who has been drinking even if he's the cutest one in the world." And the omnipresent *"Don't* talk back." Yakety-yak.

The world according to a middler is overrun with rules, regulations, and restrictions. This is especially grating because these young adolescents are old enough to make many of these decisions for themselves. When to do homework, what day to do chores, shouldn't ten- to fifteen-year-olds have some say in how they organize their lives? Furthermore, the entire agenda seems to encompass the responsibility side of life. When it comes to the fun and freedoms, the road is too long, or so it seems to them. Is it any wonder that these young people are often on the verge of revolt.

The Power of Positive Parenting

"I refuse to tolerate my thirteen- and fourteen-year-old son and daughter's disobedience and disrespect for me and their stepfather," fumed one mother. "We both work very hard to see that they are well provided for and don't deserve what they dish out. I had to install

Escapist Fantasies

We asked, "If you could do one thing on your own that you are not allowed to do now, what would it be?" The most frequently expressed desire was "to drive a car." Second choice in our tally was "to go places alone." In addition to those top two, middlers provided us with a shopping list of their fantasies. Here are some of their secret wishes:

- "Go to the mall with my friends."
- "To see what it's like to make love."
- "Go to the movies with my boyfriend."
- "Be out at midnight with no curfew."
- "Cut school for a day."
- "Go on a long vacation, just my friends and I."
- "I would ride the city bus wherever I wanted."
- "Play the lottery."

locks on our bedroom door to keep my daughter out. She's stolen money and forged checks. My son's no better. He doesn't steal, but he lies. And he's nasty (or just plain sullen) toward my husband who is supporting him, unlike his father who hasn't paid child support in years. We've tried punishment such as taking away privileges, restricting extracurricular activities as a deterrent. Nothing works. I'm just trying to hang in there and survive."

Children this age are impossible, parents of middlers universally proclaim. Sound familiar? What mothers and fathers don't know is they, too, are guilty of sour dispositions.

Parents' irritability toward children increases as sons and daughters grow from eleven to fifteen. That's what Ohio State University Professor Raymond Montemayor and researchers observed videotaping parents. The number of times parents expressed negativity in conversations rose steadily as their children grew into early adolescence, while positive expressions didn't change at all. Furthermore, the middlers were more affected by the negative remarks than vice versa.

These years are a stress inducer for parents. Conflicts are inevitable. Still, disciplining a young adolescent shouldn't be a tale of crime and punishment. Incorporate these three R's: reward, recognize, and be rational.

Reward good behavior. This rule is even more critical than punishing aberrant behavior, according to parenting wisdom based on conditioning studies. (You are reinforcing the good, rather than singling out and reinforcing the contentious.) Middlers are so hungry for approval that giving praise wisely and frequently will guarantee a replay of their successes.

"Children won't say it," reminded a New Hampshire sixth-grade teacher, "but they like parents to show they care." A nurturing family environment is also critical to fostering communication and providing the sanctuary our embattled children need.

Recognize which discipline efforts work most effectively. Start off with crystal-clear expectations. "I often tell parents, the more structure and planning you can introduce, the less punishment will be needed," advises Stanley Turecki, M.D., child and family psychiatrist, guru of parenting strategies, and author of the classics *The Difficult Child* and *The Emotional Problems of Normal Children.*

Realize that negative orders are never as memorable as positive ones. Our unconscious doesn't pay much attention to "Don't." So if your child is attached to the telephone for hours, edit "Don't stay on that phone so long!" to "Please keep your call to twenty minutes."

Moreover, negative programming can be destructive. If you tell your twelve-year-old son who has been sliding academically, "You'll never be able to handle marine biology if you don't bring that science grade up," or "You'll never get into medical school the way you're going," all the child really hears is "You'll never." Inadvertently you are internalizing this message: "You're not good enough, smart enough to do" whatever. To a middler whose psychological task is to define his identity and find his strengths, this is disastrous input. Turn the warning into a positive by saying, "If you want to go to medical school, or become a marine biologist, you have to demonstrate you can do well in science." What a difference a *don't* versus *do* approach can make!

When attempting to keep your middler in line, know which threats work best. Use them. For example, "You can either continue arguing with me about this, or you can forfeit your favorite television show, our usual trip to the mall, etc." By giving a choice, and loading it with guarantee rebellion-busters, you are improving your odds at nipping insurrection in the bud. "Use your bargaining chips carefully, and never all at once," reminded parent educator John Eddington, a licensed social worker who has spent years running parenting courses. In this way you keep a reserve of ammunition and clout.

When punishment is in order, how do you determine it? If there was one effective remedy like "no TV for a week," discipline would be simple. It's not. You know that. After consulting a number of experts, what we offer is a formula based on their combined expertise.

The most effective discipline CARES. By that anagram we mean:

C Your actions should be CONSISTENT. Punish each infraction, every time.
A APPROPRIATE. Let the punishment fit the crime.
R Make it RESULTS-ORIENTED. That means you have to decide what tactic (grounding, doing an extra chore, no TV, etc.) has worked to change your young adolescent's behavior in the past.
E Remember, EACH child is an individual, in a different development phase, and with a special temperament. Factor in these differences. (Sending a loner to his room may not work if he enjoys being

alone listening to CDs.) How you discipline a middler should be age-appropriate and temperament-oriented. If you know your child, you can figure out what she will call "punishment."

S All efforts in the discipline vein must be SWIFT. Middlers live in the now, so don't procrastinate if you want to be effective.

A parent who CARES will become a caring and efficient disciplinarian.

Punishments are consequences of actions your child takes, but not all consequences that befall your child come from you. Middlers have much to learn about this. So do parents.

Young adolescents have trouble anticipating consequences that entail thinking ahead. *If I don't study tonight, I'll fail the test in the morning*—somehow escapes their grasp and logic. "Preteens do not believe in tomorrow," insisted one teacher. To make matters worse, parents have a hard time enforcing consequences, according to John Eddington, who said, "Today's parents are often thoroughly consistent at being inconsistent."

Parents are compassionate to a fault, opting to bail sons and daughters out. *My son worked so hard on that essay, I'll just type it up for him (and make corrections along the way). I know I told my daughter she'd be punished if she failed anything, but she's such a good kid I'll forget about that sixty-five in social studies.* Divorced parents think: *I don't get to see my children as much, so I don't want to spend my time disciplining them!*

Waffling parents rear middlers who don't take parental expectations seriously. State your rules and what the consequences will be. Follow through. Don't "spring" consequences on a child. If you've never told him what will happen if he smokes a cigarette, don't be surprised if he objects to your consequences! And don't forget that sometimes the consequences (failing a test) are punishment enough.

In households complicated by divorce, all households must reinforce the same codes of conduct (especially since middlers are now increasingly capable of using their developing-thinking noodle, which means manipulating).

The truth about consequences is that they are hard for parents of all kinds to bear. Our hearts always go out to our child in trouble. However, your middler's future rests on your ability to resist the urge to rescue or excuse.

The final word comes from a West Virginia mother of three: "Teach your children to be responsible for their own actions. For every action there is a reaction . . . so think twice." Only by making the connection between expectations, decisions, and their fallout, will a middler comprehend the concept of personal responsibility and be prepared for any and all challenges, present and future."

Be rational. There are moments when we as parents lose it. We lose our temper, our patience, our reason. When that happens, give yourself a time-out. Never resort to physical measures. Did you know that twelve- to fourteen-year-olds are more physically abused than any other age group? Violence in our culture is running rampant. On that everyone agrees. Corporal punishment is still debated. Some experts note that minority parents are afraid to soften up on discipline because their offspring risk greater repercussions. But, when you use violence to discipline at home, you are giving birth to a cycle of violence that will cripple your middler, spill over into society, and further dehumanize our world. And one day it will hurt your grandchildren.

"I've written twenty-seven books—all about parenting and children—except two," announced Eda LeShan a child therapist, parent educator, and well-known author in *Mothering* magazine (Spring 1996). "When I die, I plan to be cremated, my ashes buried under the same tree where my parents' ashes are, in my daughter's garden. There won't be any headstone to mark my passing, but I keep thinking that if there were, all I'd want to say is *Please don't hit your kids.* Being hit is demeaning. Rage is a natural consequence. Hitting can only lead to abject withdrawal or hurting oneself or others."

No lie, no affront, nothing merits the physical discipline of being slapped. If you and your young adolescent are imprisoned in a pattern of endless futile punishments, chances are the lying, cheating, drinking, insubordination is a mask obscuring a larger problem. If you can't think of a better resort than lashing out, it's time to consult a professional. Talk to your child's school counselor or join a parenting group to explore your other options. When you can't change your child's behavior, you have to change your own—that's the message of many parenting education philosophies.

A Tour of the Battle Zones

The tension and confusion within the maturing process are behind many middler rebellions, tantrums, and stalemates. Our survey identified common land mines. We will explore each, along with assorted strategies, to help you deal with them in a healthy, not hurtful, manner.

Everyone's doing it or going there. "I just had a heated (to say the least) debate with my eleven-year-old son," said one mother. "He's angry because he thinks it's completely ridiculous to have to be in bed by nine-thirty on school nights. Of course all his friends get to stay up much later. I'm not buying the *all my friends* argument because I know how selective kids are about what they report. I know my son. He needs ten hours of sleep or he behaves like a cranky toddler. I doubt that every other young adolescent in the nation gets to stay up till eleven!"

"My parents won't let me date," reported a thirteen-year-old girl. "They say I'm too young. I told them all my friends are allowed to go to the movies with boys. Why are they treating me this way? If they don't let me do what my friends do, everyone's going to make fun of me. Then I'll have no friends."

The parents of every middler have to wrestle with whether to let their child go along with the crowd or whether to stick to their guns, gut instincts, and values. The issues may change. If everyone's dating at twelve or fourteen, should you let your daughter? Should your son go to a party at a house notorious for having *Home-alone* kids? What remains the same is your responsibility as a parent to do what you think is right. You, not the crowd, set the standards. This is bound to create conflicts.

The truth is that ten- to fifteen-year-olds still need structure and limits. During this stage, boys and girls think they are invincible (start the day on little sleep, in-line skating all afternoon, and *still* play tennis competitively in a match scheduled at seven). They don't see the likelihood of injury. Absolutely, they can hold their own in any social situation. ("So what if the other kids smoke pot or go upstairs in pairs!") The risk of his getting busted because he is caught with

Building a Better Middler

The Search Institute, a nonprofit Minnesota-based organization, after nationally surveying 273,000 sixth- to twelfth-graders, discovered the difference between troubled youth and those leading productive and positive lives could be distilled into developmental "building blocks." Parents need to provide these support structures and cultivate these skills and values. According to Peter L. Benson, Ph.D., Judy Galbraith, M.A., and Pamela Espeland, coauthors of *What Kids Need to Succeed* (which reports the survey findings), these assets "are resources upon which a child can draw again and again. And they're cumulative, meaning that *the more a young person has them, the better.*"

The first half were external, resources found in the environment:

1. Family support
2. Parents as social resources
3. Parent communication
4. Other adult resources
5. Other adult communication
6. Parent involvement in school
7. Positive school climate
8. Parental standards
9. Parental discipline
10. Parental monitoring
11. Time at home
12. Positive peer influence
13. Music
14. Extracurricular activities
15. Community activities
16. Involvement with a faith community

The latter half were internal, attitudes and values:

17. Achievement motivation
18. Educational aspiration
19. School performance
20. Homework
21. Helping people
22. Global concern
23. Empathy
24. Sexual restraint
25. Assertiveness skills
26. Decision-making skills
27. Friendship-making skills
28. Planning skills
29. Self-esteem
30. Hope

drug users, or her flirting with date rape because she winds up in a compromising situation—these don't factor into youthful bravado. This age group needs parental supervision.

A good strategy is to talk frequently with other parents, especially those of your children's friends. Such a network of parents can establish norms with regard to curfews, dating, chaperones, virtually any issue, and present a united front. Parent groups can be a forum in which to explore and fine-tune your values. This way when she says "Everyone's going," you can counter with "Everyone's not," and have the parental grapevine to back you up.

The messy room. This was the Number 1 source of conflict, according to our surveyed parents. Not surprisingly, middlers chimed that "Clean your room" was a major nag. Martha Stewart wannabes they're not! (Their disorganized habitat matches their nature, which we'll explore in Chapter Five.)

Living in a pigsty like a pack rat is normal. James P. Garvin, Ph.D., longtime consultant on young adolescents and author of *Learning How to Kiss a Frog,* explains, "The room is the child's imaginary world. It's filled with posters of heroes and heroines. The enormous curiosity of this age group is reflected, which means a vast array of new things and lots of unfinished projects. Stuff accumulates because likes and dislikes change rapidly. These early adolescents are collectors of information, always trying to prepare themselves because of their insecurity. If you realize that only 30 percent are concerned about structure at all, the chaos is developmentally typical."

The clash between childhood and adulthood compounds the mess. "I found my fifteen-year-old son in his room with his toy soldier collection spread out on the carpet with tears in his eyes," recalled Pat Eddington, a mother and a social worker. "He confessed it wasn't fun playing with his GI Joes any longer, but he couldn't part with them, either."

Parents, trying to reduce the clutter, may unwittingly add to the trauma their young adolescent already feels about parting with those special ingredients of childhood days.

If it's just messy, realize it's their room and it is naturally at odds with your own adult ideal. (The more structured you are, the more challenging this will be.) Parents should worry about the room, according to Dr. Garvin, "only when they see a pattern of depression or self-destructiveness in what kinds of posters or slogans appear." If the culture or climate looks troubling, talk about it with your child.

When the room gets too out of control, try these tips. Plan a shopping excursion and let your child select organizing accessories. Giving her ownership is incentive. When you want the room cleaned, be specific. Define clean: dirty clothes put in the hamper, rug vacuumed, food thrown away. Or remind them that food debris and almost-empty soda cans attract bugs. (This threat is sure to work on body-conscious middlers.)

Mouthing off. The father of a twelve-year-old, who has been teaching teenagers for years, summed up the adult-teen rapport with this quip, "In today's world the classic self-help book *I'm Okay, You're Okay* would have to be retitled *I'm Okay, You Suck!* That's how the kids talk." It's become legendary how fresh, disrespectful, and even foul-mouthed young people have become. "I never talked to my parents the way the kids do today" has become the collective gasp of adult society.

Types of objectionable middler talk can be divided into two camps: disrespectful (sarcastic and loud retorts) and cursing.

A Kentucky teacher (of two decades) blames the media for the sarcasm. "Kids try to mimic the smart sassy talk they hear on TV from sitcom teens." Contrast what TV audiences heard from Ricky Nelson and Wally and the Beaver versus what today's children get from the Simpsons or Roseanne's offspring. There is an us (children) against them (adults) mentality afoot throughout the youth culture, from Nickelodeon and network sitcoms to magazines such as *Sassy*. Its cumulative effect has influenced how middlers talk to adults.

Cursing from the mouths of these babes stops many dead in their tracks. Here's a typical tale from one parent: "I was standing on the checkout line at the supermarket. Behind me was a mother and her young adolescent daughter. The daughter wanted Mom to do an about-face and pick up items the girl wanted, apparently missing from the shopping cart. The mom, harried and tired, brushed off the pleading. The daughter lashed out with 'You Bitch!' I was so embarrassed for this woman! To have a daughter call her that! It was unbelievable. And she didn't even reprimand that child!"

Five-letter insults and four-letter words may be unbelievable but not uncommon from middler mouthkateers. Cursing has become too casual everywhere. What can a parent do to silence mouthy disrespect and cursing?

• Ask yourself: Am I responsible to any degree? If cursing, yelling, or disrespectful verbal patterns occur in your family, your middler is merely replaying what he's heard. Make a pact to change your linguistic ways together.

• Turn off the television. It indoctrinates sassiness almost subliminally.

• Counter slang or curse words with "I don't understand what you mean." When your son says, "He's a dork," or your daughter says, "The play stunk like hell," ask them to be specific so you can get their meaning. Explain colorful euphemisms aren't revealing and not very creative.

• Resist escalating the fighting words. That insulted mother on the checkout line acted wisely when she ignored the outburst. Not retorting in a heated moment is preferable to dueling name-calling. If a middler yells and you respond in kind, the volume and the anger crescendo. A later, less emotional moment is the time to discuss outrageous or unacceptable remarks.

• Take the long view. Adolescence makes otherwise good children prone to defiant, foul, linguistic practices. Middlers want the shock effect. In time they will settle down and reflect your example.

• Be plain about which words you will not tolerate but make allowances for trendy colloquial expressions, even if, to your way of thinking, "it sucks."

Privacy—rights to and invasion of. The silent treatment and cold shoulder are part and parcel of living with a middler. "Children at this age don't like to share too much information with their parents. They're secretive," agrees a New Jersey sixth-grade teacher. This withdrawal tendency increases as the middler nears the later teens.

In addition to being tight-lipped and aloof, young adolescents are big on denying. "I didn't do it. You always blame me!" Experts on preadolescents insist that this endless obfuscation is the response of a creature who is terrified of disapproval. Middlers tend to think of parents as control freaks and disciplinarians and are reluctant to set themselves up for criticism and punishment. Better not to take responsibility for the mess or not writing down the phone message. The problem arises because *denying* to a thirteen-year-old is lying to a mother or father.

Parents try to get to the truth of the matter at hand or break through the silence barrier. Children try to get away with things; parents are shocked and become suspicious. The parent pushes; the middler pulls back. The wall around your son's private life thickens. She fudges on her comings and goings. An intimacy tug-of-war has begun.

Desperate to know what's going on with an inscrutable child, many a parent stoops to snooping. Timid snoops tentatively scan crumpled notes they find abandoned on the floor. Or they nonchalantly inquire about every incoming telephone call. More aggressive snoops rifle through backpacks, drawers, listen in on telephone conversations, or raid diaries.

"I know I am a good mother most of the time," justified an anonymous mom. "But I did one unconscionable thing. When my daughter was nine, I couldn't resist her diary. It called to me from under her pillow each morning when I straightened up her room. Unable to stop myself, I read a few excerpts. When I came to a remark about how she wished she could kiss this one boy, I was horrified! Not by her secret passion but by my violating her most private sacred thoughts. She's thirteen now and still keeps a diary. But I have never, nor would I ever, intrude again."

Snooping is unethical, because every middler has a right to privacy! If you suspect your child is using drugs or getting in with the wrong crowd, snooping still isn't right. Find another way to get the information. A plan needs to be worked out, perhaps with the help of a counselor.

Planned companionship, which makes a child feel special and more likely to open up, is a far better and effective alternative to inquisitions or sneaky searches. Mothers told us about rituals like "girls night out." Fathers (of girls as well as boys) recommended fishing trips or attending a sporting event. Take middlers on chores or try cooking as a family.

"I always dreaded having dinner with my stepchildren," confessed the stepmother of two—a thirteen-year-old girl and a fourteen-year-old boy. On Saturday nights, their dad worked and we were *stuck with each other.* Conversation was hardly possible, much less intimate. Things had not been running smoothly for my stepson. I decided to try something. I announced Saturday night would be taco night. I turned my stepson over to a frying pan steaming with browning meat and told him to mix in the sauce. I gave my stepdaughter lettuce, tomato, and cheese and asked her to dice and chop. We got wrapped up in our culinary tasks, creating this kid-friendly entrée. And you know what? We started talking, really talking. And even laughing! Needless to say the following Saturday was wok night!"

The privacy tug-of-war is best mediated with sensitivity.

School and schoolwork. Parents and middlers are equally obsessed about school performance. Students want good grades and worry constantly. Parents expect as much and nag endlessly. High achievers and lesser scholars as well feel the heat.

The issues could be listed in alphabetical order. A for assignments, the unfinished variety. B for behavior, C for class clown, and D for detention. E for effort, the halfhearted kind. You see the drift. There's homework, neatness, cafeteria food fights, projects, health posters, mathematics tests. There's talking too much to your friend during science lab and not participating enough in class discussions. There is more than ample grist for the battle mill.

Not every parent will have every problem with their middler (although some will have more than they ever imagined). Chances are all parents will have at least one problem, probably a different one with each of their children. (Upcoming Chapters Five and Six will help with this battle zone.)

The look. If looks could kill (as in the fashion choices of middlers and facial reactions of parents) middlers would be dropping like flies. Outlandish outfits, bizarre hair—there are plenty of fashion statements to drive a parent wild.

"My son came for the usual weekend visitation, only this time without his usual hair color. He had dyed his brown crew cut red," recounted the father of a fifteen-year-old from New York. "I didn't flip. I remembered looking like the Messiah at his age. I couldn't resist teasing him though. Tall, skinny, carrot-red top—I told him he reminded me of a wooden matchstick. He didn't laugh, but the matchbook look was short-lived."

Experimenting with hair, clothing, and makeup is normal for ten- to fifteen-year-olds. Trying out different looks is their way of sifting through identity issues and testing out roles. Clothing defines peer groups, from preppies (stylishly ivy-league), to jocks (team logo baseball caps and Starter jerseys), to nerds.

When your child's look is testing your limits of good taste, stifle that urge to say: "You can't go out looking like that. When you walk down the street you are a reflection of me!" Focus instead on these considerations.

- *Is the choice weather appropriate?* If your child is wearing umbro shorts or miniskirts in December, object on the grounds that he or she will freeze.
- *Are safety issues being raised?* If your daughter is modeling too provocative a dress, ask what reaction such an outfit might generate. A young girl may not have made the connection that some boys will make when they see a risqué fashion choice.

Allow your sons and daughters the freedom to dress themselves their way, to be who they are and not who you want them to be. Before you criticize a child who's headed for Mr. Blackwell's worst-dressed list in your opinion, recall just how self-conscious young adolescents are about appearance and body changes. Even the worst outfits and hairdos are temporary. "You have to learn to pick your battles wisely," offers the parent of three who are now teenagers. A New Jersey parent concurs, "Say yes to as much as you can; save no for the really important issues."

A final word about clothes, music, or any other issue—it's normal for parents to endorse what they like. What happens when your middler triggers your ambivalence or disdain? You as a parent should strive to appreciate the child you have, not one in your image and likeness. The exercise that follows should help.

Crack Your Parent Code

One mom explained she recently took her fourteen-year-old shopping to buy jeans. She admitted to feeling a certain pleasure in the fact that her son's outfit of choice reflected something to which she could relate. *The kid wants jeans, I like that,* she thought. "Parent code" is how she coined her response. His dungaree preference proved that his values were in the *right* place because they were in the *same* place as hers!

Are you raising your child in parent code, trying to mold your middler to fit your style? Run through these questions and decide yes or no.

1. Have you been secretly crushed when your child shows absolutely no aptitude for the occupation (from farming to medicine to the family business) you live and breathe?
2. Have you repeatedly dismissed your child's request to take up a sport or a hobby he wants based on your attitude as opposed to his enthusiasm?
3. Even though you are a jewelry connoisseur, have you nixed your middler's design for the third hole in the ear, or some other body adornment she thinks is awesome?
4. Although you and your young adolescent converge on loving music, have you battled over CD choices, the car radio station, and concert ticket purchases?
5. Are you overly demanding about your child excelling in one particular subject, the one you were good in? Or the one you failed?
6. If your daughter exhibits a personality characteristic unlike you, for example shyness in comparison to your outgoing nature, are you constantly trying to change her personality? (The tip-off is if you hear, "I'm not you, Mom!" on a regular basis.)
7. When you critique your middler's fashion sense, is your frame of reference what you would have worn or what you like?
8. Do you nag your child to take advantage of opportunities you would have loved to have, but didn't? (Play a musical instrument, for example.)
9. Are you prone to scratching your head because your daughter has an obsession with something—cartooning, ham radio—out of left field as far as you can see?
10. Have you gotten the feeling (more than occasionally) that your child bears so little resemblance to you that he must be hosting body snatchers?

"Yes" answers should give you pause. Here is where you may be sabotaging your child's specialness. It can be hard to comprehend the tastes, opinions, and rejections that offspring possess. Two struggling entrepreneurs naturally will be disappointed if their son shows zero interest in a business they have created to pass down. Parents may discourage a child with artistic or musical leanings, fearing the cost of private lessons or future prospects. Academics may be fighting a losing battle with a jock who fantasizes about pro-ball not the Nobel.

The kernel to supporting your child in his plight toward independence, is valuing what is special or unique in him, even when it is a talent or a fixation with which you are unfamiliar, even uncomfortable. Help your middler become who he or she aspires to be. Love the child you have. Relish the surprises. Bone up on the unknown. Maybe one day you will be in the audience applauding their Emmy, Grammy, or Gold Medal.

No parent deliberately or tyrannically intends to force-feed a child a diet of hand-me-down dreams, likes, and dislikes. Yet many parents fail to recognize and encourage aspects, aptitudes, or visions that their children have and that differ from what parents know.

Liberty, Equality, Paternity, and Maternity

"Chomping at the bit" is how many parents described a middler's readiness to break away. "Independence is what this age group is all about. They're beginning their own search," explains a seventh-grade teacher from New Hampshire. Parents can launch young adolescents, take the insurrection edge out, by factoring into their child's life as much freedom, empowerment, and confidence as possible.

We've organized a question-and-answer roundup based on our interviews with experts, encompassing an array of professionals and you, the parents. This is intended to serve as a guide as you pass along the torch of adulthood.

Is there a timetable to follow in doling out later curfews, more leeway in going places with friends?

No, there is no chronological guide on the road to middler independence. The consensus of parents we interviewed believed that freedom was part of an exchange program. Middlers got it in return for demonstrating responsibility. "All privileges, such as driving, friends, out-ings, are based upon a level of competence in schoolwork and chores," began a thirty-nine-year-old father of three from Idaho. "Freedom and privileges are earned by being responsible," explained one West Virginia mom who apparently spoke the language of countless other moms and dads.

Track record is another word for trust according to most parents. The more maturity and cooperation a middler demonstrates, the more freedom he is granted. "As long as his grades are good and he behaves himself in school and at home, I try to be lenient when he wants to do something," responded the mother of an eleven-year-old boy.

Trial and error was the most common method for monitoring freedom and maintaining the independence parameters. It involves a certain measure of risk, but parents seemed to take that chance. "Until he gives me reason for not trusting him, freedom is awarded," promised one single mother.

"There is a time and a season for every level of independence," philosophized a Missouri fifth-grade teacher. "Some kids fail at independence because they have skipped the prerequisites." Parents seem committed to apportion freedom in a way calculated to teach middlers to handle independence well.

How can a parent make a powerless middler feel more powerful?

At no other time in their lives do children feel as powerless as they do between the ages of ten and fifteen. No wheels. No salaries. No say. There are concrete ways parents can give power to the powerless.

Give your child an allowance. It puts power into middler hands, spending power, as well as autonomy. It can provide the seeds for learning the fiscal skills of saving, using purchasing power wisely, delayed gratification, and discretionary spending.

These skills are critical considering that middlers come with a huge media-driven appetite for consumer goods ranging from computer software and games to electronic equipment and designer fashions. Everything today's kids want costs a bundle, from sports gear to concert tickets. An allowance can help your daughter deal realistically with advertising pressures and designer-label allure, and teach your son how to distinguish between his wants versus his needs.

By handing over a certain amount of money, a parent is handing over control in equal measure. What items bought, what events planned, what savings accumulated . . . these decisions are now in the realm of the middler and out of the domain of the parent. There is no better way to invest in your daughter's money-managing mentality or to give your son a return on his decision-making skills.

How much allowance? According to a recent Nickelodeon/ Yankelovich *Youth Monitor U.S. Survey,* nine- to eleven-year-olds received an average of $4.17. What amount you decide upon will be up to you. Take into account your middler's age and what expenses the allowance should cover (lunches, church donations, class trip expenses, weekend entertainment, such as movies or a day at the mall).

Chores and $$

Nearly 70 percent of our young adolescents surveyed said they had enough spending money. Allowances given to young adolescents (9- to 13-year-olds) add up to $1.3 billion a year according to researchers. Yet our parents didn't register as big spenders in the allowance department: 40 percent of those we asked *did not* pay out regular allowances.

Of the parents that did give out weekly stipends, nearly all did so as payment for doing chores. The mothers and fathers we talked with believed "earning" one's allowance is good.

Do you agree? If you do, you are WRONG, according to a host of financial experts who advise parents on teaching children the value of a dollar. Hardly any of the experts recommends attaching a "salary" in the form of an allowance to chores. As one parenting columnist remarked, "Children are part of the family and not our employees. They should help not because they will be paid for services rendered, but because they are part of a family."

All experts endorse children helping out. Despite this, it is a declining trend. Children in dual-career families with two college-educated parents do a meager 11 percent of chores, compared to 20 percent in less-educated households. The learned consensus on chores says *more children should be doing more chores* because helping with household tasks teaches domestic skills, responsibility, a sense of service, and provides opportunities for building self-esteem. So keep insisting that your middler pitch in ("Do your chores" is a major nag from parents, report our middlers), but keep money out of the bargain.

Respect middler protocol. Middlers have their own strict rules and definite no-nos. Loving a middler can take on all the intrigue and secrecy of an illicit romance. The mother of an eleven-year-old boy or a fifteen-year-old girl knows what it's like to be a clandestine parent. No kisses or hugs on Main Street. No using pet names. No rendezvous in the halls at school.

"Drop me off at the corner, not at the front door of the school," begs a fourteen-year-old. "You can come to the movie with me and my friends, but would you mind sitting in the back by yourself?" Concert arenas in some large cities now have a place called the Parent Room to accommodate chauffeur parents whose children don't think it's cool to be seen at a concert in the company of anyone over thirty! Sleepover parties are especially tricky. You have to be there, of course, but you have to remain invisible, too, or at least out of earshot. Your role is like a downstairs maid in upstairs society: keep passing the tray of snacks, but don't intrude.

You can see the slippery dilemma with protocol. How your middler instructs you to act changes from year to year (even from child to child), which makes it difficult for parents to discern and adhere to their foreign customs.

"My sixth-grade daughter surprised me when she insisted I walk her to the bus stop her first year in the middle school. Wouldn't she be afraid she'd get teased by the other kids? She said no. All that year I schlepped around the block with her at the crack of dawn, with umbrellas, in snowboots. I was the only mother in a gaggle of a half-dozen kids. More than once on my way back home, freezing or wind-blown, I reminded myself that every such day might be the last."

There is no surefire do's and taboos guide that applies to all middlers. Parents must look for the secret society rules and avoid the faux pas as a way of according a child respect and a measure of authority in her world.

Can the family be adapted to help the middler thrive?

Invite your middler into the inner circle of power in the family. Families are so hectic these days. Pass some of the decision-making responsibility over to your young adolescents. What to plan for dinner, which restaurant for Saturday night, ideas for spring break or summer vacation, how to rearrange the garage or the basement to accommodate all the stuff accumulated—the challenges in a parent's life are many. Managing the family's time, social calendar, daily needs, recreational goals, extended family gatherings—these require problem-solving on many levels. By delegating some decisions to your middler, rotating others around the family, you are according your children regard, reaffirming their sense of belonging, and lavishing that coveted commodity—control.

Allow your middler supremacy over his leisure. Between school, homework, sports practice, religious instruction, and music lessons, middlers have very little leisure time. Avoid committing them to appointments without asking permission. It's a courtesy. Check first before you schedule the orthodontist, the ride in to visit grandparents. In so doing, you are giving your child the same consideration you would like in return. If a middler is given maximum control over his free time, he will give you a minimum of lip.

Last, but not least, add humor to the independence battleground whenever possible.

"One night at ten-thirty, I told my thirteen-year-old to go to bed for the fifth time. She pleaded with a nasty edge, 'I want to watch the end of this movie.' I said 'no,' again, louder this time than the previous four. 'Oh yeah, watch me!' she retorted. I was stunned. I could've strangled her, but I just repeated 'Watch me?!' 'Watch me?', each time glancing her way with a tone of incredulity. She looked out of the corner of her eye. Slowly our mutual rage mellowed into a giggle." This mother turned a potential showdown around by letting humor negotiate a stalemate.

A joke, a laugh, a hug—these are indispensable items to keep in your parental toolbox. After all, middlers are just getting the hang of flexing their humor muscle, which makes them very receptive. When all else fails, try approaching issues from the light side. When all fails, remember this story from the burned-out mother of two, a teen and a middler:

On a Monday in May, Lark, a war-weary single mom, announced she was going on strike! Henceforth, she declared her son and daughter could do their own laundry, get themselves to wherever they wanted to go, and do their own cooking for the week. Did it work? NOT! Much to her disbelief they didn't care. They ordered pizzas from their savings—no dishes or cooking, and decided to spend all their free time watching TV instead of going anywhere. Lark said, next time, rather than going on strike, she'll go on vacation.

Middlers are wily. As their little bodies and minds are stretching and straining, trying to escape your grip and grasp, they are edging toward what will one day be total independence. As you encounter the insurrection campaigns of your middlers, make certain you don't win short-term battles and lose the war by forfeiting their affection.

The forward-looking nostalgia of this mother's remark gets to the bottom line:

"It's not easy being a parent, and unfortunately this, too, shall pass. They'll grow up and move away." The breaking away years (the good, the bad, and the ugly) in hindsight will be the good old days.

Strategies: Is Your Parenting Style Too Nice or Too Negative to Be Effective?

As we strive to become positive parents, it can be helpful to examine our style. Read each of the situations below, choose one answer, and mark it in the space provided. Then proceed to the scoring section, and on to evaluating your responses.

1. Your daughter has come home from school clearly upset. She confesses to being excluded and ridiculed by girls she thought were her friends. Would you

   (a) empathize by sharing a similar memory and advise her to take a wait-and-see approach; (b) telephone the mothers of the girls causing your daughter's distress and ask them to intervene; (c) dismiss the episode by telling your daughter that she has you as her best friend; (d) label those so-called girlfriends "catty," "bitchy," and not worth her time. _____

2. Today is report card day. Your child's grades are satisfactory overall, maybe even wonderful, except for one or two. Your strategy would be to

   (a) call the teacher immediately for a conference to discuss the low grades and what can be done to improve them; (b) commend overall performance, but ask your child to explain the poorer grades; (c) focus on the positive aspects of the report card only, because to do otherwise would only cause trouble; (d) figure one or two low grades are nothing compared to how badly most children this age do in school. _____

3. Your son seems down these past two weeks. When you probed "What's got you down?" he dismissed your efforts with monosyllabic responses. Your next step would be to

(a) chalk it up to the moody blues of youth and give up trying to cheer him; (b) read his diary, E-mail, scour his backpack, eavesdrop to ferret out the truth; (c) observe him for signs of sleep or appetite irregularities, withdrawal from social routines, and in the meantime be available in case he wants to talk; (d) get tickets to a sports event or plan a weekend to get his mind off his problems. _____

4. Your daughter has brought home a new friend to whom you take an instant dislike. How would you handle this?

(a) arrange to include this new friend in a family outing so you can overcome your first impression or collect ammunition to blow her out of your daughter's life; (b) figure out what bugs you so much— her fresh mouth, rebellious attitude; (c) interrogate your daughter about this new friend: where they met, what have they in common, what her parents do; (d) give your daughter's judgment the benefit of the doubt while following the friendship from a distance. _____

5. There is a rumor going around that an upcoming school dance is going to have alcohol on hand on the sly. Your son wants to attend. You would

(a) allow him to go, pointing out that the alcohol is going to create problems for some at the dance, but you trust him; (b) suggest he and his friends have one beer at your house as a compromise before the dance; (c) prohibit him from going to the dance because fourteen-year-olds plus alcohol equal disaster; (d) contact the school principal and insist an alcohol search-and-seizure policy be initiated for this function and any others. _____

6. It's Tuesday morning and your daughter comes into the kitchen with what you consider too much makeup. When you object, she tells you all the girls wear makeup. Your next communiqué most closely resembles this

(a) "I don't care what the other girls look like, you are not going out of the house looking that way!"; (b) "You could use a little help, so how about we both get a cosmetic makeover at the mall this weekend?"; (c) "It's not the makeup I take issue with as much as how much is appropriate for school."; (d) "Where did you get that eye color, lipstick, and who taught you how to line your brows?" _____

7. You have heard through the grapevine that one of your child's oldest friends from grade school has a problem with marijuana. You know your child still has contact with this problem child. Which approximates your strategy?

(a) you would forbid your child from seeing this old friend because of the new drug problem for fear your child would be lighting up next; (b) you would wait for the right moment and then confide to your child what the grapevine has been saying and ask what she thinks; (c) you would launch into a search-and-destroy mission—search your child's room for signs of marijuana and destroy that friendship by tattling to the child's parents and the school pronto; (d) you would tell your child about the times during your youth when you experimented with drugs like this friend in question. _____

8. Divorce is on the horizon. It is a difficult time for you and you suspect it will affect your children. How would you broach the issue? (If you have no divorce experience, try and put yourself in the shoes of a parent going into a divorce.)

(a) you would tell your children the truth about the impending divorce, assure them they are not to blame, and encourage them to share their feelings; (b) you would warn the teachers, ask the school social worker to begin seeing them, get a detailed visitation schedule in place, and be ready for any signs of distress; (c) you would brace yourself for the hysterics, the cold shoulder, and the blame game; (d) you would have a heart-to-heart chat with each child and tell them how this marriage has become unbearable, how the spouse has become intolerable, and how much you need their love and understanding. _____

9. There's a bully on the school bus. Your son has not been targeted yet, but others have. Would you

(a) find out who has been harassed, the details of the incidents, and call the bus company and the school to have the offender lose bus privileges; (b) see if your child volunteers any details about the bully and if he doesn't ask him what his take on the situation is; (c) give your son instructions on how to bully the bully; (d) do nothing because all boys get aggressive at this age. _____

10. Someone you know casually remarked your daughter is feeling her hormones. When you pressed, she repeated your daughter's

reputation for making out in the halls with her boyfriend. You didn't even know she had a boyfriend. Your next step would be (a) get the boy's name, the rumormonger's names, confront your daughter, and demand an explanation; (b) ground your daughter for kissing and not telling; (c) look for an opportunity to bring up the subject of young love and sex and see where the discussion leads; (d) sit your daughter down and tell her about your first romantic or sexual experience, tell her what you heard, and that you know how she feels. _____

Scoring: List your answers below. Look for the point value in the table provided. Write your points for each answer. Total your score. Proceed to the evaluation section.

Answers	*Point Values*				
1._____	(a) 20	(b) 15	(c) 5	(d) 10	1._____
2._____	(a) 15	(b) 20	(c) 5	(d) 10	2._____
3._____	(a) 10	(b) 15	(c) 20	(d) 5	3._____
4._____	(a) 5	(b) 10	(c) 15	(d) 20	4._____
5._____	(a) 20	(b) 5	(c) 10	(d) 15	5._____
6._____	(a) 10	(b) 5	(c) 20	(d) 15	6._____
7._____	(a) 10	(b) 20	(c) 15	(d) 5	7._____
8._____	(a) 20	(b) 15	(c) 10	(d) 5	8._____
9._____	(a) 15	(b) 20	(c) 5	(d) 10	9._____
10._____	(a) 15	(b) 10	(c) 20	(d) 5	10._____
					Total_____

Evaluation:

(50–75 points) ***The Confidante Parent*** If you scored in this range, you want to be your child's best friend. Your reasoning: if you forge a confidential rapport, then no harm can come. Criticizing grades or makeup is not good for your relationship, so you think. You don't want to be the authority figure laying down the law. A sanctioned beer before a dance, to your way of thinking, is a shield. Hearing you wax nostalgic about getting high, making love in your VW may establish rapport, but at what price? Your messages may sanction the very behavior you intend to discourage. You want your child to understand your divorce, but will she find the revelations burdensome? You may want too much from and you may be inclined to share too much with your child. Middlers need rules, role models, and yes, even authority figures. You mean well but your parenting style is too close for their own good.

(75–125 points) *The Negative Parent* If you scored in this range, you believe all the negative images about middlers. Catty. Rebellious. Hysterical. Expecting only the worst, you have little—if any—faith in your child's ability to rise above the temptation of alcohol or the influence of a troubled friend. To you, peer pressure is trouble. You risk pigeonholing your child's new acquaintances. Assuming everyone and everything is out of control, especially yours, your parenting approach is neglectful. By neither intervening nor guiding your child to sort through dilemmas, your absentee-parenting style handicaps your child. Worst of all, your attitude robs you of any joy in appreciating young adolescents.

(125–175 points) *The Micro-Manager Parent* If you scored in this range, you are in an eternal quest to make the world safe for your child. Of course, your child is precious, but you go overboard—always on the lookout for trouble, asking too many questions, scanning your child's private life for the slightest hint of scandal. You want to know everything, run everybody, control every situation. A bully on the bus or alcohol at a school dance, you take it upon yourself to remove these dangers. Why? You are mistake-phobic. The problem with your micro-managing is that you are depriving your child of decision-making and problem-solving opportunities. These are essential to survival in middlerville as well as later on in adulthood. And chances are you are driving your middler crazy with your twenty questions and perfectionistic ways!

(175–200 points) *The Effective Parent* If you scored in this range, your style is most effective. You are not bent on running your child's life, but helping her develop. You are not biased about this age group. When you see depression or stress, you don't dismiss it but look further. You don't try to make all the decisions in your child's life, whom she befriends or rejects. You solicit his thoughts, her opinions. Do grades reflect ability? Require more work? By letting your child explain, you foster his creating a plan of action. By allowing your child to go to a dance where there may be risks, you are giving him the opportunity (and show of good faith) to exercise good judgment. You know that no parent can protect a child from all the danger all the time. The best we can do is behave securely, nurture the skills and confidence children need to survive and, in good time, flourish.

Trying to stay too connected, on top of things, and getting turned off to young adolescents—these are occupational hazards for parents of middlers. Keeping nonproductive urges in check will make well-meaning, loving parents more effective.

Five

Three-Ring Circus

Why Your Middler Is Distracted, Disorganized, and Disinterested

"Believe it or not, these kids are trying. Trying to cope with more and more. Too often we see so many of the problems they face and forget about the honest effort they are making."

(Teacher from New Hampshire)

Your middler's life is like a three-ring circus with its sensory overload of sights, sounds, smells, and feelings. Not even the most extravagant production by Ringling Brothers could compete with all the excitement and drama. So many spectacular events unfolding! Remember how it is at the circus. Focus on the acrobats in ring one and you may miss the dancing bears in ring two or the trained horses in ring three.

Is it any wonder your child finds it impossible to concentrate on just one activity at a time? As adults we have learned how to juggle our work and responsibilities. (Although some of us accomplish this balancing act more easily than others!) Middlers have not yet acquired that coping mechanism so necessary for survival. And if any age group needs help adjusting, this one is it.

As we have learned, they are going through a tremendous growth spurt that can leave them sore, tired, and cranky. Their hormones are raging and are responsible for their varying moods. They toil under an increased load of schoolwork and extracurricular activities. They are forging new relationships with their peers, discovering the opposite sex, and attempting to exert some independence from their parents. It's exciting, to be sure, but dizzying and overwhelming, too.

How do they react? The responses, while as individual as the children themselves, can best be described by three adjectives: distracted, disorganized, and disinterested. In this chapter you will view your middler in 3-D and learn how you can help him to maintain his focus.

The First D—Distraction

Concentrating on a task for any length of time is something that your middler will have trouble doing. His tapping pencil, drumming fingers, squirming body, and wandering eyes will probably drive *you* to distraction. You can help yourself and your middler by remembering that much of this fidgeting is beyond his control. No doubt he is frustrated, too, by how his body is behaving. On top of that, he is developing the ability to ponder weighty matters. And there is so much to think about—school, friends, sports, fitting in, doing well, what to wear. His circuits are overloaded. No wonder he appears distracted.

It's not easy living with a child who seems to have a permanent case of spring fever. Your middler may appear to be constantly daydreaming—gazing into space, staring at the TV, lying on his bed looking at the ceiling. He is caught up in his own little world, one that, at the present time, does not seem to include you (or many other adults, for that matter). Capturing your child's attention will often seem to be an effort in futility. Even if he *looks* at you, he may not *hear* you. Even if he *hears* you, he may not *listen*. So your entreaties to take out the garbage, walk the dog, clean his room, will probably be ignored.

This generation of middlers has become particularly adept at tuning out unwanted noise. They have grown up surrounded by electronic pandemonium—arcade games, CDs, Walkmans, music videos, TV. This cacophony is so much white noise to these young people. Amazingly enough, they don't find it bothersome. Only 13 percent of middlers who answered our survey report doing their homework alone in a quiet room. The majority say they have no problem concentrating with a radio, CD player, or a TV on, often in a room filled with other people working and talking. If your daughter can screen out all that noise and distraction while doing her algebra, what chance do you have to break through?

A very slim chance indeed. Don't take it personally. Middlers are often indifferent to their surroundings. A messy room will drive you crazy, but your son will barely notice the empty soda cans, candy wrappers, and soiled underwear that litter his environment. Nagging him to clean his room is a conflict you are destined to lose. Yet most parents are unwilling to concede defeat. More than one-third who answered our survey placed messy rooms at the top of their "battle zone" list.

While you may be willing to overlook the fact that one-fifth of your home has turned into a landfill, you will probably have more trouble dealing with another symptom of middler distraction: a poor academic performance. "My daughter was labeled gifted in elementary school," said one mother. "She was always ahead of the others. Then in middle school, she stopped working. She didn't hand in homework, forgot assignments, failed tests. She'd claim she was doing her homework, but if you walked into her room while she was studying, she would quickly shuffle her papers to hide the letter she had been writing." This mother mused: "I wondered if it was because the learning always came so easy, then she got kinda overwhelmed when it required real studying so she just tuned out."

Some of that mother's analysis is probably true. Research shows that between the ages of twelve and fourteen, a child's ability to learn slacks off. Your son may no longer be able to absorb material at the breakneck pace he exhibited when he was younger. Unfortunately, this slowing down in brain power occurs at exactly the wrong time. Sixth, seventh, and eighth grades are demanding. Not only is there a greater volume of work, but also the assignments themselves become more challenging. Advanced subjects may have been added to your child's course load. Perhaps he is now learning a foreign language. Algebraic equations are creeping into his math work while chemistry and physics are being introduced in his science class. With the move to middle school comes a new routine, changing classes with each subject, requiring your child to deal with many more teachers, each with a different teaching style.

A temporary lag in homework or a disappointing grade here and there is to be expected during this transition. But if your child's school performance changes dramatically and continues to slide for longer than six months, those bad marks should serve as a red flag to warn you that something more serious is going on.

Helping Without Harming

Your child may be rebelling against your authority. Are you a hands-on parent with respect to homework, constantly looking over your daughter's shoulder, correcting her misspellings and addition errors? All your double-checking may be sending her the powerful message that you don't believe she can do the work herself. Why be surprised when she gives up and brings home poor grades?

As hard as it may be for you to let go, it will be even harder if you don't. You will suffer because your child will demand larger chunks of your time at the worst possible intervals, before dinner when you are busy or after the evening meal when you are looking forward to a few moments of relaxation. This pattern will injure your child because she will never learn to do the work herself. Unless you plan on attending college with her and later following her into the workplace, she will at some point be on her own. Better for her to make mistakes now, in middle school, where the stakes aren't so high and she still has time to learn how to approach her work responsibly. A good middle school has plenty of support systems—afterschool study halls, homework hotlines, adult mentors, to name just a few—built in to help children who need extra support. Find out what is available in your school and community and help your child tap into it when necessary.

Listen to one mother who managed to step back: "I finally, really, truly gave my seventh-grader ownership of her work. I had to let go of trying to protect her from failure. Last quarter was a disaster, but I didn't even ask to see her report card. She told me what her marks were. Inwardly, I winced. I asked her how she felt about them. She told me she wanted to bring them up. Since then she has made a consistent effort to get her homework done on time and to do better in school. She tells me (without my prying) how she is doing. She is starting to develop an inner motivation—pride in her accomplishments—that will keep her going long after she's on her own. She seems happier, and I feel more relaxed around her. Yes, I still have to keep her on track a little tiny bit, but she knows the responsibility is hers."

Of course, where your child's schoolwork is concerned, there is a midway point between being intimately involved and totally ignorant. "The parent should be a support person, more an encourager than any other kind of role taken," said a seventh- and eighth-grade teacher from New Jersey. "The parent should help the child develop a 'can do' attitude, be willing to hear problems, and help the child become a good problem-solver."

"At this age, a parent needs to be an overseer," added a sixth-grade teacher from Louisiana. "The overseer or foreman certainly steps in when he/she sees problems."

Be sure that your child has a space in which to work where he can be physically and emotionally relaxed. Selecting this location is a personal decision. Your son may prefer to be alone in his room, while your daughter would rather be in the kitchen or den where she can solicit your assistance whenever needed. No matter where the child is, make sure study supplies are plentiful, lighting adequate, and seating comfortable.

Beyond creature comforts, however, the emotional atmosphere in your home should be free of conflicts so that your child can concentrate on schoolwork. "Some students have so much garbage going on in their home environment, there is no way they can concentrate on math, etc.," said a fifth-grade teacher from Idaho. A teacher from Maine summed it up succinctly: "Bad home life equals difficulty concentrating at school."

Some of these conflicts, of course, may be beyond your own power to control. A family crisis may be sopping up all your emotional energies, leaving you with little resources to help with homework. Check out what help is provided at your son's school. Tutors (oftentimes parent volunteers) may be available to pinch-hit for you temporarily. In the meantime, try to carve out a quiet time each evening when your child can work. Through your words and actions, convey to your child that you consider school important. "If these young people feel their parents do not care if they fail, it's so *tough* to get them to care for themselves," said one teacher. "They feel unworthy."

Roadblocks to Learning

"My fourteen-year-old son is not doing well in school," confided one mother. "I know he is capable of the work. He was tested two years ago and is in the 95th percentile. Is it time to go to a psychologist? Am I coddling him? He seems genuinely upset."

Experts agree that the years from ten to fifteen are often when a learning disability, either one diagnosed when the child was younger or one to surface for the first time, can seriously impede your child's ability to progress in school. Many times these learning problems may be subtle ones, so subtle that they may escape the notice of parents, teachers, even the child. It may be that the remedy will merely involve enlisting a tutor or stressing study skills more. But discovering what the obstacle to learning may be—whether that obstacle is a rock or a boulder—can help all concerned address the issue.

These impediments may include:

Language difficulties. Your son may have no trouble understanding or following written instructions. But if the teacher gives directions orally, he may find himself lost. He may also have trouble expressing himself verbally. His embarrassment may lead him to become disruptive in class or to skip class altogether.

Spatial orientation. Your daughter may be just the opposite of your son, able to understand verbal instructions, but unable to process information given to her visually. How does this show up in schoolwork? Look for a child who has poor reading or spelling skills, can't remember how words look, and is apt to reverse letters that look the same, such as *p* and *g*, or *b* and *d*.

Memory. Your son's brain is a large repository of information. But he may be having problems getting to that information when he needs it. This retrieval problem becomes more noticeable in middle school, when coursework demands that students regurgitate data quickly, particularly on timed tests. Your son may study for hours for a test and still fail. The right answers were in his head. He just couldn't get to them.

Fine motor control. Your son may be smart, but if something interferes with the mechanics of putting down on paper what he knows, he's in trouble. He may begin to think of a pencil as his worst enemy. He can't remember how to form his letters, and, when he does, he can't get them to look right. His schoolwork will tend to look sloppy, and he may be easily embarrassed over the final product he must hand in. Is it any wonder that he tends to lose his papers?

Sequencing. "Class, open your textbooks to page fifty-six. For the next twenty minutes, read from pages fifty-six through sixty-six, answer questions twelve through twenty-four on page sixty-seven. Double-space your work and make sure you are writing with a black or blue pen, not a red pen or a pencil. If you finish early, you may get started on your homework assignment on page forty-five in your notebook."

Phew! A child who has a problem with sequencing would have lost the teacher right after opening her textbook. And while the above illustration is an exaggeration, it's not unusual for middle school students to be given a series of directions and be expected to follow them properly. Imagine the confusion and frustration experienced by a child who can't remember what she's supposed to do next. Children with sequencing problems also have trouble estimating time, making classroom life even more vexing.

ADD and ADHD. Much has been written about Attention Deficit Disorder and Attention Deficit Hyperactivity Disorder and the number of children who are being medicated to help them perform better in school. It is estimated that more than one million children now take Ritalin—the drug most widely prescribed to help children settle down. While many doctors, educators, parents, and even children themselves praise Ritalin and other psychoactive drugs for their effectiveness, others condemn medication as a quick fix that fails to address underlying problems.

Thomas Armstrong, Ph.D., an outspoken opponent of Ritalin, believes that other solutions besides medication—behavior modification, a teaching approach that addresses the child's individual learning style, removing allergens from the diet—can be equally effective in helping a child to focus. "I wonder whether there aren't hundreds of thousands of kids out there who may be done a disservice by having their uniqueness reduced to a disorder and by having their creative spirit controlled by a drug," he writes in his book *The Myth of the A.D.D. Child.*

Ritalin has staunch support, too. "I am the mother of a ten-year-old son with ADD/ADHD disorder," one mother typed onto a bulletin board in cyberspace. "He was diagnosed four years ago, and, like most parents, the thought of giving a child 'drugs' was scary to us. I just want to say it was the best move we ever made. My son, now in fifth grade, is a straight A student and loves to be at school. He has many great friends now and is such a joy to be with. The fighting we went through in the past with schoolwork, his impulsive behavior, and many other problems all seem to be forgotten. Don't be afraid to try meds if recommended by the doctor. It helped here more than I could ever say."

Because middlers naturally have difficulty focusing, they are prime candidates for being diagnosed as ADD/ADHD. Prescribing medication for a middler is particularly troubling to some parents. There have been reports that Ritalin is being sold illegally so that users can snort or inject it. While widespread illegal use of Ritalin is a remote possibility (it is too complex a drug to be manufactured illegally and its high nowhere near that produced by other substances such as cocaine), it still sends middlers a double message about drugs at a critical juncture in their lives.

So how does a parent decide whether to medicate a child or not? The decision is very personal and should never be made without consulting qualified physicians, educators, and other experts. Read available material and ask questions. Most important, bring your child into the decision-making process. Middlers are not five-year-olds who can be told Ritalin is a "smart pill" that they then eagerly swallow. Middlers are apt to ask questions and, if not convinced of Ritalin's usefulness, refuse to take it. They also will be more aware of the medication's side effects, which may include insomnia, weight loss, stomach pain, and irritability when the drug wears off.

The controversy over Ritalin is just one mental stumbling block a parent may encounter when trying to decide whether to investigate the possibility of learning disabilities for their child. What are your concerns? The reasons are many and varied:

You worry that your child will be labeled "slow" or "retarded." Learning disabilities are not the same as mental retardation, autism, deafness, blindness, or behavioral disorders. In fact, most children and adults who have been diagnosed with learning problems have higher-than-average intelligence.

You feel your child's learning problem may be the result of something you have done (or not done) as a parent. Learning problems are neurological in origin. Some of these disabilities may have been caused by alcohol or drug abuse during pregnancy, premature delivery, or low birth weight. Aside from that, even the most conscientious parent would not have been able to prevent such a problem from surfacing eventually. "In the same way a child comes into the world with large ears, a tendency to go gray in his twenties . . . a child is born with a brain that functions in a particular way because of its chemical composition," said Dr. Harold S. Koplewicz in his book *It's Nobody's Fault: New Hope and Help for Difficult Children and Their Parents.* "It is brain chemistry that is responsible for brain disorders, not bad parenting."

You are waiting for your child to admit he is having trouble. Chances are he is as perplexed as you are about his inability to perform well. On some level he may sense that the work is beyond his ability, but he is not apt to conclude logically that he is having difficulty because something is interfering with his thought processes. Rather, he is more likely to feel that he is "dumb," and become defensive. The result? Lost homework papers (preferable to lose them than hand them in and get a poor grade), forgotten homework assignments (even better, skip the work altogether!), rejecting the work as "boring" (in fact, the work may be boring if he doesn't understand it).

You are waiting for the school to pick up on your child's problem and notify you. That may happen but, then again, it may not. With large classroom populations, teachers have less opportunity to observe each student. Once a child is diagnosed with a learning disability, special accommodations must be made. Oftentimes making such adjustments may put further demands on a school's already overtaxed staff. And the more time that goes by, the more ground your child will lose. If you suspect there is something going on, then you're probably right. Don't wait to take action.

You hope the learning problem will go away. Learning disabilities never go away. An individual can be helped to compensate for the problem by being taught new ways to read and write. Ignoring the disability, however, won't cure it, but will lead to anger and frustration on the part of the child.

You worry about the cost of getting help for your child. Federal law IDEA (Individuals with Disabilities Education Act), mandates that all children with learning disabilities are entitled to a "free" and "appropriate" education in the "least restrictive environment." You have the right to request that the school conduct a comprehensive assessment of your child's skills. You also have the right to examine all your child's records and see the results of the evaluation. If your child is found to have a learning problem, he would be eligible for special services.

What might these special services include? Accommodations range from regular classes with certain in-class remedies or supplementary help all the way up to a special day school or homebound instruction.

One mother said that after her sixth-grade son, Nicholas, was found to have language difficulties, he was assigned a consultant teacher. This specialist goes into his classroom on different days and works with him and other students. "He is never pulled out of his work group," said Nicholas's mother. "His level of support is invisible."

You worry that your child might react negatively. In the beginning, it's possible your child will be upset at the idea that he has a learning problem. After all, your son is eager to fit in among his peers. He's not going to be happy with the idea that he is different in some way. Yet because children with learning problems are usually intelligent, they know there is something wrong. Oftentimes their imaginations run away with them and their initial anger over the testing process comes more from fear than anything else. "In my experience, once a child goes through the testing and has his parents and teachers explain to him what needs to be done, he relaxes," said one teacher. "The reality is never as bad as the child's own fears."

If you need further convincing, consider this: Adolescents who have learning disabilities that are not addressed are more apt to abuse drugs and alcohol, commit crimes, drop out of school, and compile a poor employment history. At the same time, early diagnosis and successful intervention can turn the situation around. "If a child is not progressing at an appropriate rate—don't be complacent!" advises a pamphlet from the National Center for Learning Disabilities. "The frustration and consequences of living with an undetected learning disability can be profound."

Your first step should be to schedule a meeting with your child's teacher. Go to this meeting prepared to discuss specifics. Vague comments ("Heather just doesn't seem to be into her work anymore") won't provide the teacher with meaningful information she can act on. Instead, try to supply the teacher with concrete examples that can illustrate the struggle your daughter is having. "I know Heather studied very hard for this history test, but she still received a bad mark." If the teacher wasn't aware of Heather's problems, she will be sure to keep a watch now that you have brought the situation to her attention.

Once your teacher has been consulted, you may request a comprehensive assessment of your child to be done by the school system at no cost to you. If your child is found to need special education services, within thirty days you have the right to have what is called an Individualized Educational Program (IEP) put in place to help your child.

Your rights extend throughout the time your child receives these special services. If at any time you are displeased with the program that has been devised, you may request a hearing. At some point, if the school decides your child no longer needs extra help, you may contest that decision, too. (For contacts to help determine what your rights are in this area, see the list of resources at the end of the book.)

The Second D—Disorganized

With so much to do and think about, it's inevitable that some ten- to fifteen-year-olds will let things fall through the cracks. How could it be otherwise? Their workload has increased both in volume and difficulty, and they have a lot to learn about managing time and work. (Many top corporate executives still haven't mastered techniques to work more efficiently.) The following characteristics of a disorganized middler may be all too familiar:

Constantly forgets things.
Messy room.

Constantly loses things.
Underestimates the amount of time it will take to complete a given task or chore.
Does homework but fails to turn it in.
Seems oblivious of time.

Unfortunately, your daughter's procrastination and forgetfulness may mean headaches for you. Chasing down lost sneakers and missing homework papers can be aggravating. Your middler needs help and both of you will be the beneficiaries of your intervention.

Begin by reevaluating your daughter's schedule. In light of her increased amount of homework, can she still manage her extracurricular activities? During the middle school years, these after-school pursuits become more intense. Serving as the goalie on the school soccer team or nabbing a lead in the seventh-grade play will be exciting for your daughter. But she will expend more energy at a time when her body is demanding that she rest more. She is apt to come home physically and mentally exhausted, wanting nothing more than to flop onto the couch and watch TV for two hours. Instead, she faces mounds of homework. Is it any wonder she may have difficulty keeping up? Failing grades will no doubt produce sagging spirits.

Talk with her to see if there are some things she can drop. Perhaps you can rearrange the timing. If she tends to have more homework at the beginning of the week, you might shift some extracurricular activities to the weekend.

Once you have helped your daughter to pare down her workload, approach her with a plan for getting organized. Language is important during these discussions. Avoid being judgmental. Try to present it as a team effort, the two of you working together to help her do her work in a more orderly way. Point out one advantage that will no doubt appeal to her: the better organized she is, the faster she can get to her work and complete it, the more time she will have in the evening to relax and enjoy herself.

What strategies can help get your middler organized?

Arrange a good place for your child to work. It bears repeating: Make sure your child has a comfortable, well-lit place to do her homework. She should have ready access to whatever supplies she needs.

Know your child's study habits. Remember body rhythms. Some children like to unwind, play outside, have dinner, before they settle in to do work. Is that your child? Then you will have no success insisting that he attack his homework seconds after walking in the door.

Make a list. Every night write up what he needs to do. Have him estimate and jot down the amount of time each task will take to complete. He no doubt will be astonished when that ten-minute math assignment actually took thirty minutes. Making a list also will give him a sense of accomplishment when he gets to cross off the items as he finishes them.

Use visual reminders. A list is one way a child can actually see what needs to be done. If your child is in the habit of forgetting things he needs to take to school, write up a checklist and post it near the door where he won't fail to see it on his way out. Lucy Hedrick, a time-management consultant and author of *365 Ways to Save Time with Kids,* has helped organize more than one middler. For one of her young clients who kept forgetting to take his glasses to school, Hedrick made a huge sign—JAMES! REMEMBER YOUR GLASSES!—that he had to pass each morning. "I also got him a secretary chain—one that was cool with love beads—so that he could keep his glasses around his neck," said Hedrick.

Use verbal reminders. Ask your daughter before she leaves if she has her lunch, history homework, permission slip for the class trip, etc. Be specific. Asking a general question like, "Did you pack everything you need?" will almost certainly earn an affirmative response, whether it's true or not.

Invest in an oven timer. One reason middlers waste so much time is that they believe they have an endless supply of it. Your daughter may spend an hour on the phone and think it was five minutes. Suddenly a whole evening has evaporated, and she still has unfinished homework. An oven timer can be a handy device to help keep your middler on time. If you limit phone calls to ten minutes on school nights, for example, have her set the timer to warn her when her time's up.

Break big tasks into manageable pieces. Hedrick calls this "eating the elephant one bite at a time." Say your son is given a week to complete a science paper. Ask him to write up a schedule detailing when and how he will complete each part. For example, he may spend the first day reading research material, the second writing up note cards, the third writing a rough draft, the fourth polishing that draft, and the fifth making final corrections and adjustments. If he sticks to his schedule, the project should not be overwhelming.

Give your child a checklist of things to do before a test. Studying for a test is challenging for a middler, mostly because there is no concrete way to measure progress. If your son has a lot of material to cover (a lot could mean two pages of notes, ten pages in his textbook, and five pages in his workbook) he may not know where or how to begin. Most middle schools stress study skills and so your son has probably been given some guidance on preparing for a test. Aid him at home by suggesting that he make flash cards that he can use to study by himself and then have you test him when he has mastered the material. Or reinforce some of the techniques presented at school and see which ones are most effective with your child.

Back up written assignments. Are lost homework papers your child's problem? If she does her assignments on a computer, have her keep backup copies on disks. If the homework is handwritten, photocopy important work at a local shop.

Set aside a day each week to clean out his backpack. Your middler's backpack soon becomes a repository for the detritus of his life—past tests, forgotten notes to parents, empty soda cans, candy wrappers, pencil stubs—you name it. "My son is a walking disaster and so is his backpack," reported one mother. Over the weekend, help him sort through this collection. File old homework papers and tests, toss out the garbage. On Monday morning, he can start with an organized backpack.

Enlist the school's help. You may do everything possible at home, but somehow homework papers are not handed in, textbooks needed for homework are left at school, and upcoming tests are forgotten. Talk with the school's guidance counselor about setting up a tracking program for your daughter. Here's how it works: every day, she would be required to have each of her teacher's sign a sheet verifying that she has turned in all her homework and participated in class. If she misses any teacher's signature, she would get detention (or any other consequence the school deems appropriate). After several weeks, if she has been successful, the tracking sheets could be signed weekly rather than daily.

Use rewards. All work and no play will produce an angry middler. After your daughter has put in a hard night, reward her for her effort, verbally and materially. Be sure to commend her effort with praise and a hug. Then give her a break or suggest a special outing to celebrate.

Set a good example. The "do as I say, not as I do," argument holds no weight with this age group. If you expect your child to complete homework in a timely manner, then don't allow her to see you procrastinate. In fact, one study done by Rhodes College in Memphis found that parents who put off schoolwork when they were students didn't change their habits when they grew up. Procrastination breeds procrastination. So if you tend to stall, work to improve so that your daughter will imitate your good habits, not your bad ones.

Prepare the night before. Again, using yourself as a role model, let your son see that you pack your briefcase and leave it by the front door before you go to bed and that you try to place your keys and watch in the same place every day. Show him that you need reminders, too. Use the oven timer yourself when your time is at a premium. Ask him to remind you to take the roast out of the freezer in the morning.

The Third D—Disinterested

While some children appear to be whirlwinds of activity during the middler years, others seem to shut down. Your son's friends may stop calling. He may seem to be spending long amounts of time on his own, sitting in his room, watching TV, reading.

Interests shift during this period. Your daughter may become bored with a hobby that once consumed her. Privacy is a major issue with middlers. They want and need time alone.

Within reason, these middler reactions are normal ones. Your son does have a lot to think about, and there's nothing wrong with him taking time out to reevaluate where he's going. Your daughter may be on the verge of taking up a new activity to replace the one she abandoned. The problem is, she hasn't yet found the activity that interests her.

Don't panic. A closed door alone does not signal that your daughter is depressed or your son is doing drugs. Preadolescents are expected to put some distance between themselves and their parents.

When does your middler's withdrawal become abnormal? Trust your instincts. If you are uncomfortable and fearful for your child, something more serious is probably happening in your middler's life.

Begin by making sure you aren't part of the problem. Are you unconsciously pushing your child away, assuming he needs more privacy than he wants? Failing to include him in a family outing because you assume he wants to be with his friends? Oftentimes, parents are the ones to initiate separation, or, at the least, do little to resist their children's efforts to pull away. There's nothing wrong with sticking with some of the old traditions and expecting your child to participate in a family social event once a week, for example. You may have to try a little harder to plan something that your middler will find enjoyable.

Many middlers live in rooms that are so well equipped with food and entertainment they find little reason to leave and join the family. If this is the case in your house, think about creating a gathering area someplace else where your middler will want to come and sit. One mother said she has resisted her daughter's requests for her own TV set. "The only set in the house is in my bedroom," the mother explained. "Even though it's sometimes inconvenient having my daughter in there watching while I'm doing something else, I always know I can count on having her near me at some point during the day. While she's watching TV, she's relaxed and will open up to me about her day."

Rekindling the interest. "My lovely, talented thirteen-year-old daughter is *sooo* unsure of herself despite all the encouragement and support we give her," said a mother. "She refuses to try anything new, for fear of failure. So she does nothing. How can we get her more involved? I'm trying to remember what it was like to be that age, and I know it is difficult for her. If left up to her own devices, she'd be perfectly happy to sleep, eat, and watch movies."

You can hear the frustration in this mother's lament. She looks at her daughter and sees someone who is "lovely, talented." Her daughter, on the other hand, views herself as a failure and is afraid to take risks, however small. Girls in particular experience a crisis of confidence as they approach full-blown adolescence. Those who work with middler girls often comment on this phenomenon, which was first detailed by Harvard researcher Carol Gilligan. A girl who was secure at eleven seems to crumble at thirteen. A piano teacher commented: "I've had girls who at eleven were unafraid to experiment with music and attempt difficult pieces suddenly freeze when they turn thirteen."

This reaction is pretty typical for middlers who feel self-conscious about themselves and their abilities. But a middler's withdrawal may be more complicated. What are some reasons that might explain middler withdrawal?

These young people often allow one setback to contaminate their overall outlook. The old adage, "If at first you don't succeed, try, try again," is not one your middler will be quick to embrace. Instead, one misstep or failure is apt to sour him on the class or activity forever. Remember your son is very concerned (perhaps even obsessed) with how others, particularly peers, see him. If he strikes out every time at bat during a baseball game, he will decide he wants to quit. A failing mark on a math test will cause him to neglect his homework for the next week. "Out of sight, out of mind." If he doesn't have to look at his math book, he won't have to remember his failure.

Of course, he probably won't tell you outright the reasons behind his actions. On one level, he may want to spare you the truth. On the other, he may not know himself why he is behaving the way he is. Don't take his explanations at face value. He may justify leaving his baseball team with, "Baseball is boring," but the real truth may be, "I'm afraid of striking out again in front of all my friends."

Deal with each event as it occurs. Over time, however, this stopgap method will be too time-consuming and energy intensive to work. What you need to do is think long range and work to change your child's outlook. Watch your language when you comment on your child's successes or failures. Avoid focusing your criticisms or praise on him. Did he do well on the math test? Don't say, "Boy, you're a real math whiz!" Instead say, "You studied really hard for that test. You must be pleased with your mark." Thus, you will be reinforcing the idea that actions have consequences—good or bad—that your son can control. Soon this message will sink in and he will develop the resiliency he needs to persevere.

A middler may become discouraged because her skills have plateaued. How many adults have you met who regret their youthful decision to drop the piano, ice skating, horseback riding, tennis, or whatever? Too many to count, probably. Chances are the decision to quit was made during the middle school years. This time is one when many children reach a skill plateau with these hobbies. And without those feelings of advancement and fulfillment, your child will probably become discouraged and want to quit.

There's a reason your child may not be progressing, and this lack of progress has everything to do with your middler's development. Physically, your daughter's body is changing. She may find ballet movements, for example, are difficult, even awkward for her to master at this stage. Your son's inclination to fidget will make it difficult for him to sit and practice the piano for thirty minutes a day. There's nothing wrong with exerting some parental authority here and advising your child to stick with the activity for a certain length of time. Chances are, he will soon make the progress he has been looking for and will want to continue the activity himself.

A great surge of discouragement and declining interest in sports and fitness begins in the eight- to ten-year range. When physical education shifts to team sports and competition, preadolescents begin the painful process of measuring their athletic abilities against their peers. Boys and girls are haunted by the nightmarish image of being the last one chosen for a team, or the possibility of striking out, missing the goal, the kick, the hoop in front of everyone. So they drop out.

That was the experience of supermodel Kim Alexis, who was a champion swimmer in her youth. "When I was twelve, I wanted to stop swimming competitively," Alexis recalled. "I told my father I was tired of the pressure, the schedule of practicing so often. He said to me, 'You're not a quitter.' I stuck it out and was glad that I did." Alexis has followed the same strategy with her own sons, advising them to stick with hockey, for example, when they wanted to stop pursuing the sport.

If one pep talk doesn't do the trick, however, here are some other ways to reengage your child:

Remind her why she took up the activity in the first place. Did your daughter take up field hockey to get exercise and make new friends? If the activity still meets those needs, then she shouldn't be concerned that she hasn't increased the number of goals she scores in each game.

Remind her of an upcoming event she was looking forward to. Was her chorus planning a special concert? Was her art club going to exhibit its work in the library? Focusing on a special happening may be all she needs to get her through.

Help him to establish a new objective. If he took up karate with the idea of being a black belt by the time he was ten, he needs to see that his original goal was too ambitious. On the other hand, he may have surpassed what he had hoped to achieve and does not feel challenged. Whatever the situation, focus on what he has already accomplished and help him formulate a new target and game plan.

Find a new way to pursue the interest. This tactic can be particularly effective with music lessons. "My daughter has played the piano for several years, but as soon as she hit eighth grade, she told me she wanted to drop her lessons," said a parent. "Instead, I suggested that she take up another instrument so that she could play in the school band. I went to meet with the school's music teacher and he agreed to start her on the flute. Because she has such a solid background in music, she had no difficulty picking up a new instrument. Now she's playing in concerts and even doing some traveling with the band. She still plays the piano and might take lessons again in the future. But right now she's continuing to enjoy music and have fun. That's what's important."

Focus on fewer activities. Parents tend to follow a shotgun approach, signing their children up for too many activities at once, without following through on any one activity for an extended period of time. By the middler years, your daughter may have tired of doing so much and not seeing expected results. So she may decide to drop out of everything. Discuss with your daughter which avocation she really enjoys and would like to continue. Drop the rest.

Remember the commitment. One middler father has this complaint: "This year we signed our son up for a Saturday basketball league. Each team was made up of twelve boys, more than enough to keep the game going. My wife and I stressed to our son that if he signed up for the league, he was making a commitment and, barring sickness, would have to be at the gym every Saturday at nine a.m. We were proud that he honored his obligation. Unfortunately most of the other parents felt otherwise. After two games, boys started to drop out. By the last game, our son's team was down to only five boys. It really made me angry. We heard that one boy dropped out because the team wasn't winning. It wasn't fair to the boys who were playing and to those boys who were shut out of the league. And what kind of a message were those parents who allowed their boys to quit sending out? I see this with too many parents. Then they wonder why their kids don't develop a sense of responsibility!"

Find a role model. If your daughter is struggling to make progress with a sport or a hobby, show her someone who has beaten the odds.

Serve as a role model yourself. Children who see that their parents are involved and have many interests will follow suit. Expose your middler to different activities without being obvious. Play the piano, garden, help out in a shelter for the homeless, do woodworking, fix airplane models, cook, knit, take up a foreign language, read a book of poetry aloud after dinner. Something, somewhere, somehow will pique your child's interest.

Master Middler-Speak

One of the most frustrating experiences about parenting a middler is finding the right words to begin a meaningful conversation. This challenge becomes Herculean when you are dealing with a preadolescent who appears to be disinterested. Every time you ask a question, your child answers with another question, an objection ("stop the third degree") or worse, invokes middler-speak. Middler-speak is the use of words that convey absolutely nothing. The three most commonly used forms are "fine," "nothing," and "I don't know." There are probably times when you can overlook these nonanswers to your questions. But when you are looking for ways to motivate your child, you want and need more information than you routinely receive.

Parent: How was school?

Middler: Fine.

Parent (taking another approach): What's new?

Middler: Nothing.

Parent (refusing to give up): Is anything wrong?

Middler: I don't know.

That signals the end of the conversation (we use the term "conversation" loosely here). If knowledge is power, then you are a dead battery. How can you begin to help if you haven't a clue as to the problem? You can't. Is it possible to rekindle your child's passion for school, a sport, or a hobby when he won't tell you what turned him off in the first place? Not likely. You must first learn how to decipher middler-speak, break through the barriers that isolate floundering middlers from their parents. It's as easy as stop, look, and listen.

First, STOP. Refrain from the frantic firing of twenty questions, ten orders, or five pieces of advice. "Are you having trouble in math?" "You'd better practice the piano more before your recital." "If you studied harder you would have done better."

Take a time-out. Look at your communiqués from a middler's perspective. To a thirteen-year-old, questions are prying, reminders are nags, advice, railroading. You might disagree with this translation, and maybe rightly so. Nevertheless, the fact remains that communication is a two-way process, and if it isn't happening, it's time to try something new.

Second, LOOK for windows of opportunity. All middlers give cues that reveal their readiness to open up. When we asked parents, "What moment works best for you when you are trying to talk to your child?" the resounding tip was bedtime.

"Bedtime is when he's relaxed," said the mother of a twelve-year-old. "He still needs that closeness and affection at night that he seems not to want during the day."

One place where the window cracks open is in the car. Automobiles have some kind of magic formula that drives straight to the heart for middlers and parents. There's something about being comfortably seated, strapped in, and not facing each other but looking straight ahead, that greases and accelerates intimacy. You can gently probe and your child may squirm, but can't bolt. Extended car trips have treated parents unexpectedly to weighty discussions and once-in-a-lifetime exchanges. But even short jaunts may produce surprises.

Third, LISTEN. Listening well means giving your middler the opportunity to talk and a license to say a range of things, without jumping in to offer advice and criticism. "Substitute comments with lots of head nods," advised a Florida parent. All parents want to be good listeners. Few of us succeed without lots of practice.

When you see your child is obviously upset, a better alternative to "What happened?" is to say "Something happened," said Adele Faber, a communication expert and coauthor of *How to Talk So Kids Will Listen & How to Listen So Kids Will Talk.* "You offer empathy, thereby encouraging your child to go on," she said.

Allow your child to finish the story before you rush in with opinions. Then, if he asks you your opinion, turn the tables and ask, "What do you think?" Chances are he will tell you.

Above all, emphasize hope. No matter how bad things are, you always want to give your child confidence that next time the results will be better.

The STOP, LOOK, and LISTEN approach to communication will provide a medium in which your young adolescent can reveal himself, admit his problems, and mistakes and begin to arrive at solutions. Neither the *I-don't-want-to-know-parent* nor the *I-want-to-know-everything-parent* is well equipped for the communication challenges ahead. The parent who will succeed will practice patience, gentle prodding, and restraint.

Bringing It into Focus

Living with a middler in 3-D will not be easy. Just when you think your child is on the right track, he is suddenly derailed. You may have pulled back from the hands-on involvement you used to have with schoolwork and outside activities. Getting geared up to commit yourself once again will obviously require some time and effort.

Be comforted by the fact that you are not alone. Many middler parents are having the same experiences, whether or not they are open to discussing them. The good news is that there are many support systems available in school and the community to assist you and your child. With attention to the right details, it won't be long before your child is back on track, moving full steam ahead.

Strategies: Follow These Three Rules for 3-D Middlers

No matter which of these 3-Ds your child is exhibiting (perhaps all three!) there are three important bits of advice for you to keep in mind:

Don't retreat. Let's face it. Your daughter may go through some days when she's not a joy to be around. When she shouts, "Leave me alone!" you may be only too happy to oblige. Back off, but don't go too far. Whether she tells you or not, your daughter needs you now more than ever. You may have to show her how to get organized. You may be the one to help her discover a new hobby or interest, although she would probably be the last to give you credit for your input.

Control your reactions. This advice may sound like psychobabble but it's true: You can't control your child's reaction, but you can control yours. Sure it's easy to hit the roof when he's misplaced his homework paper for the third time in a week. But blowing your top won't find the paper and it won't help him get his act together, either. Ready to explode? Go for a jog, clear your head, and then come back with some helpful suggestions.

Be an advocate. Sometimes being supportive involves more than words or pats on the back. You may have to assume a more active role with the school, for example. If your daughter has always been a straight-A student, it may not be her fault that she is now bringing home Cs. If your son has always done his homework with little complaint, there may be a reason he is now falling behind. Don't be so quick to slap a "lazy" label on your child. Investigate, ask questions. If your child won't answer your queries, arrange a school conference. It's possible your daughter is the victim of a clique and her falling grades a symptom. She may need your guidance to put things in perspective. Or you may find that a learning problem is behind your son's sudden school troubles. If that is so, you will have to remain an advocate for quite some time to ensure that your child gets needed assistance, some of it mandated by a recent law.

Six

Ringing the Bell

Helping Your Middler Succeed in School

"A good parent's involvement is always welcomed when it leads to a partnership among parent, child, and teacher."

(Middle school teacher)

Midway down the arcade, a strapping young male (half of a twenty-something couple) looks at the mallet and the stump he's supposed to pound in order to ring the round golden bell and win the prize. He watches the man ahead of him grab the hammer, but alas, his swing only pushes the meter up halfway. Now it's his turn. He takes the hammer and WHAM—GONG! He rings the bell. It was a matter of strength, yes, but not entirely. Lots of strong men fail along the arcade. The secret to winning, to ringing the bell, is in the effort. It must be focused.

The metaphor applies to education. For schools to succeed and for the students within their walls to achieve, all effort needs to be focused, balanced, and targeted.

When parents step up to the kindergarten door hand in hand with child, each wants their child to do well. When the bell chimes, parents want everyone involved in education to hit the mark of excellence with no less than Pavlovian precision.

But at the middle school juncture, many parents lose their way. Middle school is often a mystery, raising more questions for parents than providing answers. "What goes on?" Where do they fit in? In this chapter we'll outline how middle school operates and the ideal role for parents. Knowing the hallmarks of what makes a good middle school will enable you to access it as a primary (and wonderful) resource for your child's learning. Finally, as a parent what can you do to improve your middler's educational experience, or your middle school if it is not making the grade?

A Revolution in Learning: Hallmarks of a Good Middle School

When was the last time you were inside a classroom-in-progress in a middle school? You've never been? You are not alone. Most parents are not well-versed in the revolutionary changes that have taken place in young adolescent education. These changes were set into motion after researchers, looking into why this age group held a record for poor performance, recommended the grade six through eight middle school configuration.

If you went into a middle school you would *see* some of the innovations. Teachers writing on blackboards, lecturing students all in a row reading from textbooks—that was the reality of the past. Now, students bustle about in noisy classrooms where Geography Jeopardy is being played, or work groups argue over math equations. Furthermore, there are a host of new dimensions that you can't see.

The National Middle School Association (NMSA), which stands at the helm of this movement, outlines exactly what elements make a good middle school in their report *This We Believe*. Here is a roundup of their hallmarks.

Educators who are "middler experts." All teachers are trained to understand the characteristics of young adolescents so that they can individually and collectively meet the particular needs of middlers. How does this come into play? Here's one way. Once teachers learn young adolescent boys can't sit still for more than fourteen minutes (sixteen minutes for girls), they adjust the pace and span of lessons to accommodate their antsy learners.

These teachers have a backup staff with whom they interface on a regular basis. This includes specially trained guidance counselors, child psychologists, social workers, special education specialists, and school nurses (a larger group than you may recall). Add to that more administrators. Principals now work with at least one vice principal.

An agenda that is both academic and "developmentally appropriate." Young adolescents need to master mathematics, language, and science, but they also need training in order to cope with all the changes they are undergoing, and the changing world as well. Middle school offers a variety of programs to address developmental challenges.

Nutrition, media literacy, drug prevention, and family skills are just a few of the subjects pertinent to middlers, which are interwoven into health class or social studies, science and English. An appreciation of ethnic cultures, their own and others, might be cultivated in music class, as students perform or play a tape of ethnic music that reflects their heritage.

A smorgasbord of extracurricular activities—sports, drama, instrumental bands, language, and environmental clubs, to name a few—are offered so that young adolescents can explore their interests and satisfy their vast curiosity.

In this context, educators can zero in on issues that young people need to address. Our survey recounted the story of a sixth-grade teacher from Alberta, Canada, who suspected one of her students was in the grip of an eating disorder. She said, "I discussed this with her parents, then I assigned the child a research project on the topic of anorexia nervosa." Another seventh-grade South Carolina teacher did a unit on the subject. She added, "I invited a young girl who was recovering from bulimia to talk to the class."

Another example is teaching students to resolve their differences in an orderly manner through peer mediation. In this "student court," trained middler mediators help their contemporaries work out interpersonal conflicts.

Teaching methods that are flexible. Because students learn at different rates, in varied styles, and favor interacting with one another, lots of different teaching strategies exist in midlevel education. For example, cooperative learning logistically groups students together to conduct science experiments or put together video slide shows. Learning styles are explained and lessons try to accommodate each. Hands-on activities are popular because, although some of us learn by *listening* to a lecture, others absorb material more effectively by *doing*. Still others learn best by *seeing*. Independent study, block scheduling (longer periods), and team teaching are employed at middle school. Team teaching assigns the same students to a group of teachers for all subjects so that the teachers can confer with one another and effectively follow the progress and problems of the young adolescents on their team.

Our survey illuminated the many ways NMSA teachers approached getting students to learn. Academic planners were an organizational tool used by at least one-third of teachers. An academic planner is a notebook in which students list daily homework assignments, weekly tests, monthly project due dates—all their expected schoolwork. Planners keep naturally disorganized middler students targeted, parents informed, and serve as a communication bridge among student, teacher, and parent.

Counseling as a focus. Since we have explored how tenuous and fragile the middler mind is, take comfort in knowing middle school is customized to help young adolescents adjust to the stresses and strains of growing. "Advisory programs" (going beyond mandated school psychologists) are self-esteem builders and stress reducers. Advisory is like a homeroom period, a daily time (twenty minutes or so) linking a small group of students with an adult (teacher, specialist, or administrator). The sole purpose is to establish rapport between a caring adult and the middler. If a student wants to talk out a problem, or if the advisor senses one, a support system is in place to help, or guide the student to the appropriate counselor.

The last two hallmarks are *a positive school climate* (which we'll get to later in the chapter, with a focus on violence, gender bias, and sexual harassment) and *flexible evaluations*. Do grades make the middler? Yes and NO!

(Too) Great Expectations

The pressure of new technologies, global competition, and the downsizing of corporations has made these hard times economically for an unprecedented number of American parents. Computer stress

Turn to Your Middle School When You Need Help

Throughout our pages we describe many instances in which middle school teachers and staffers intervene on behalf of a student with a problem. Nearly one-third of teachers in our survey spotted eating disorders. Teachers (67 percent) recognized substance abuse and referred the child to a school counselor. Use your middle school as a resource. Watch for speakers and programs geared to particular concerns you may have (learning problems or parenting classes). The school is there for your children, and you, too. Take your worries to school if any of the following register:

- your daughter appears too thin; you worry she could be developing an eating disorder.
- your son blows up about the smallest things, and his anger seems to be getting more intense.
- you suspect your child has been experimenting with marijuana.
- you feel marital, money, or family problems may be troubling your child.
- you see your daughter hiding her voluptuousness in baggy clothes and she has implied others tease her about her body.
- your child is afraid of being hurt by another student.
- your child is experiencing great frustration with schoolwork.

Start with your child's advisor or homeroom teacher. Get that outsider's opinion. Together you can decide which other professionals (child psychologist, social worker, special education specialist, etc.) might be helpful.

drives us over the edge as we scramble to get our techno skills half as good as our childrens'. Layoff paranoia plagues more than half of us, according to one *New York Times* poll. White-collar managers worry about losing their jobs. Manufacturing workers do, too, as industries disappear only to surface somewhere else on the globe. "The number of people experiencing work-related stress is probably greater now than at any time since the Depression," quipped a Boulder, Colorado, management-consultant firm president.

With "job security" out and "outplacement" in, parents bring baggage of serious anxiety to school. A major concern expressed by the parents in our survey was whether or not their children would graduate equipped to compete and succeed in the future. "I'm afraid that even with a college degree, jobs will be limited," worried a Missouri mother who continued, "Choosing the right career that will offer security, happiness, and financial security gets harder and harder." A Texas mother of three had a less ambitious frame of reference but the same level of fear: "My greatest fear is after high school education, will my children be able to support themselves?"

Such high anxiety influences how parents see their child's academic performance. Mothers and fathers are not in class watching emerging ethical consciousness or developing social finesse. The one thing all parents see is the report card, which now comes through the mail. It is the yardstick parents use to measure their child's success (or failure). Grades become the focal point of parental angst, the battleground pitting parent against middler, and a source of contention between many parents and teachers.

For some parents, grades are never high enough nor are teachers good enough. How well public schools are performing is a controversy that has fueled an exodus to private schools in many parts of the country. This despite the fact that nationwide more than 70 percent of parents rate their neighborhood public school "good" or "excellent," according to a survey done by Public Agenda, an independent think tank.

Teachers take issue with parents' obsession with numbers on report cards. NMSA educators insist that grades alone do not define a successful young adolescent. "Often parents want only to see the child's grade higher, without any thought to the other needs of the child," said a teacher from Hawaii. Middlers have a lot on their psychic plate. Here are five "brain drains" that affect middlers:

1. *Middlers are entering unchartered territory.* The middle school is new for them, too. It is different from elementary school. Teachers (and more of them) operate differently. Students change classes for every subject and get homework in all these classes from all these teachers!

2. *During young adolescence, brains grow at different rates.* This creates a rhythm of intellectual spurts and plateaus. For instance, if your son never had difficulty with math before yet seems stumped by geometry, it could be his abstract skills have not kicked in yet. Remember middlers mature according to different timetables. Consequently, all middlers cannot grasp a lesson at the same moment in time. Thinking skills do fall into place, in time. Teachers know this and give students academic leeway.

3. *Doing well in school is eclipsed by popularity.* We asked students: "Why do you work hard?" Wanting a good grade was the motivating force, according to 65 percent. Being turned on by the subject matter (20 percent), liking the teacher (5 percent), and pleasing parents (5 percent) paled by comparison. In reality, that well-intentioned goal gets lost during the pressing social agenda. (Peers is the subject of the next chapter.)

To make matters worse, very high academic achievement is risky. Remember when girls were advised to play dumb to get the guys? Well, things have changed and they haven't. Being smart still isn't cool in some parts of Peertown. Will a middler's A+ make his friends look like Dumb and Dumber? Since friends reign supreme in the middler value system, underperforming may be preferable to the honor roll. Doing lackluster work oddly can become a matter of honor among peers.

It takes some middlers time to sort through their priorities. A level of security and maturity has to be reached before some will risk the Dweeb label, which comes in both genders now. Many a teacher works hard to teach kids that smart is cooler than smart aleck.

4. *Boys and girls discover the opposite sex.* Puberty, hormones—a major distraction, say all teachers. Who's going out with whom. Who's been dumped. Middle school trysts are a living soap opera. It isn't easy concentrating when you go to school at Heartbreak Hotel.

5. *Many families are raising their middlers in complicated times.* Divorce, remarriage, blended families, job loss, relocation, eldercare, women reentering the workplace—these are always stressful. To a middler who is encased in enormous developmental turmoil, this added burden can be the straw that breaks the good student's back.

Taking into account the hurdles that go along with middler territory, you can see why many need a bit of slack. You've already gotten some suggestions about combatting the 3-D liabilities—distracted, disorganized, and disinterested. Parents need to balance their urge to push too hard with not taking the initiative soon enough. Getting extra help or giving a longer rope, your child's performance and standard pitfalls both need consideration.

What can parents do to help keep middlers on track academically? We polled, from coast to coast, NMSA teachers for their consensus of ideas. Add these to your tutorial arsenal.

STAY INFORMED. Too obvious? Countless teachers told us that parents do not know what their child is expected to master. "Parents want good grades without really asking themselves 'What is my child learning?' " argues an articulate young Colorado teacher. Keep track of your child's assignments. Read her academic planner. Respond to notes and progress reports from the teacher. Attend parent-teacher conferences and be prepared to ask for tips to help your child in his weak areas.

"At the middle level, some parents let go, stop monitoring homework because they think children are old enough, mature enough to do it on their own," said one South Carolina teacher. "But middle level students need as much involvement as elementary students, sometimes more."

PREPARE YOUR CHILD FOR LEARNING. Make sure your child gets enough sleep. This isn't easy since middlers need more sleep and yet school begins at the crack of dawn for many. When they are sequestered in their room, plugged into dance music, they aren't watching the clock or thinking how exhausted they'll be at 6:30 A.M. Watch the clock for them.

MAINTAIN HIGH EXPECTATIONS. There is a simple, 100 percent proven correlation between what parents (and teachers) expect and what students deliver. Parents teach motivation. Put a premium on education. If you believe education is important, your student will bring that value to his schoolwork. Teachers said this over and over.

Don't sabotage your child with lowered expectations. In a new book *Beyond the Classroom* by Laurence Steinberg, he analyzes why Asians always top the class, followed by Caucasians, while students of color lag behind. Asian parents, you see, expect *all* offspring to get As, slower students merely have to expend *more* effort to do so. Other parents often label some children early on as "not as bright as so and so." Teachers can do this, too. In this way students are programmed *not* to achieve! So if your child is not measuring up, get him help or remind her to put in extra time.

NURTURE YOUR LEARNER. It's easy to fall into the trap of only remarking on schoolwork when it falls short. We're busy, side-tracked, and tend to tune into a child's efforts only when they don't measure up. Praise good work more often. "If a child feels loved and accepted at home, this carries over into school," insisted a Washington eighth-grade teacher. "A loved child feels more confident. A confident child feels comfortable in school and does better."

A gentle touch will prevent your student from resorting to cheating, which is epidemic. Eighty percent of New York teachers in a recent study described cheating as "rampant, among great students as well as poorer ones."

Nurturing is more critical if your family is in the throes of crisis or hard times. Nothing ruins a child's concentration at school like family problems. If you are in a take-one-day-at-a-time mode, carve out a portion of each day to hug your son, apologize to your daughter for all the unavoidable tension. Reassure your child that better days are coming. Even when your family life is caught in a hurricane, you can whisk your child occasionally into the storm's eye.

MAKE LEARNING A MULTIMEDIA ADVENTURE. Did you buy educational toys for your infant? Picture books or educational videos when your daughter was learning to read? When was the last time you supplemented your middler's learning with "toys"? Young adolescents are still children! Take advantage of a new frontier of educational alternatives. There are Civil War trading cards and U.S. presidents playing decks. Adorn your child's room with posters. A budding sax player will appreciate legendary saxophonist John Coltrane's fingering exercises. Use CD-ROMs to teach language skills. *Games in French* (Syracuse Learning Systems) teaches language with bingo and puzzles. Software such as *Where in the World is Carmen Sandiego?* can teach geography. Board games can fine-tune language arts, science, and math skills. Try Aristoplay's *Nova True Science* (a trivia challenge) or *The Play's the Thing* (you're an actor trying out for parts in Shakespearean plays). Free Spirit Press has books such as *Psychology for Kids* featuring experiments—an instant science project.

These are only a sampling of products that give students of all skill levels the message that learning is FUN.

Access your local library (and librarian!) for books, videos, and programs to supplement your child's education. Visit local museums, aquariums, planetariums, and historical sites such as a president's or poet's birthplace, a Civil War battleground memorial. *Books on the Move* (Free Spirit Publishing) matches travel destinations with topics.

KEEP CRITICISM OF TEACHERS AND SCHOOL TO A MINIMUM. Parents have lots of axes to grind nowadays. In many places there is a war going on between teachers and parents. Some parents unfortunately had rotten experiences with school when they were young. This is not solely a history reserved for immigrant or minority parents, either. Be careful about badmouthing education because this will seep into your child's head and erode his effort. A sixth-grade Florida teacher asks parents to remember, "School is only six hours. Home is eighteen. It takes a lot of convincing during school time to overcome negative vibes at home."

In these strained economic times, in some parts of the country parents are inflamed over teacher salaries. Historically, teacher's pay scales were low, but currently they can appear enormous compared to downsized corporate salaries, loss of health insurance coverages, and pink slips. Don't let your payroll-envy thwart the parent-teacher partnership good education demands. If you feel strongly, take your objections to the Board of Education.

If you heed this advice from our NMSA teachers (along with our 3-D tips on helping your child), master monitoring (and not meddling), your child is sure to make a better grade.

Parents Should Be Seen, Not Heard . . .
(at Least in a Middler's Presence)

As your son or daughter heads off to the middle school, for the first time many a mother or father feels left out. When your little one was in elementary school you knew what was expected. You baked birthday cupcakes or cooked up ethnic delicacies for holiday class parties. You volunteered for the PTA's fund-raiser or the car wash. You felt welcome in your child's classroom. An open invitation was extended

for you to read a children's story to second-graders, cook with kinder-
gartners, or talk to fourth-graders about your job on career day. You
knew the teacher and how your child was faring even before the
standard November conference. You were in touch and involved.

The middle school is different. Parents often don't see the same
welcome mat. Young adolescents certainly don't light up at the
thought of Daddy or Mommy coming to school. There is no single
teacher with whom to communicate. If you're lucky, you get flyers or
newsletters signaling upcoming events, but more often than not, those
get lost in the Bermuda Triangle portion of your child's backpack.

Data from the U.S. Department of Education and the National
Center for Education points out that three-quarters of American parents say they had high to moderate involvement in schools when their
children were eight- to ten-years old. By the time children reached
sixteen, high school age, active parental participation dropped to 50
percent.

Parents bow out not because they don't care, but because they
erroneously think they are supposed to. Many mothers and fathers
don't know what role to play during the middler years. One mother
said she made an appointment with her sixth-grader's team of teachers
after the first report card. Her concern was not academics. She simply
wanted to know, "Where do I fit into my daughter's middle school
experience?" The sixth-grade New York teacher explained, "Parent
involvement is vital, but at this age harder to finesse. The essence of
your new role is a twist on an old adage: *parents should be seen but not
heard.*"

NMSA teachers agree that a parent's role is to become a young
adolescent's backup, advocate, and audience. Here are job descriptions
waiting for you to fill them:

• *Cheerleader.* Mark your calendar because your attendance at
school events such as talent shows, concerts, sports matches, and science fairs is extremely important to your child. You are the one he or
she wants to impress. If you have to work, ask someone to videotape
the event for you.

• *Chauffeur* may not be glamorous, but it becomes critical. Your
middler has places to go—dances, special rehearsals for clubs and
plays, field trips, community service activities. You are charged with

transportation. Car pools help, especially with working-parent schedules.

• *Chaperone.* With so many women in the workplace, teachers are often hard-pressed to find adults who will volunteer for class trips, social events, and fund-raisers. Try and juggle your work schedule to fit in at least one of these activities.

• *Committee member.* Middle school has any number of committees and task forces that rely on parent participation. For example, site renovating or landscaping projects need designers. Special themes, such as acknowledging diversity or educating the student body about the abilities of the disabled, require committees to plan programs and contact speakers. Curriculum reviews and evaluations warrant parent input.

• *Resource.* You are an invaluable resource, the artifact for a history report, interview subject for a psychology experiment, or guinea pig for a science project. Who else will be the research assistant at the library or computer? Subscribe to lots of magazines and the newspaper in order to set a literate example.

• *Volunteer.* The PTA has numerous fund-raisers and specialty groups that finance sports or the arts. Become an active member, a committee head, or an officer.

• *Club sponsor or assistant.* If you excel at a hobby such as computers, gardening, kayaking, see if you could start up a club for students to share your expertise. Are you an amateur theatrical director, lighting technician, musical arranger, carpenter? If so, you could contribute to the musical productions, concerts, or stage plays. The possibilities are only limited by your imagination and commitment to play a part in your middler's school life.

NMSA teachers from coast-to-coast in our survey wanted to see more parental involvement. And you know what? The parents' wish list featured more opportunities to get involved! The discrepancy is obviously a communication gap. If you are out of touch with your middle school, look for the following. If they don't exist, get together with similar-minded parents and get them rolling.

Is there a school newsletter? A newsletter is a great way for the school to communicate with the community. Student accomplishments can be featured. The administration can use it as a promotional device to amplify good news, solicit volunteers, or test out new ideas. Teachers can explain to parents what's happening in their classrooms as well as what parents can do to help. Special inserts could advertise fundraisers or special-interest group agendas.

Does a school calendar of events go out to every parent in the community? If parent attendance is down at parenting classes, sports, or fund-raising sales, perhaps it's because parents do not know the details—the when, what time, where, who, and what! Be sure a detailed calendar is drawn up and circulated throughout your community. (Your school district may have one, and it may be languishing somewhere in your middler's messy room.)

Telephone chains are an up-and-coming communication device. In Maine's Freeport Middle School, the administration set up "a calling tree." One parent was chosen to be a liaison between the school administrator's office and parent representatives for each grade. Then once a month the reps call any participating parent to convey the latest school news.

The phone tree can be tapped to get parents' opinions or to voice teacher's concerns. Too much homework? Not enough? Surveys like this were done in Maine and proved very beneficial to both teachers and parents. The telephone chain can easily locate chaperones for upcoming class trips, judges for contests, or volunteers for computer labs and library.

A calling tree helps everyone—parents, teachers, and administrators—work together more effectively. And in this context, the phone call from school is not something only to be dreaded because it spells trouble.

Get to know other parents because in numbers there is shared knowledge and a stronger voice. Taking an active role in your child's school sends a clear message that school is important. You are making that invaluable point with your time, your attention, and your presence.

Is Your Middle School As Safe As It Could Be?

The climate in a school "teaches" lessons, according to NMSA. Those lessons should be respect, caring, and optimism. In this less-than-perfect world, the positive-school climate is endangered. While the academics have been busy implementing a kinder, gentler educational experience for middlers, the outside world has been equally intent upon bringing anarchy into the schools.

In the 1940s, the top seven school problems were (1) talking out of turn, (2) gum chewing, (3) noise, (4) running in halls, (5) cutting in line, (6) dress code infractions, and (7) littering. They seem quaint compared with the list compiled as the 1980s wound down: (1) drug abuse, (2) alcohol abuse, (3) pregnancy, (4) suicide, (5) rape, (6) robbery, and (7) assault.

In Virginia recently, of 2,016 weapons confiscated in public schools, 853 were toted by middlers. Immature adolescents think a weapon is an equalizer if they are small or feel inferior. Weapons, gangs, and bombs have made school halls and playgrounds potentially lethal. The firearms homicide rate for ten- to fourteen-year-olds has doubled since 1985. Middlers are victims of assault more than any other age group. Almost three million crimes occur on or near school campuses every year, according to a National Crime Survey. "So many kids are bringing guns to school I worry about getting killed," confessed a Nevada seventh-grader.

Racism glares from lavatory walls in the shape of swastikas and slogans of hate. Sexism threatens the self-image of both boys and girls subtly, according to the American Association of University Women's 1991 report, *"Shortchanging Girls, Shortchanging America,"* and overtly as students grope or roust one another in lewd gestures and humiliating language.

You send your sons and your daughters off every morning to school, to face the best and the worst society has to offer. "All places where hundreds of seventh- and eighth-graders congregate have safety issues," explains an eighth-grade teacher from Hawaii. "Arguments can quickly escalate into assaults. Being a witness to a breach of school rules can turn into *school-a-phobia.*" A Minnesota teacher added, "Some students are time bombs!"

Violence is an equal-opportunity threat. Inner-city youths risk being killed in drive-by shootings. Even remote country communities turn out to be survivalist covens.

Violence is not a school problem. It is society's problem, which children bring to school, reflecting our collective failings as citizens, parents, and lawmakers. If a positive school climate is to be created, safety must be paramount.

How can you ensure a safe learning environment for your middler? Start by becoming informed about the rate of violence at your child's school. Not all schools are the shooting galleries portrayed by the media. Look for these anticrime guidelines.

Adequate security at building entrances and exits. Other targeted areas require vigilant personnel, such as playgrounds, cafeterias, and any other areas where students congregate.

Well-defined rules for unacceptable behavior. A "zero-tolerance policy," becoming popular in many schools, deals swiftly and assertively with aggressive students and weapons.

An emergency plan (notifying police and alerting teachers) to handle crime.

Peer mediation to defuse clashes and arguments before they escalate into fistfights.

An antiviolence "curriculum." Teachers develop "emotional intelligence" skill training to teach the controlling of impulses, and how to assess intense feelings (an excellent resource here is *Emotional Intelligence* by Daniel Goleman, Ph.D.). Other programs aim for harmony with ethnic appreciation agendas or teach media literacy so that students can examine and discuss the impact of violence, seen on television and in video games, upon society.

An atmosphere of trust so students feel comfortable reporting or witnessing episodes of violence to teachers and administrators.

Coordinated rapport between middle school and local law enforcement. In communities around the country, administrators are joining forces with local police departments to build better community relationships and impart to students trust in and respect for the law. Antidrug programs often use police officers as guest speakers. Vermont's Milton Junior High School sends eighth-graders to court to observe a trial. Then they go to jail (and actually get locked behind bars) to experience real-life consequences for criminal behavior.

If your middle school falls short on violence prevention, work with other parents to implement these guidelines. Keep in mind that school administrators and teachers share your concerns. Establishing and maintaining a disciplined learning environment that is SAFE and RESPECTS the dignity of young adolescents scored highest in an itemized list of sixteen features examined by NMSA in a 1995 study of principals and teachers nationwide.

Students (of all colors) want order in the classroom. Hispanic students are almost 30 percent more likely than Caucasian students to feel that classroom disruptions interfere with their learning, according to Education Department statistics.

Don't forget to examine yourself and your household. On a personal level fight against the groundswell of aggression. If you have registered firearms in the home, make absolutely certain they are not accessible to children. (Schools are an easy target to blame when children are found carrying a gun, but aren't parents ultimately responsible if it was their gun?) Educate children about firearm safety. Set an example by not resorting to violence as the solution to any problem. Discuss television depiction of violence and what characters could have done differently.

If you live in a high-crime neighborhood, organize a neighborhood safety watch so youngsters can come and go to school under the umbrella of adult supervision. Ally yourself with community organizations to provide activities for young adolescents, such as midnight basketball, to keep them from joining the competition: gangs. All adults need to mentor, but this is especially needed in minority communities.

"I have spent eleven years working with poor, minority children from some of New York's most dangerous communities," says Geoffrey Canada, president of Rheedlen Centers for Children and Families, award-winning African-American leader, and author of *fist stick knife gun.* "I spend time teaching kwon do, a means of self-defense.

Martial arts offer not only a respite from fear and a sense of personal power, but a way of teaching discipline . . . a forum for discussing violence and strategies for avoiding violent confrontations."

There are so many ways to fight back. However, if we are to beat violence, we need to address the root causes, look deeper at our attitudes and values. As parents we have to inculcate our children with tolerance, empathy, and genuine respect for all races and religions. We have to *model* brotherly love, harmony, and maturity in expressing our anger and resolving our problems. We have to become whistle-blowers when we see racism, injustice, and violence, and active participants in making the world a better place for those less fortunate than ourselves.

This is a tall order, a life's work. Don't be overwhelmed. A manageable way to approach this philosophy one day at a time is to order *100 Ways You Can Stop Violence,* a poster available for free from the National Association of Social Workers (750 First St., NE, Washington, DC 20002). It has suggestions such as "Curb disparaging remarks." "Take a friend to dinner at an ethnic restaurant." "Speak out against hate." "Let someone get ahead of you in line or traffic." Each little step taken by a mother or a father, imitated by a middler, multiplied by all parents and their offspring can stem the tide of violence.

Gender Bias—Not for Parents of Girls Only

Creating a positive learning climate demands equality. The mother of a fifth-grade girl got a letter from the new teacher the first day of school, inviting any questions parents might have. Hearing all the bad news about gender bias in classrooms, this mom's major question, "Will my daughter be treated equally?"

Yes, feminism has gone back to school. In *Failing at Fairness: How America's Schools Cheat Girls,* education professors Myra and David Sadker claimed boys calling out answers were called upon and encouraged more often than girls in an 8–1 ratio! Peggy Orenstein spent a year in middle school classrooms testing out the AAUW shortchanging girls theory and wrote *SchoolGirls: Young Women, Self-Esteem and the Confidence Gap,* detailing what undermines girls' well-being academically and psychologically. Our schools are sexist. And during the middle school years the deleterious effects are the most devastating.

Do teachers unwittingly give rowdier boys more attention? Encouragement? Are girls typecast as superior verbally but simultaneously as mathematically inferior? These are the years many girls tune out math and science and experience a downward spiral in feeling confident. Experts suggest that a girl's spirit is being broken with a hidden curricula that teaches silence and compliance, preventing many from stretching intellectually, taking risks, and asking questions. Some are pushed into perfectionistic crusades for the perfect academic record.

Parents of boys should pay close attention to gender inequities, too. It has been pointed up that teachers unconsciously reinforce expectations that *all* boys exhibit physical prowess and big personalities to match. This hurts the less boisterous and less extroverted middlers as well as the ones who haven't hit their growth potential. When boys are called on more often, they learn being the "squeaky wheel" works and don't get the lesson that collaboration can be as valuable a skill as being competitive. Many male students, stereotyped as poor readers, are not pushed to attain excellence in language arts, vocabulary, and reading. A disproportionate number are assumed to be candidates for ADD and not likely to be held to tight enough standards of discipline and achievement.

The difficulty with the issue of gender bias in education is the constant contradictions produced by conflicting survey results, for example, are teachers sexist? One school of thinking defends teachers as fair but in need of better discipline techniques for handling boisterous boys. The opposite camp insists teachers need sensitivity training to cure their sexist tendencies.

How can parents sort through well-meaning but divergent information on gender bias?

Ask your school district for a gender breakdown of enrollments in courses such as math, science, and honors; of participation in extracurricular activities and sports; and of test scores and scholarships. The numbers will show either gender parity or inequity. If your district needs upgrading, marshal support from other parents and spearhead action. Some schools are trying girls-only math and science classes because in them girls feel more confident and can employ a more cooperative learning style. (Note critics say this "mommy track" approach smacks of a lesson in inferiority.)

Bring up the issue of gender bias at parent-teacher conference time. It will support progressive teachers and give less activist-minded ones something to ponder. If your child mentions any discrimination in the classroom, take it up with the teacher. Be careful to question not attack. "All too often parents arrive at school ready to behead a teacher rather than befriend and assist," remarked a seventh-grade male teacher from Oklahoma. Be diplomatic even in the face of wrongdoing.

Examine your own homework approach. Do you admit to math anxiety? Are math problems deferred to the male members of the household? Some studies suggest parents behave in a sexist fashion on the homework front. Boys get instruction and permission to work alone. Girls on the other hand tend to get the problems solved for them. The underlying message is *they are incapable or inadequate* or *math is just for men.*

Be your child's academic supporter as well as intellectual stretcher. Don't believe the old saying about girls, which goes *good in writing then bad with numbers.* If she's doing well in language arts but not in math, prod her. If your daughter is science-shy, broaden its definition and change the context for her. Remind her a day at the beach is a living lesson in marine biology. Cooking is chemistry. So is love. Make her feel science is a natural part of her life, not some incomprehensible subject. If she lags behind in mathematics or computer skills, get her to join a club where the camaraderie makes learning fun. Point out examples of female scientists and mathematicians in history and in today's headlines.

Similarly, if your son does poorly in English literature, don't assume that's normal, either. Help him improve his skill level by providing reading material that reflects his interests, such as *Sports Illustrated.* If he prefers the arts to sports, nurture that cultural sensitivity. Take him to concerts or exhibits to see artists in action. Then he can be comfortable with his talent whether it is ballet or violin. The point is that all stereotypes stunt our middlers' potentials.

Continue to critique the media. Let your sons and daughters know that the media doesn't always portray men or women fairly and equally. Only boy pictures on the chemistry set packaging, the documentary that doesn't have one female voice in it, turn your middlers into sexist-detectives, who recognize sexism at a glance.

No matter how far women come, there always seems to be room for improvement in the battle for equal rights. Even *Sesame Street* and the *Cat in the Hat* needed a gender-bias overhaul. So if your middle school needs work, just get in there and do it!

Where Violence and Sexism Meet . . . Sexual Harassment

At a corner table in the cafeteria, a group of sixth-grade girls alternate between giggling and arguing, periodically squealing out consensus. Having written a rating system to judge all sixth-grade boys, they are dissecting every suspect: "Nice buns. Pimplepuss." Meanwhile, in the boys' locker room, several seventh-grade boys are pulling off the ultimate gag: pulling down the pants of an unsuspecting boy as he enters. What a hoot! In another part of the building, a couple is locked in the aftermath of a romantic fallout. The willowy eighth-grade girl is crying. A boy has her pinned to a locker. "We're through, I told you!" she cries. "NO!" he pleads. "I won't let you go. You are my life. I'll beat up anyone who asks you out."

Are these episodes respectively harmless fun, run-of-the-mill antics, and simple unrequited adolescent crush stuff? Not any longer. What were once dismissed as immature shenanigans are recognized now by society as sexual harassment. It runs the gamut from lewd remarks, unwanted attention, on up to groping and rape. Dirty jokes, pornographic doodling on notebooks, the spreading of sexual rumors, obscene T-shirts—any number of components can create the hostile environment that is also part and parcel of sexual harassment. Many young adolescents, including yours, may be an unwilling victim or become an unwitting perpetrator.

Sexual harassment is widespread, polluting the school climate for 81 percent of students, including Caucasians, Latinos, and African Americans. That's four out of five in the recent and much publicized poll of 1,600 public schools, (grades eight to eleven), conducted and reported by the Education Foundation of the American Association of University Women (AAUW). Although some incidents involve a school employee victimizing a student, by far most episodes are student to student. Boys (76 percent) reported being victimized nearly as often as girls (85 percent). Classrooms and hallways are where girls are targeted, generally for how they look. Locker rooms and playgrounds are the danger zones for boys, ridiculed usually for how they act.

The effects are equally disheartening. Twenty-five percent of victims no longer wanted to go to school or speak up in class. Grades dropped in 16 percent of the cases. To make matters worse, most students are reluctant to report being subjected to it. Middlers often are confused about the definition of the issue. They blame themselves. They are afraid of the harasser or just plain embarrassed about the whole episode.

According to Charol Shakeshaft, who headed a Hofstra University study of 1,000 middle and high school students, "Sexual harassment is most potent and damaging in the middle school."

Middlers are not inclined to stand up to peers, harassing or otherwise. They feel powerless to begin with and can ill afford the added feelings of powerlessness that intimidation heaps. It is another nail in the coffin of an already anemic self-image. Moreover, they are notorious for not wanting to bring attention to themselves (what an attention-getter a sexual harassment claim would be!).

See that your middle school is not a hotbed of this kind of dehumanizing behavior. How?

Be sure sexual harassment is on the administration's agenda. It should be. Sexual harassment, defined as sexual discrimination, is against the law (Title IX of the Education Amendments of 1972). Schools are legally responsible and liable for episodes.

Have you received mailings about sexual harassment policy and reporting procedure? Has your child been given a handout? Has the school newsletter featured an article? The issue needs to be publicized so that middlers understand the issue and how to make a complaint.

Examine how complaints against teachers or other school employees are handled. Sexual harassment charges against a teacher or other employee are always an explosive affair. A thirteen-year-old California girl told us, "A custodian always hits on me." Be certain school officials research a complaint thoroughly. Both students and teachers are entitled to fair hearings. All proven breaches deserve appropriate responses. Researchers say that students feel the schools do not protect them, and should. Students are correct to expect educators to stop the harassment.

Bring the issue to the forefront in parent groups. The PTA should examine the school climate for sexual harassment. Survey students. Is sexual harassment a problem? Do students feel comfortable about reporting it to teachers, the administration, or guidance counselors?

Parent groups should be asking: "Are teachers receiving the appropriate training to ferret out this behavior?" If not, they can pressure the school board to finance in-service seminars. "Are students being educated and coached on how to confront the abuser in a harassing situation?" If not, hire a speaker.

Introduce sexual harassment awareness efforts. Sponsor an activity to increase visibility of sexual harassment. Plan a poster competition or an essay contest. Schedule a program of skits or readings on the issue for a school assembly or during the advisory period of the school day. Set up an awareness booth at the next sports event or school play. These can be done by the PTA, in conjunction with special clubs, or sponsored by local business or community groups.

Talk with your child. "Boys have grabbed me and said things," a fourteen-year-old girl from Maine claimed. We found girls complained about bra-snapping; boys about name-calling. Explain what kinds of behavior constitute harassment. Ask boys and girls if insults or actions have made them uncomfortable.

If your child tells you about an incident, don't advise, "Ignore it." Victims say that has been the standard advice from teachers, counselors, and parents. Children know ignoring such attacks does *not* make them go away or ease the humiliation. Instead, tell your child to call the offender on sexual harassment or report the incident. Stress that it is equally important to report witnessing an incident in which another student is victimized. Assure your child that there is a difference between snitching and working to create a school environment without sexist intimidation. A harassment-free school is every student's right and responsibility.

When it comes to helping our children succeed in school, we—parents, teachers, administrators, and students—are all in this together. Good middle schools, motivating parents, and effective educators share an agenda that stimulates young adolescents intellectually while nurturing them emotionally, taking into account their special challenges and handling them with respect and caring. We have to pull together, take aim collectively, or else we will fail to hit the mark.

Strategies: Think of Yourself As an Educational Consultant

Now is the time to reinvent your role in your child's education. Be the best activist you can be at school. Bring the hallmarks of a good middle school into your home.

Become a middler expert. (You are on your way by reading this book.) We have peppered our text with many resources to educate you. Begin dialogues with other parents. Join the National Middle School Association to receive the latest information on issues concerning middlers.

Help your young adolescent develop many skills. Work on *more* than academics. Have ethical discussions. Explore controversial topics (from the news) such as sexism, immigration, and racial discrimination. Ross Burkhardt, past NMSA president, reminds us that success is more than intellect. "Look at Hitler and Nazi Germany, Mussolini. Intelligent, yes, but failures when it comes to what makes good human beings and societies."

Make homework hands-on. Empower your child with new ways to study and learn. Determine the learning style of your child. A quick way: Does he/she prefer listening for directions (auditory), reading a map (visual), or getting in the car and exploring (kinesthetic). Visual learners trying to memorize New World explorers or science theories would like flash cards. Verbally quiz an auditory learner, Jeopardy-style. Let the kinesthetic learner write a *matching column* or *fill in the blanks* test to master vocabulary words or foreign language.

Evaluate more than grades. Take a broader view of achievement. Expect and assess grades, but look further. Is he behaving conscientiously regarding homework? Is she motivated to study for tests, expending enough effort for projects? Grades may be erratic, so allow leeway, especially if your child is trying hard. Be more of a counselor than a critic.

Make the home-learning environment a positive, nurturing one. Tell your child, "You are the client and I am your personal educational consultant. Together (with your teachers), we can turn you into a lean, mean learning machine." Put your heads together to identify challenges and overcome hurdles. Above all, put caring, respect, and (yes) fun into the learning process.

A Report Card for Middle Schoolers—Parents, Students, and Teachers

According to *Metlife's Survey of the American Teacher, 1984–95,* many teachers believe aspects of public school have improved considerably in the last ten years. What did our survey reveal? [E—excellent S—satisfactory U—unsatisfactory]

Grade Subject

E *Approval* Middle schools are doing a good job, say 75 percent of parents.

E *Academics* Academics and sports are well-balanced, say 87 percent of teachers.

U *Safety* Fifty-eight percent of teachers admit safety issues exist (from rowdy middlers to violent episodes). Thirty-five percent of teachers have been threatened or harmed.

U *Equal Opportunity in Sports* Boys are favored in sports programs, say 40 percent of parents. Only 35 percent thought programs offered equal opportunity.

U *Parent Involvement* Teachers (95 percent) want to see parents *more* involved.

U *Parent Awareness* Teachers feel parents are not well-informed about the lives of their middlers. (More in the dark on their child's private life.)

U *Student Performance* Getting middlers to do homework and meet responsibilities is a battle zone in one-third of families, according to parents.

S *Reading* Middlers read for pleasure, according to 60 percent of parents. Children say they like horror best, followed by fantasy, sports, romance, biographies, and history. Magazines—66 percent read them. *Sports Illustrated* and *YM* top their list.

E *Useful education* Students believe (75 percent) what they are taught helps them in life.

S *Student schedules* More than half of middlers feel their schedules (homework, sports, and activities) are just right.

Congratulations on your achievements. Keep up the good work. Buckle down to do better in the areas that need improvement.

Seven

Enduring the Bumper Cars

Sibling Rivalry, Peer Pressure, and Other Obstacles

"At this age, friends are extremely important sources of support, a 'measuring stick' of how well they are developing."

(Teacher from Texas)

As parents we would like our children's ride through young adolescence to be like a pleasant, leisurely drive down a scenic country road. Unfortunately, the journey is more apt to resemble a teeth-jarring turn in the bumper cars. The overall experience is exhilarating. But the jolts that strike can throw off even the most determined driver and send him careening out of control.

What are these obstacles that crash into our children during these middler years? First and foremost are other children—siblings and peers. This chapter will examine the love-hate relationship that exists between middlers and their contemporaries. Be prepared for head-on collisions and fiery explosions.

Peer relationships are the ones that we dread as our children rely increasingly on their friends for advice, guidance, consolation, and support. Yet there is much that we can do during these years not only to continue to influence our children but also to ensure that both sibling and peer encounters will be positive ones.

Siblings: The Ties That Bind

Middlers are liable to treat brothers and sisters (particularly younger brothers and sisters) with disdain. Looking at the situation from your middler's point of view, that feeling is not surprising. Siblings seem destined to thwart a middler's every attempt toward independence:

Middlers crave privacy, but with siblings around, it is often difficult or impossible for middlers to be alone. "Stay out of my room!" or, if the siblings share a room, "Leave my things alone!" will often be the battle cry that starts the war.

Middlers, on the threshold of the adult world, have mixed feelings about leaving behind childhood things. Suggesting that some of these items be turned over to a sibling may bring a strong reaction. "When my daughter turned thirteen, I didn't think she would mind if I let her younger sister play with her Barbie dolls," one mother recalled. "She hit the roof! She took them all back and locked them in her closet, leaving my eight-year-old in tears. I was going to reprimand her for being so selfish, but then I realized that the simple act of passing on those dolls was very painful for my older daughter."

Middlers are self-conscious. Your daughter is overly concerned with how she looks and must contend with the scrutiny of peers at school each day. Having to deal also with a sibling who is critical rather than sympathetic will add to her misery.

Middlers are insecure. Your son is filled with self-doubt. Will he make the basketball team? Did he do okay on the math test? If he goes to the dance, will any of the girls want to dance with him? During these anxious years when he is constantly evaluating himself to see how he measures up, comparison with siblings is inevitable. Even if you refrain from making comments, others may not be so thoughtful. Teachers, friends, and siblings themselves (who, after all, are engaged in their own struggle with self-esteem) may remind your son that his brother or sister is superior to him in some way.

Middlers are sensitive to injustice. The ten- to fifteen-year-old will scream if he suspects a sibling is receiving preferential treatment. Whether the argument is over something trivial—a younger sibling getting the bigger slice of cake or being allowed to select the evening's TV show—or substantive—an older sibling being allowed to stay out later—you will find yourself in the unenviable position of arbiter.

Middlers really do crave emotional closeness and are apt to have deep feelings for siblings, even if the siblings are young pests. The old saying, "You always hurt the ones you love," can best sum up the relationship. After all, your daughter is not going to take out her anger on a classmate whose friendship she may lose forever. But she can be sure that her sister will still be there tomorrow, no matter how much she tortures her today.

Where relationships are concerned, however, yours is the one most important to your middler. Remember the children's story, *The Runaway Bunny* by Margaret Wise Brown? The little bunny seemed determined to run away from its parent, conjuring up numerous scenarios, everything from turning into a crocus to joining the circus. In every case, the parent bunny offered the assurance the little bunny was seeking that, no matter what, she would always come after her child because "You're my little bunny."

There's a reason for this book's popularity. Children like to be reassured that their parents will always be there for them, no matter what they do. In her own way, your middler is seeking a reaffirmation of this parent-child pact. That may seem strange to you, because she may be sending you the opposite message, preferring the company of her friends. Those friendships, as important as they are to your daughter, are constantly in flux. She can't depend upon them the way she can depend upon you. That is why most of the fights between siblings are actually fights for your time or attention. Shift your focus to one of your other children and she will sense the abandonment and react, usually with anger against the favored sibling. It's a hard task you face as the parent, attempting to meet each child's needs, particularly if you have more than one middler to deal with at the same time.

Parental Control

For many of us, sibling battles are nothing new. We may have fought with brothers or sisters when we were younger. We may still be actively engaged in these struggles. Although the fights themselves are no longer physical, they may be every bit as painful. And, consciously or not, our own sibling relationships may affect how we react when our children engage in power struggles. If you were constantly picked on by an older brother, you may come down hard on your middler when he picks on his younger sibling. Similarly, if you were the older child and resented having a baby sister who always interfered with your privacy and plans, you may be favoring your older child in these situations. Were you an only child? Then you may have no frame of reference for sibling squabbles, and your reaction may often be out of proportion to the problem.

It's not an easy task to examine our own biases and attempt to set them aside. A sibling relationship that was particularly troubling may be one for which you have sought professional help. Simply recognizing the pitfalls may help you to step back and remember that your current position is different from the one you occupied as a child. This may be your opportunity to affect your children's lives in a positive manner so that, years from now, these sibling bonds will be supportive rather than restrictive.

What can you do? Be realistic. You may not be able to stop the fighting, but you can establish some ground rules. Make it clear what types of behavior are off-limits—name-calling, physical violence, unwanted touching, damaging personal possessions. Your children cannot be forced to like each other, but they should still treat each other with respect.

Talk with each child to determine what is important. Privacy? Possessions? To stress that you are taking these concerns seriously, interview each child separately and write down what is said. "Now, let me see if I understand you, Johnny. When you have friends over, you would like Mark not to disturb you. Is that right? And Mark, when you are doing your homework, you would prefer that Johnny not play his radio. Correct?" This system, because of its inherent fairness, will appeal to middlers. And once you have in writing what the rules are that govern behavior, it will be easier for you to enforce them.

Some sibling fights are not fights at all but merely the manner in which your children play or work out their disagreements. Constantly stepping in will prevent your children from learning how to resolve their problems. Also, your authority will be weakened if you exercise your discipline muscle too often.

How do you decide whether to step in or leave well-enough alone? There are several tactics you can use. Time is one. Set a kitchen timer or glance at your watch. If the tiff lasts longer than four or five minutes, intervene. You will probably be surprised to discover that very few of your children's free-for-alls last that long. These rows only *seem* to go on for hours!

When the action is physical, learn to tell when someone is at risk. Doing so is not always as easy as you would think. Say you walk in on your two sons wrestling. You may be frightened because an aggressive activity such as wrestling makes it look like someone is being physically harmed. Yet children, like bears, often roughhouse as a way of play. Your sons may be having fun and will resent your intrusion. On the other hand, if you find an older sibling tickling a younger one who is rendered helpless with laughter, you may laugh, too. Ironically, this situation might be one where a child is feeling violated and wants to be rescued.

When you find one sibling being overpowered, ask if the child would like the action stopped. If the answer is no, set some ground rules (not in the house, watch the lamp, no kicking), step back, and let them go at it for a while. Your middler is a bundle of energy and oftentimes initiating a fight with a sibling will be his way of dealing with his inability to sit still. When you sense he is restless, suggest another physical activity—basketball, in-line skating, bicycling—to keep him occupied.

How do you deal with the verbal battles? "I know my thirteen-year-old daughter loves her nine-year-old brother, but you would never know it by what she says to him," said the mother. " 'You're stupid,' 'You're fat,' 'I hate you!'—sometimes I can't believe the things that come out of her mouth. With everyone else she is gentle and kind. Our poor son! He thinks his sister hates him."

There is a great deal going on here besides the bad words. Call a family meeting to discuss the situation. Pick a time in the evening when the entire family can sit down at a table with no interruptions. Turn off the TV, turn on the answering machine. Start by describing the situation as you see it and make it clear you are prepared to hear all sides of the story. Each child should be able to talk uninterrupted by the other. Chances are you will discover your middler is grappling with another issue (no privacy, for example) that triggers the verbal abuse. After you have heard both sides, establish some guidelines for behavior and punishment. Be sure to follow through. Drawing lines won't work if you don't deliver on your promise to reprimand the offender.

No matter how frustrating your middler may be to parent, don't discuss him with one of his siblings. Even comments made in a fit of anger ("Your brother drives me crazy! He never does his homework!") will serve no purpose other than to damage your relationship with everyone. Remember that your other children are not dispassionate observers. They are members of your household, and, as such, also fall under your authority. In a game of one-upmanship, one child may repeat the comment to another to gain an advantage. ("Mom tells everybody you're a slob!") Even if she keeps the remark to herself, she is apt to wonder what comments you make about her!

Exercise discretion in what you tell other adults. You have no assurance that good friends won't relay something to their own children. When the comment comes back to your son, you will have seriously damaged your credibility with him.

It's tempting to compare your children, not only to each other but also to their friends. "Why can't you be more like . . . ?" "So-and-so wouldn't do that!" Perhaps you refrain from making such blatant comparisons, but may, through your words and actions, imply that your child's behavior, achievements, or whatever fall short of his brother's or best friend's. This ploy is destined to backfire. Your daughter's self-esteem will take a major blow. At the same time, whoever is being held up as your ideal will incur your child's wrath. If this model child is a sibling, you have ensured that the sibling wars will enter a new and bloodier stage. And you will not achieve your goal of motivating your daughter. She is liable to become even more angry, bitter, and uncooperative.

Admittedly, when a mother and father talk about their children, it seems natural to make comparisons, particularly in the younger years with so many developmental milestones. "Amy didn't walk until she was fourteen months old, but Ben was running around before he turned one." Even if Amy overheard these remarks, she probably wouldn't be upset. She had little control over when she began to walk, so she can remain detached. However, substitute "read" for "walk" and add some years to the ages, and you can see how Amy's reaction might change. Some parents who are used to comparing their children, even sharing these thoughts with the children themselves, fail to recognize that as a child matures these comparisons become more meaningful and thus have the power to inflict great psychic harm.

Comparing your children isn't an easy habit to break. You can enlist the cooperation of your spouse or another parent and make a pact to stop each other before doing so.

Avoiding comparisons will help you recognize that each child is different with his or her own characteristics, talents, temperament, and needs. "There is a great sibling rivalry in our household," said a forty-two-year-old mother of two from New Jersey. "My children are only twenty months apart and are forever comparing what one gets to the other. I see this as a serious problem in our house. My older one is athletic, very personable, and really does not have to study hard to get good grades. Whereas my younger one is not as athletic, extremely shy, and really has to study to get good grades. I find myself trying to give more personal attention to my younger one to help her feel good about herself."

Sometimes one child needs more attention. In the future, your children's situations will change and so, too, will the amount of time you spend with each. Don't feel you must always be fair. Explain the disproportionate use of your time in a way that does not portray one child as being less capable. "Mary has a math test tomorrow and I am going to help her study. If there's something you want help with, I can be with you afterward."

Dividing up your time among your children is a tricky thing because to a child time equals love. The situation becomes more complicated with middlers because these children are now spending more time with their friends, but when they want to be with a parent, they become very possessive of the parent's time. Again, those of us who grew up in families with other brothers and sisters have faced this dilemma. Our parents swore on a stack of Bibles that they loved all of us equally, but we always suspected which child Dad favored or Mom liked more. Now that we are on the other side, we can see for ourselves how difficult it is not only to love all our children equally but also to demonstrate that equality through our actions. At the least, we can avoid making statements that imply we do favor one child. Ideally, we can plan time alone with each child where, for a short while, this child will feel special.

Whenever possible, plan time together as a family away from home, school, and friends. With their friends out of the picture, they will be forced to rely on each other for companionship and fun. No doubt, a family vacation with plenty of suitable activities available can be an opportunity for everyone to get reacquainted and remember their similarities rather than their differences.

When Your Middler Is a Stepchild

With stepchildren who are middlers, two issues will loom large over your relationship—their territory and their parent's time. They are apt to be extremely possessive about both and become angry when their needs are not met. It helps to remember that this anger is really about something entirely different, the fact that the family structure has changed. Middlers, who are already trying to figure out where they fit in, will struggle with finding an acceptable place within their blended family.

"Territory was always a big issue with my stepchildren," recalled one woman. "After my husband and I got married, we lived in the original house, and his children would visit us on weekends. I know it was hard for them coming back to their home, seeing that I had changed the decor and setup. I had turned my stepdaughter's room into my office, and she was upset about that."

Shortage of space may not allow you to provide each middler stepchild with his own room when he visits. But, if possible, help him to carve out a space where he can feel at home. Equally important is ensuring that he will have sufficient time with his primary parent while visiting. While the stepparent may feel she wants to be with them throughout the visit to create the feeling of family, the child may want time alone with his parent.

Many of the fights in stepfamilies erupt when the adults involved have different parenting routines. The ideal situation is to have all the parents and stepparents reach some sort of consensus on the important issues—freedoms, curfews, dress, homework. If the child must spend time in two different households, it would help her to have the rules in each be relatively similar. If her mother wants her in at 10:00 P.M. but her father lets her stay out until midnight when she visits, conflicts may result.

On other issues that may be less critical but equally disruptive to home life, discuss with your partner what you are willing to compromise on. Perhaps you don't care if your son plays his music loudly, but it bothers his new stepparent. In most cases, it would be best not to create too many changes in your middler's life. After all, he has been living with one set of guidelines. To have a stepparent come in at this stage and establish new ones is bound to cause resentment.

Because middlers are already questioning authority, they will not eagerly accept an additional adult in their lives who represents yet another layer of government. Whether the stepparent has been on the scene for a long time or a short one, he or she should tread lightly. As we've already said in Chapter Three, trust between the child and stepparent must be built slowly. In blended families, the first few years are the most difficult.

Peer Review—A Painful Process

Friends are everything to a middler, a fact that parents will be reminded of loudly and often. Your daughter, who once refused to go anywhere without you, now can't seem to exist without constantly being in touch with her friends. How, you wonder, can she spend an hour on the phone talking to someone she was with all day long? Easy. Middlers never run out of things to discuss with their friends. The conversations might seem trivial and repetitive to you, but to these young people the topics are compelling.

Because a friend means so much to your daughter, she will automatically assume that she is the most important person to that friend, too. Unfortunately, the middler years are volatile ones where friendships are concerned. Middlers mature at different rates. Some friends may move on, leaving others in the dust. "My daughter is at that horrible in-between stage," said one mother. "She still wants to be a child, but she is enjoying being a teenette. She has managed to stay friendly with two groups of girls, one interested in boys, the other not. It's a tough assignment she's given herself, trying to please two different groups."

It is a painful time for many young people who may be excluded from cliques and ostracized by former good buddies. The desire to fit in may become overwhelming, and some children may end up making foolish choices just to be accepted by peers.

Other obstacles crop up. The middler years are ones when children first begin to understand racial prejudice. In this age of political correctness, even young children are being called to account for their actions. How do we educate our children to stay safe on the streets while avoiding racial stereotyping? How do we equip middlers who may be in the minority to handle the prejudices they will encounter?

The situation is not as bleak as you might think. Contrary to popular parental opinion, not all peer pressure is bad. In our survey, 62 percent of middle school teachers said that peer pressure can be good as well as bad, depending upon the situation. One teacher from California said that peer influence was so positive in her classroom that she routinely employed peer-tutors. "Peer pressure can be positive," observed a seventh-grade teacher from Oklahoma. "When a class has one or two disruptive members, usually the others can control the situation because they want to learn. It's an interesting dynamic to watch."

Peers can encourage one another to work hard in school, say no to drugs, smoking, alcohol, and sex, be responsible, help others, and, in short, be the ideal children we all want them to be.

Good News—and Bad News

The area of friends is one where parents feel the loss of control most keenly. After all, since our children were crawling, we selected their friends. We met other parents in the park or at the day-care center and, based on the behavior we saw, decided which children would be appropriate playmates. An aggressive child who threw sand or bit stood little chance of being admitted to our inner circle.

As our children grew, so did our role in their friendships. You may have selected your child's school (or your community) with the intention that the other children there would come from families with similar values. You met other parents and arranged playdates and sleepovers. If there was a friend you didn't approve of, you could gently steer your child away from him. In many cases, our friends' children became our children's friends, thus giving us even more control.

With your child's move to middle school, all that has changed. Your role as your daughter's social director has come to an end.

Some parents, however, refuse to step aside. They continue to voice their opinions—unsolicited, of course—about various friends. In extreme cases, a parent may issue an ultimatum, forbidding friendships with certain boys and girls. Such heavy-handed behavior is destined to fail. We are all acquainted with situations where an adolescent has sneaked out to see friends behind a parent's back. Essentially a parent is telling a child, "I don't trust your judgment." Why should a parent be surprised when the child then rebels, and not just against a parent selecting his friends, but to protest the parent's overall authority? At one point, an adolescent may decide for himself that his friend is not a good influence and drop him. But it isn't likely he will do so to please his parent.

Don't feel helpless, though. Even if you can't pick your child's friends, you can teach him how to exercise his own good judgment, no matter who he is with. As one mother expressed it: "Some parents will attempt to build a fence around the ocean. Others will teach their children to swim." We want to teach our children to be good swimmers, to stay afloat no matter what forces are trying to drag them down.

Swimming Lessons

A strong swimmer stands a good chance of making it through rough, stormy seas to the safety of shore. Similarly, you can help your child build up his resistance through what happens in your home.

• Establish a respectful environment in your household where everyone is treated fairly. You may not be able to quash every single sibling battle, but make it clear you do not approve of behavior where one child is belittled or picked on. If you look the other way when these fights erupt, your middler may look the other way (or, worse yet, participate) when a group gangs up against someone in her class.

• Be tough with older siblings who swear. Tolerate the language in your home, and you should not be surprised when your middler uses that language outside of home. Tell your middler that George

McKenna, deputy superintendent of schools in Compton, California, has called obscenity "the language of powerless people." When a swear word is used in frustration, help your child find another way to deal with his feelings.

• Don't see it as your role to entertain your middler after school and on weekends. Teach him to be a self-starter with activities. Most kids who get involved with drugs, alcohol, and sex, do so because they are bored. A child who has hobbies and interests to pursue as a means of relaxation will find other ways to occupy his time. He won't be so quick to follow a peer who is engaging in negative behavior.

• Turn off the TV (or be prepared to discuss) when programs portray adults as dumb and out of control. Many shows use the "us against them" (children against parents) as a theme that negative peer groups can use to their advantage.

• This age group is big on celebrity worship. Point out behavior by rock singers, athletes, and movie and TV stars that is disrespectful. In the real world, a person has to earn another's respect and adulation. Cite examples of famous people who are worthy of praise because of their accomplishments. You are putting across the message that your son's friends, too, must earn his loyalty through positive deeds and not just because they are in a cool gang or wear the right brand of sneakers.

• Make it clear that your house rules apply to your daughter's friends, too. Don't be afraid to reprimand a visiting child even if it risks embarrassing your child. One mother told this story: "My daughter brought over a new friend who I thought was very sassy and disrespectful. I let some of it go, but when she made my younger daughter cry with a very mean remark, I stepped in. I told her that if she expected to come back to my house again, she had to shape up. Initially, my older daughter was mortified. But later on she confessed that she was upset about her friend's behavior, too, and didn't know how to handle it. She was glad I stepped in."

• Children who are able to look at the facts and arrive at a decision on their own are children who will resist being mere followers. Encourage your son to participate in discussions at home. Show your appreciation for his opinions. Give him a chance to defend his point of view, but don't let him off the hook easily. "Everyone says," or "I just know," cannot be substituted for the facts.

• Teach through example that each person should be valued for his exceptional qualities. Middler mentality often dictates that these young people should do everything alike. This attitude gets them into trouble when they opt to go along with the crowd rather than be viewed as different. Point to friends that you have who are nothing like you. You might share stories about when you disagreed with your friend. It's possible to be loyal to a friend without always following his lead.

• The best defense against negative peer pressure is for a family to have strong values that are known and observed by each member. Talk about the tough topics—smoking, drinking, drugs, sex, AIDS, race relations. Let your child know how you feel about these issues. Yes, these subjects are being discussed at school, but your child still needs to hear your opinion. Middlers want to please their parents. Knowing that you strongly disapprove of drinking, for example, will register, and when your daughter is being coaxed into drinking by a friend, a gong will go off in her head.

When your child sticks to his guns, reward him. It may be a painful experience for him, and he will need your consolation and support.

Swimming Against the Tide

Peer pressure is a powerful force. There is strength in numbers. When your daughter is the only one who disagrees with something her friends are doing, it takes great resolve to say no and walk away. She risks losing face and friends. Chances are she will be reluctant to do anything where she alienates them. This is where a parent can help. Role-play with her by creating different scenarios and asking her how she would respond. "Say I tell you that my parents aren't home today and that I have a pack of cigarettes. Want to come to my house to smoke with me? What would you say?"

Just say no. If your daughter feels comfortable doing so, she can just say no. This situation is one where those discussions at home will come in handy. "I'm not going to smoke. Did you know that cigarette smoke contains fifteen known carcinogens?" She might even wind up talking her friend out of the activity!

Ignore it. Perhaps the friend made the request during lunch when the cafeteria was noisy. Your daughter can decline to acknowledge that she understood her friend. "Oh? Did you mean today? I'm sorry. I didn't understand."

Use humor. Your daughter can make a joke about it. "Oh, right! Me smoke? What will I tell my uncle, the surgeon general?"

Make an excuse. She can always tell her friend she'll get back to her if she feels she needs time to formulate an excuse. Chances are, with a middler's schedule being so full, some other activity will intervene.

Blame your parents. As a last resort, your daughter can lay the blame on you. "I can't come over today. I promised my father I would rake leaves." Or, "Are you kidding? If my mother ever caught me, I'd be dead!"

Love Me, Love My Friends

What happens when your child falls in with the wrong crowd? We're already said that your son probably won't listen if you try to tell him to give up these friends. Is there anything a parent can do?

Start with the school. So much peer influence begins in the classroom that a teacher who is on top of matters can be a valuable ally. In our survey, teachers reported that they frequently intervene in these situations. "If a really nice boy or girl was being pulled into a potentially less desirable group, I have talked to the student and, at times, called the parents," said a seventh- and eighth-grade teacher from Nevada. The teacher may arrange to have your child's seat or group assignment changed. And because these things are happening at school, away from your authority, your child will have less reason to blame you for being separated from his crowd.

Get to know other parents in the class. They, too, may be concerned about their children. Your child's middle school may sponsor social events where parents can talk. Make sure to introduce yourself to the parents of your son's friends. Establish a rapport with these other parents and it may be possible to work together to turn the situation around.

When you approach another parent about a situation that may be causing you concern, use language that is nonjudgmental. Never assume that your child is blameless. Rather, present the issue as one where, as parents, you have mutual concerns. The goal should be to come up with a solution that will satisfy all parties. Here is one example:

You find marijuana in your son's dresser drawer. Upon questioning him, he tells you that he was only holding it for his friend, Mike. You could call Mike's parents and accuse him of leading your child astray. But chances are your son is not guiltless. A better approach would be to call Mike's parents, talk about what happened, and then enlist their support. Both boys should be held accountable. This time would be a perfect one for discussing drugs.

It's easy to become alarmed when your child starts hanging out with friends who have pierced noses, tattoos, and spiked hair. Appearances may be deceiving. Many middlers go through phases where they try to shock adults with their bizarre clothing and jewelry. Underneath, these children may be no different from yours and, indeed, six months from now will abandon this form of self-expression. Invite your son's friends over. See for yourself how these young people interact. You may find that some of your fears are groundless. If you do see behavior that you disapprove of, you will have some concrete issues to discuss with your son.

How do you tell your son you don't like his friends? Tactfully. It may be better to present your criticism as observations. "I wonder why Jonah always says such negative things about the other boys in your class. Does he have many friends?" Or, "Why do you suppose Marsha wears so much makeup? She really doesn't need to, because she is so pretty. Do you think she's trying to send a message?"

No doubt these theories will cause your child to reflect on his or her friend's motives, too. Try to point out some of the friend's positive points, too. That way your child won't believe you are being overly critical and just look for the bad in his friends.

The only way you will observe your child's friends is to spend time with them. Encourage your daughter to have her friends over. Even if you don't like the friends, it's better to have them in your home than elsewhere. Create a kid-friendly environment where they will like to gather. If they decide to go out, volunteer to drive them or pick them up. Stay close without being intrusive.

Get on the list to chaperone school events or, if possible, sign on as a parent coach, tutor, or library helper. Your middler may not want you near him, but you can find a way to be in the school where you can observe his friends and get to know them better.

Working parents may find it more challenging to get involved. School functions many times are scheduled during working hours. Talk with your child's teacher and study your child's upcoming calendar of events. Look for ways to put yourself on the scene.

What we said earlier about addressing negative situations immediately still goes, however. If you witness behavior that is off-limits—in your house or elsewhere—make your feelings known. These are times when it would be helpful to know the friend's parents so that you can enlist their help in handling any problems that crop up.

Try not to be judgmental of parents and their children. "My daughter, who just turned fifteen, wrongly earned a bad reputation," said one mother. "We live in a small town, so it has really affected her. She made some bad choices about who she runs around with, and now she can't get back into the crowd she was with because the parents have decided she is a bad child. What can I do?"

None of us can ever assume that we won't be in this mother's position someday. We would want our child to be given the benefit of the doubt. Middlers are constantly changing. Today's rebel may be tomorrow's hero.

Hurtful Cliques and Bullies

The middler years are a time when your child may first be confronted with cliques and bullies. Because we have all survived similar ordeals, we are apt to dismiss these fears and complaints. Yet think back to your own middler years. If someone had been able to help you handle your own situation so that the outcome was more positive (and you weren't forced to relive the trauma every time you dealt with an abusive boss or were ignored at a cocktail party), wouldn't that have been better?

There is another reason for parental intervention. Cliques and bullies today are rougher and meaner than they were in the past. Childhood has lost its innocence. We have all read the headlines where children as young as six have shown they are capable of unspeakable violence against other children. Being picked on used to mean someone tied your shoelaces together or stuck gum on your seat. Today it means a classmate may threaten your child with a knife or a gun. So the wise parent will stay informed and stand ready to get involved.

Anatomy of a clique. What is a clique? The dictionary defines a clique as "a small, exclusive circle of people." Cliques are different from mere groups of friends, because there is a concerted effort to keep certain people out. And very often those left on the sidelines are ostracized. These social enclaves occur among both sexes.

Many characters play a role in the drama of cliques and, at one time or another, your child will no doubt be cast. These players are:

The aggressor. One person (or sometimes two) usually dominates a clique. Young people are naturally attracted to an aggressor because he is charismatic and persuasive. Yet the aggressor often lacks self-esteem and needs the support of the clique to bolster his self-confidence.

The joiners. These young people are extremely susceptible to negative peer pressure. They probably have no strong feelings of loyalty for the aggressor but have joined in merely because they are afraid not to.

The spectators. Even though these students are not actively participating in the clique, they are just as responsible for letting it happen. They are inclined to look the other way and not get involved. Yet, if they are approached by the clique, they might easily turn into joiners.

The victim. The person who finds himself excluded is often someone the aggressor sees as a threat. The victim may be the smartest, most attractive, or most athletic student in the class. The aggressor, fearing that he will be left behind, convinces the others to gang up on this person.

Who gets singled out as a victim? It's hard to predict, but here are some general observations:

• *Anyone who looks different.* In a homogeneous school, someone who is of a different ethnic background stands out.
• *Anyone who stands out in a physical way.* This often means some-

one whose looks make them noticeable, either because they are "too pretty," "too ugly," "too fat," or "too thin."

• *Anyone who stands out in an academic way.* A student who does very well in school may be ridiculed. "Many students think it is not 'cool' to do well in school, so there is pressure on the good students not to risk looking too different from the average," observed an eighth-grade teacher.

• *Anyone who is well-behaved and tagged as the "teacher's pet."* "Students do not get any peer attention for positive behavior," noted a teacher from Vermont. "If they do, it is in the form of razzing." Another teacher agreed. "Some students ridicule and put down well-behaved or academically motivated students, calling them 'school boy or girl.' "

• *Anyone who is new to town.* A new student makes a perfect target because he has not yet made any friends, so who will come to his aid?

• *Anyone who is easily upset.* The aggressor hopes to get a reaction. A victim who cries or worse will satisfy that need.

• *Anyone who mingles with kids of different races.* In schools where racial prejudice rears its ugly head, students who are color-blind will be singled out for criticism.

• *Anyone who doesn't follow strict codes of gender behavior.* Girls who are athletic or boys who shun sports may be jeered at by other students.

You can see that cliques are complex, with many personal dynamics being played out. The rules governing who is in or out are established arbitrarily by the aggressor. Your daughter, the victim, may find that although all her friends have been accepted by the clique, she has not. Soon, these former friends (joiners) not only avoid her but may side with the aggressor and others who make fun of her and spread rumors that try to damage her reputation. Any attempts your daughter makes to reach out to new friends (spectators) may be rebuffed. The other girls may fear the wrath of the clique. And, after all, some of these girls may be striving for acceptance themselves. Associating with someone who has already been rejected seems foolhardy.

Cliques operate slightly differently for boys. While girls are subjected to shunning and verbal attacks, boys may be targets for physical violence.

You can easily see how a young person, who already is struggling with issues of identity and acceptance by peers, can be seriously harmed by the actions of cliques. A middler who is isolated from her classmates and made to feel like a freak may become depressed, even suicidal.

Rest assured, at some time or another, your child will have a role to play in the clique drama. No doubt you will find the experience painful, whether your child is the victim, aggressor, joiner, or a mere spectator. No parent wants to see another child targeted for this type of abuse. With good communication and cooperation among parents, cliques can be dismantled.

The best precaution you can take is to be aware of your child's friendships. A young person who is being tormented by a clique may not confide in a parent. There are warning signs a parent can look for though. Obviously, the big tip-off is a lack of friends. Something is going on when the phone stops ringing and friends never drop over. A child being tormented at school will be reluctant to go. A parent may let a few headaches or stomachaches go by, but soon enough will become suspicious.

What do you do when you find out your child is the victim? Your first step should be to talk with the teacher. In our survey, we found that teachers felt it part of their job to create a classroom environment that is fair and equitable. "I make sure all students feel welcome in my classroom," said an art teacher from California. "We are all artists in here. There is no room for cliques."

Teachers report that they use a variety of tactics to make sure students work with different groups. "I change seats every three weeks," said a teacher from Vermont.

On the occasions that cliques do form, teachers are not reluctant to intervene. Here are some strategies we heard about:

The teacher sits down with the students involved and talks about the harmful nature of cliques. "I explained that they were excluding a part of our team and that it was hurting the individual and all of us," said a fifth-grade teacher. "I gave suggestions about ways they could include the student and they did."

Focusing on the victims, the teacher finds ways to make them feel special. "I involved shunned students with activities that showed their talents and skills," said an eighth-grade teacher from Maine.

Using role-playing, the teacher asks the leaders of the clique to imagine how they would feel if they were excluded. "I try to get them to live in the other person's shoes," said a teacher from Vermont.

The students involved might participate in peer-mediation. Because students feel less threatened talking with their peers, these sessions, where both sides are given a chance to talk out their problems, have had much success.

The teacher can arrange a meeting with the students and a trained counselor. "I was approached by a group of girls who were struggling with one girl," said a sixth-grade teacher. "I asked them to think of ways they could communicate their issues. We sat down with a guidance counselor and hashed things out."

Parents of the students involved can be called in to school. "The discord between a group led to violence and spilled into the classroom," said a fifth-grade teacher from Missouri. "I contacted all involved parents and we held conferences."

Oftentimes being confronted by the teacher will be enough to stop the aggressor, or at least intimidate the joiners, so that the clique will be dispersed. Chances are, by the time you talk with your child's teacher, she will already have noticed the clique and taken steps to deal with it. If not, you might help her formulate a plan based on your child's feelings.

Should you be unsatisfied with the teacher's response, take your concerns to the middle school's counselor or psychologist. These trained professionals are accustomed to handling peer-related problems. The next step up the ladder might mean approaching the school's vice principal, who is usually in charge of discipline, or the principal.

Should you call the other parents yourself? This tactic may not work if the aggressor's parents are uninvolved or inclined to be defensive about their son's behavior. Still, because cliques usually involve a group, you might have success enlisting the support of other parents whose children are participating as joiners or spectators.

Whatever steps you take, throughout the ordeal you should offer your child, the victim, a great deal of love and support. His self-esteem will no doubt be battered by this experience, so he will need extra encouragement from his parents. Talk with him about the other children and why they might be engaging in this type of behavior. While he cannot control their actions, he can control his reactions to them. Try to steer him to other classmates outside the clique who might be mere spectators at this stage. Are there friends outside of school, from camp or church, for example, who could provide needed companionship?

The good news about cliques is that they are short-lived. Soon the developmental winds will shift and those acting as the aggressors will either move on or get left behind.

Bullies—Beyond Eddie Haskell

Bullies are different from cliques. While cliques involve groups, a bully usually acts alone. A bully doesn't necessarily need a whole group behind him to feel powerful. He singles out one child to torment, someone weaker than himself, and he sets to work making that child's life miserable.

As with cliques, bullying is not the harmless taunting that existed back in the *Leave It to Beaver* era when Eddie Haskell would tease the Beav about his haircut. The phenomenon even has a new name— child peer abuse—signifying that authorities no longer consider it insignificant. These days tough boys and girls are making life not only unbearable but also dangerous for other children. While it is hard to get a handle on the number of bullies operating, as many as 20 percent of school children may be victims. Bullying includes everything from name-calling, taunting, and teasing to shoving, kicking, and more violent physical assaults, some with weapons.

The good news is that bullying, which often begins in third grade, wanes by high school. The bad news is that the intense bullying occurs in middle school, peaking in the eighth grade. One study showed that as many as 58 percent of students say they skipped school once or more because they were afraid of being picked on at school by a bully.

Parents, whose ideas of bullies were formed from their own days in junior high, often give their children outdated advice on dealing with the school yard menace:

Fight back. Taking a swing at a bully is not a good idea. He might be armed with more than his fists.

Ignore him. Today's bully is the "in your face" variety, not likely to go away just because you try to shrug him off.

Feel sorry for him. It's only in the movies that the bully comes from a broken home and needs your compassion. More often than not, the bully is after power and not pity.

He's really after your friendship. Usually the bully has other friends and just wants to make your son's life tough for other reasons.

So who is the bully? Sometimes he does come from a dysfunctional family. More often than not, he has been impressed by the way he sees people get ahead by using power. He's seen all the R-rated action movies where the hero achieves his goal by threatening others with physical violence. He sees the way society worships those who have power and know how to use it. He may grow up to be the next drug pusher or the CEO of a major corporation. But right now, he's your son's worst nightmare.

What do you do if your son or daughter is the target of a bully? First off, don't dismiss any grievances you hear from your child. Take them to heart. Most middlers are not inclined to whine about being bothered by other children. If your son comes to you with specific complaints, treat them seriously.

Get the facts from your child, complete with the bully's name, the time, place, and details of each encounter. Armed with this information, go to school. As with cliques, start with your child's teacher but be prepared to go higher if your concerns are not addressed quickly. Let the school know that you are concerned about your child's safety. Also approach your PTA and encourage them to sponsor safety training workshops where all parents can talk about the issue of violence in the school.

Current thinking is that bullies are stopped not by heavy-handed disciplining techniques but by engaging them in activities where they must be caring and helpful toward their fellow students. A good middle school will have such programs in place. The entire student body needs to be involved, because bullies don't exist in a vacuum. If the school environment is one where bullying is tolerated, no one is safe.

Where the school is not helpful, you may be able to pursue a legal remedy and obtain a restraining order to keep a bully away. If the abuse could be interpreted as being sexual harassment, there are other legal remedies you can avail yourself of. (See Chapter Six for more information on sexual harassment.)

While the school works on the bully, you can give your child some help at home:

Teach him to walk away from confrontation. The most effective defense against a bully has been found to be walking away to avoid escalating the conflict.

Teach him self-defense. Most self-defense courses stress self-discipline and self-control, not aggression. Enrolling your child could help his self-esteem.

Help him build other friendships. It's harder for the bully to harass someone who has a lot of friends.

Help him to avoid being a target. If all the kids in school wear jeans and T-shirts, and your son wears chinos and a button-down shirt, he will stand out and make a convenient bull's-eye. Sometimes fitting in can be as simple as buying a pair of jeans.

As with cliques, children mature and move on, leaving the bullies behind. You can help your son by telling him his current situation will not last forever. Hopefully, you can help him get through it without sustaining any physical or emotional scars.

Racial Harmony

"Physical violence's hurt and pain goes away, but prejudice and racism, especially blatant prejudice and racism, stays with you forever," said an eighth-grader. "People are going to say things I don't necessarily like or agree with. It's their right to hold an opinion, but, on the other hand, *nobody* has the right to demean another because of materialistic stupidity."

By the time children hit fifth grade, they are aware of racial differences. If they don't hear about race in their home, they hear their friends talk about it, see it portrayed on TV and in movies, and read about it in the daily headlines. They study the Civil War and learn about blacks and slavery. They study World War II and learn about the Holocaust and the Jews. All the while, they are thinking and beginning to form their own opinions. These children have a tremendous curiosity and openness to accepting other people's points of view.

The world is becoming a smaller place and in order for our children to live and work in the next century, they have to develop an appreciation and tolerance for people who are different. Racial slurs, derogatory remarks, stereotyping—these are things that will doom our children from the start, whether they are on the giving or receiving end.

How do you prepare your child to handle racial issues? Begin by talking about race. Many parents avoid the subject with their own children. But as the comment that opened this section shows, young people are thinking about and are affected by race. Your child wants to know how you feel. Once you open up the discussion, the questions may be tough and unending. They may cause you to reexamine your own feelings.

Avoiding the topic won't make it go away. And, rest assured, your child must deal with racial issues in school. There may be peer pressure to "stick with your own kind." Students who have friends who are a different color may risk being ostracized by others. Many children are ignorant about different races and may accept the stereotypes they see on TV. Counter these prejudices by pointing to people of different races who have succeeded in their careers. Set a good example by talking about people based on their accomplishments, not on their color.

Use books, art, TV, and movies to get across some of your ideas. Books like *I Heard the Owl Call My Name, Johnny Tremain, The Giver,* and *I Remember Mama* were all cited by teachers in our survey as ones that can help children understand those whose background and beliefs are different.

Middle school is a microcosm, a lively environment filled with all the excitement, challenges, conflicts, and opportunities your child will experience on a large scale once he moves on to high school, college, and then the real world. He is learning that human relationships are complex and disagreements not always easily solved. He must learn to negotiate and compromise. She must learn to be persistent, tolerant, understanding, and compassionate. These years are the critical ones where experiences—positive and negative—will burn themselves into your child's memory and could affect her future relationships. It is a challenging time for parents as we learn painful lessons, too, that we cannot protect our children from every sling and arrow that comes their way. We can help them, however, develop the talents and skills they will need now and later in life.

Strategies: Understanding How Your Middler Chooses Friends

WANTED: One best friend for a thirteen-year-old. Must be nice, a good listener, and be able to keep secrets. I enjoy in-line skating, soccer, and music and want someone who shares my interests.

Middlers don't advertise for friends, but if they did, most would probably express their desires in this manner. In our survey, we asked ten- to fifteen-year-olds to describe the glue that held their friendships together. The vast majority of middlers (43 percent) said a good friend's most important qualification was to be a good listener. Another important quality (named by 15 percent) was the ability to keep a secret.

The old adage that opposites attract does not apply where middler friendships are concerned. Nearly one-third (29 percent) said they were attracted to young people who shared their interests.

As a parent, you need to keep up-to-date concerning your child's friendships. If your child, for example, is hanging out with a group that smokes but insists that he doesn't, be wary. Middlers rarely sustain friendships with peers whose likes and dislikes are decidedly different from their own.

Eight

Video Arcade

The Promise and Peril of the Electronic Media

"Kids expect to be entertained, have short attention spans, and resent having to respond to what they hear. Because of what they have seen on TV and in movies, they know an awful lot about sexual matters for their young ages."

(Fifth-grade teacher from Missouri)

Like a brightly lit midway, the electronic media beckon to middlers, enticing them with flashing images and mesmerizing sounds. Most parents are savvy enough to realize that there's no turning back the clock. Television, radio, movies, popular music, and computers are ubiquitous, their influence profound. Technology continues to move forward at a breakneck pace, and with each innovation, the media increase their reach, communicating faster, farther, and to a larger group of people. The world is being transformed right before our eyes.

Technology has changed the way we communicate (E-mail has replaced the paper letter), do research (CD-ROM reference works have replaced the bulky encyclopedia), earn degrees (on-line classrooms and videotaped lessons have caught on), and even relax (virtual reality rides are delivering a bigger jolt of entertainment than can often be had by visiting the real thing). Computer literacy is more than a catch phrase; it is a bona fide skill essential to anyone who hopes to live and work in the next century.

Middle schools across the United States and Canada have responded enthusiastically, integrating the new technologies into the curriculum. Computer labs are now an accepted part of the school setup. Many schools have taken it a step further, installing computer networks so that students and teachers can communicate with one another. Increasingly, schools are going on-line, giving their students access to the Internet and the World Wide Web, which together encompass a wide range of information services. Hearing the morning announcements read over the PA system is fast becoming passé. In some schools, on TV monitors in classrooms, middlers watch a morning news program totally produced by students. As students become media literate, understanding how commercial programs and messages are put together, they are able to grasp the media's power for influencing viewer opinions and attitudes.

In our survey, parents applauded these advances in curriculum in the middle schools. They want their children to be able to compete fully in the workplace of tomorrow. Yet, these new technologies do not come without their problems. As our children become more proficient with computers, they become less proficient with the basic disciplines that we were taught as being so important. Our children read less. "My students don't recognize words on the printed page and spell poorly," said a seventh-grade teacher from Oklahoma. "They've *heard* it not *read* it." Good penmanship is as alien to middlers as calligraphy. Basic math—multiplication and division, for example—seems a waste of time to these young people. "Why can't I just use my calculator?" Spelling? "My computer can check my spelling."

There's no doubt that the new technologies are exciting and fun. Adults, too, are attracted by the packaging and the promise of a better life. We buy a TV set because we like the wide screen and the fact that it will receive so many channels. We install a computer and go on-line to work and bank at home. But once we have let the Trojan Horse into our midst, we cannot always control what comes pouring out, threatening to engulf our children.

Ten- to fifteen-year-olds are the most vulnerable age group. These children are struggling with identity questions and cannot help but be swayed by what they see, hear, and read. We can rail against violence on TV, R-rated movies, pornography on the Internet, and obscene lyrics on CDs. Congress can pass laws, mandate V-chips, institute labeling, set up rating systems, or whatever, and still our children cannot be sheltered. Even a child whose home is TV-free will be exposed to MTV and the latest shows in a friend's home. So parents must teach their children how to deal with the electronic revolution that is now and ever will be part of their lives.

In this chapter we will learn more about the electronic media and their effect on middlers. We will learn ways that we can protect our children while we teach them media literacy, helping them learn how to analyze and evaluate the messages they receive for themselves so that they can utilize mass media and the new technologies in positive ways.

It's a Small World After All

In 1967, Marshall McLuhan predicted that electronic technology would re-create the world as a "global village." McLuhan died in 1980, too soon for him to realize his prescience. Indeed, the world has become a smaller place. Across the United States and Canada, we watch the same TV shows, visit comparable cineplexes to see the same movies, and cruise the same sites on-line to chat with one another. The result has been a remarkable homogenization of society. This phenomenon is strikingly apparent among middlers. No matter where they live, they are plugged into the same cultural sources. More than ever before, this age group talks, walks, and dresses alike.

There are extremes in behavior and appearance, of course. But the middlers making bold statements with tattoos, body piercing, and spiked dyed hair are just as likely to be found in Nebraska as in New York. Similarly, alcohol, drugs, and premature sex are not issues that only urban parents must deal with. The midway, with all its temptations, can be found in every town.

Technology has played a major role in bringing the cultural revolution into our living rooms. What has caught many of us off guard, however, is how quickly our lives are affected. When Guglielmo Marconi sent a radio signal across a room and made a bell ring in 1894, it took another twenty years until the radio was within reach of the average household in the United States and Europe. Now, technological changes are occurring so rapidly, it is difficult to prepare ourselves in advance.

Why even bother? Unless you need to become computer proficient at your job, isn't it possible for you to ignore cyberspace? If you find R-rated movies objectionable, isn't it better to stay home? Can't you keep your radio dial tuned to an easy-listening station? Is it really necessary for you to listen to hard rock (or worse yet, watch music videos) just because your children are?

No one cares about your children as much as you do. In order to be an effective parent in this area, you need to place your own media prejudices aside. You may loathe TV, but you will not be able to guide your child unless you first watch yourself.

Those who work with middlers have long ago recognized how important it is to tune into their culture. "I require all my teachers to watch one-half hour of MTV (Music Television) every week," said the principal of a middle school. "They need to know what their students are watching."

Beaver and Wally vs. Beavis and Butthead

Perhaps the first thing you need to know is that the various media your child is exposed to these days are like nothing you remember from your own adolescence. Whether we are talking about radio, television, movies, or recordings, the differences are profound. The language is rougher. The images tougher. The action is often violent, sexual, and sadistic. Very little is left to the imagination.

Most media companies have not set out to corrupt the youth of America. Their focus is to make money. A TV network wants to attract large audiences for its programs, which in turn will attract major advertisers willing to spend millions to advertise on those shows. A record company? Its eye is set on hitting the top of the charts with its latest release from a star recording artist. A movie company wants to produce the kind of film that will pack the theaters and generate millions of dollars in ticket sales.

Isn't it possible to produce TV shows, recordings, and movies that are both child-safe and successful? Sure, and each year we have a few such hits that you will probably feel comfortable taking your child to see. But in the great majority of cases, what sells to a mass audience are those productions that push the limits of good taste. *Pulp Fiction*, not *Pocahontas*. "It takes more now to stand out," observed an advertising official whose agency has produced racy TV ads. Often that extra ingredient added to the mix will be controversial.

One media executive probably speaks for many of his colleagues when he points out that his company's products are aimed at adults over eighteen, not middlers. "Parents are ultimately responsible for what their children watch at home," he said. But herein lies the problem: Even the most conscientious parent could not possibly monitor everything that a child is exposed to at home and everywhere else. "There's just too much stuff out there," one father complained.

But rating systems, warning labels, and the V-chip for TVs are not foolproof. "My daughter wanted a CD she had heard at a friend's house," said one father. "The salesperson told us that the offensive records have warning labels and this one didn't. So we bought it. After we gave it to her, I reviewed the lyrics. I found songs about drug dealing, oral sex, simulated orgasm, and the word 'nigga.' She has already memorized the lyrics to one song and I am worried about the effect on her. I want to un-give this gift, but don't know how to do it. I also want to take it back to the store and give them a piece of my mind about this piece of trash."

As crazy as it sounds, that particular recording probably didn't warrant a warning label because, compared to everything else on the market, it wasn't viewed as that outrageous. Unfortunately, after a steady diet of violence and bad language, we become desensitized. As a society we are numb.

Perhaps you remember the controversy in 1993 that accompanied the introduction of the video game *Mortal Combat* where an unlucky warrior may have his head chopped off, his spinal cord ripped out, or his heart torn from his chest. These severed appendages continue to twitch and beat as the triumphant hero holds them up in victory. Following news reports showing the game's violence, the game was toned down, although not enough to suit some critics. However, the controversy has died out. Not only has the game sold millions of copies, it has spawned at least three even bloodier sequels. Guess what? Even decapitation seems dull. "Blood, gore, broken bones, mayhem— usually this stuff gets me all excited," said one reviewer for *Game Players* magazine. "But somehow I'm starting to care less and less." Exactly.

The Medium Is the Message

In our survey, parents and teachers alike were outspoken in their condemnation of the messages being sent to their children through the mass media. "The media doesn't always portray reality," said a forty-year-old mother of two sons from Arizona. "There are consequences for people when they use and abuse drugs, and there is a lot more to life than going through it in a stupor."

"Remember that children are easily influenced," said an eighth-grade teacher from Hawaii. "They have not had enough experience to know the long-term effects of some of the decisions they make. Imagine your child making a decision about whether it's right or wrong to spread false rumors if her nightly viewing includes shows like *Beverly Hills 90210* and *Melrose Place*. Imagine some student making a decision on whether to use violence based on so-called reality TV."

Who is responsible for shielding our children from offensive images? A lot of fingerpointing goes on. Parents look to government officials to pass laws. Congress asks the industries involved to police themselves. The media companies say that parents should be responsible for deciding what their children view.

No matter who is right, we as parents have the most at stake. Yet many of us give up too soon without fighting hard enough for what we truly believe is best for our children. We are influenced by our peers, too, other parents whose standards may not be as stringent as our own. Do any of the following situations sound familiar?

Your son has been invited to see an R-rated movie with a friend and the friend's dad. You and your spouse saw this movie last weekend, and you believe it to be inappropriate for a ten-year-old. You are reluctant to voice your concern to the other father, so you allow your son to go. It's only one movie, right?

Your son asks for a certain video game for his birthday. It's the only thing he's asking for and you know he will be disappointed if he doesn't receive it. It's obviously a popular game because you must visit five stores before you find it. You ask the clerk if the game is violent. He shrugs. You study the package. It doesn't have a warning label and it is the last one. You buy it. Your son is ecstatic when he opens it up. But later on when you watch him play it, your worst fears are confirmed. It is violent and you don't like it.

Your daughter is going to a sleepover birthday party where the girls will watch videos. You know the hostess's parents and believe they will make good choices about which videos to select. The next day when you pick up your daughter you discover that the evening's viewings consisted entirely of slasher films. Your daughter was laughed at when she refused to watch and spent a miserable evening by herself reading in the bedroom.

Rare is the parent who hasn't encountered one or all of these situations or others. Controlling your child's media intake is a difficult and thankless task. You are met with resistance at every turn, especially from your child. Yet it is a job that you need to do and do well.

In order to exert some influence over what your children watch, hear, and read, you need three things:

Time. Monitoring the media involves a commitment. It's much less time-consuming for you to let your children watch whatever they want whenever they want. Think of it as an investment in their intellectual development. Somewhere down the line, the hours you put in will pay off.

Information. Would you buy a new car without reading up on the current models? Would you use a new medication without carefully reading the warning labels? Controlling what media our children come into contact with is nothing more than being a well-educated consumer. There are several ways to evaluate shows, records, movies, or games in order to determine whether they are okay for your child. (Later in this chapter you will learn how.)

Resolve. In Chapter Four you learned all about picking your battles. Well, if you decide that keeping your child away from objectionable media fare is something you want to fight for, then don't surrender too easily. There is a lot you can do not only to control what your children see and hear but also to help them analyze, accept, and, in some cases, reject these messages.

What Parents Can Do

Think of your middler's media consumption in terms of a diet. The key is variety and balance. You wouldn't feed your child three meals a day that were totally made up of sugary desserts with no protein or vegetables. So why allow him to watch five hours of TV sitcoms? Everything in moderation is the best course to follow. Similarly, a middler should not live by TV alone. Besides her schoolwork, your daughter should be enjoying sports, hobbies, friends, and family.

What follows is a menu of the media offerings your child may select from. We have included our own analysis. The pluses discuss ways the medium may benefit your child; the minuses, ways the medium may harm your child.

TELEVISION

Coaxial cable and satellite TV have made it possible for the average set to receive 100-plus different services. There is a channel for everything—history, science fiction, cooking, arts, comedy, women, music, religion, and children. Pay services deliver movies and specials for a special cost added to your monthly cable bill. With pay-per-view you can order up a movie fresh from its play in the theaters.

The television landscape has changed so much since the advent of cable and independent stations, it is virtually impossible to predict when an objectionable show will crop up. The late-morning and early-afternoon schedules include talk shows that often delve into topics not appropriate for young ears. Soap operas, whose plots have always revolved around infidelity, have become bolder, showing love scenes that would be considered steamy in prime time. Reruns of violent hour-long police dramas that were once shown after 9:00 P.M. have been sold into syndication and may turn up anytime, anywhere. Reality-based shows that depict police officers tracking down fugitives and making arrests are particularly upsetting because these scenes are purported to be from real life. Even the nightly news might be considered off-limits depending upon that evening's top stories.

Because the top-rated TV shows generate the most publicity, the lead actors and actresses landing on magazine covers coast-to-coast, those are probably the ones your middler will want to watch. Will these shows be okay for middler sensibilities? That depends. One factor is when the show is on. At one time, the hour from 8:00 P.M. to 9:00 P.M. was considered the family viewing hour and TV programmers at the three major broadcast networks (ABC, CBS, and NBC) made up their schedules with that in mind. Although that hour is no longer held sacrosanct, in general, the earlier in the evening a show is on the less objectionable it is likely to be. Television executives argue that after 9:00 P.M. they program for adults. If you check your national TV listings, you will see the later the hour, the higher the quotient of sex and violence. But, as we've explained, with 100-plus services to choose from, not all of them will be child-safe all the time.

Pluses. So much of the debate over children and TV is negative that it is easy to lose sight of the fact that television has a lot to offer young people, particularly middlers. Think of the events—both good and bad—that have been brought to us via TV. How many of us watched Neil Armstrong take the first steps on the moon and still remember the excitement of seeing the event as it happened? Events that will similarly shape the lives of our children will come to them through the TV.

Used responsibly, TV can allow your child to venture to faraway lands or times past, gaining a greater appreciation of the world, its people, and its history. A total ban on watching TV may make it more difficult for your child to find common ground with peers. Like it or not, we are defined by our popular culture. Middlers, in particular, with their evolving identities, need to feel a membership within this culture.

Minuses. Children watch too much TV—an estimated 28.5 hours per week, on average. That's more than one day per week spent watching rather than doing. On a typical school day, according to a report from the Carnegie Council, seventh-graders spend an average of 135 minutes watching television, ninth-graders spend 173 minutes, and eleventh-graders, 150 minutes. The same report showed that seventh-graders read for schoolwork 57 minutes a day, ninth-graders read 63 minutes, and eleventh-graders, 69 minutes.

Aside from quantity, it's quality that matters. A steady diet of "junk TV," like junk food, will do nothing to nourish your child's intellectual side. A middler who spends a disproportionate amount of time in TV land will begin to compare her own life to the fantasized lives she sees in TV shows and commercials. In this fantasy world, everyone is thin and beautiful, lives in lavishly furnished homes and apartments, wears only exclusive designer fashions, drives expensive cars, and spends little time working and most time playing. Real life pales by comparison. On TV, most of life's vexing problems are wrapped up and solved in thirty-minute segments. What a shock when your middler discovers she can't dispense with her own traumas as quickly!

TV's unrealistic portrayal of sex may confuse your son at a time when he is just beginning to discover his own sexual identity. According to *TV Guide* statistics, each year viewers are exposed to 9,230 scenes of suggested sexual intercourse or innuendo, and fully 94 percent of sex on soap operas involves people not married to each other. Abstinence and safe sex, topics that you are beginning to discuss with your middler, are not likely to be given proper attention.

Based on the most popular TV shows, middlers may develop misconceptions about adult life. Bad language is viewed as widespread and acceptable. Successful women are shown to dress provocatively. Smoking and drinking are regarded as cool. Men and women are often portrayed in stereotypical fashion. Ethnic groups—African Americans, Hispanics, Asians, and Native Americans—are not adequately represented. The minority characters that do show up will do nothing to increase our understanding and will merely reinforce existing prejudices.

Realistic police and rescue programs only add to the confusion because, although a show may depict one isolated incident, the message that comes across is that such an event is not unusual. Children begin to pick up on one of TV's major themes, that it's possible to solve problems through the use of violence. "Don't let them watch shows in which the solutions are always violent, even if the 'good guy' wins," said a teacher from Maine. Trouble is, on TV the bad guys often win and manage to escape punishment for their crimes.

Controls. Broadcast TV comes under the purview of the Federal Communications Commission. Federal law prohibits the broadcasting of "obscene or indecent programming." The FCC has the power to revoke a station's license, levy fines, or issue warnings to broadcasters who break this law.

While the federal law seems straightforward enough, defining what is obscene or indecent applying "contemporary community standards" is difficult. The FCC does not monitor broadcasts but acts on complaints it receives from the public. In general, the FCC can threaten and cajole the networks in terms of what is broadcast, but is prohibited from acting as a censor.

Cable TV has made the situation more complicated. The courts have ruled that because individuals must become subscribers in order to receive cable service, they are accepting whatever that service delivers to their home. The cable company, however, is required to make available a lock box that enables a subscriber to block out certain channels. You could punch in a code, for example, to prevent your children from watching MTV or a premium channel such as Home Box Office, where an R-rated movie might be playing.

The V-chip will operate as a screening device, too. As envisioned, parents will be able to block out programs that have been deemed unsuitable for children because of high levels of violence, sexual activity, or other objectionable material. The V-chip proposal was part of a massive telecommunications bill that President Bill Clinton signed into law in 1996. Parents must program their sets in order to activate the device. Whether parents will take the time and effort to do so (on all the sets in a household) remains to be seen. And we haven't solved the main problem of reducing overall violence on TV. It's possible that TV programs might become even more violent, since television officials can now argue that the V-chip will allow parents to keep these shows away from children.

Where middlers are concerned, the cable box and the V-chip have obstacles to overcome. These screening devices may end up creating a "forbidden fruit" situation, increasing the appeal of those tainted programs. Cynics are placing bets that decoding any device will present little challenge to the technologically savvy middler. Beyond that, we have to examine the message we are sending to our middlers at a time when we are attempting to teach them how to be independent and make good decisions on their own. How can they do that if we make a preemptive strike? How can we build an environment of trust if we begin with an act that tells them we don't trust them?

What you can do. A far better strategy is to work with your middler to decide together on what are appropriate choices for TV viewing. Begin by agreeing how much TV you are comfortable having him watch each week. Having a loose rule such as, "No TV until your homework is done," won't be useful if your middler winds up rushing through his assignments in order to plop down in front of the set as early as possible.

• *You might want to restrict TV to the weekends.* Don't feel you are depriving your child. TV isn't necessary for life, like food or oxygen. It is perfectly possible for him to relax and have fun without watching TV. Better in fact. You might find that if you restrict TV on certain days, your child will find other activities to pursue during those times.

• *Help your middler to plan which TV shows he will watch.* TV viewing shouldn't be an activity that just fills up time. Rather, when your child sits down to watch, it should be with the idea of enjoying a particular show or special. When your daughter asks, "Can I watch TV?" don't give an automatic yes. Ask, "What program do you want to see?" Once she gives you a specific answer, you can then make a decision. This approach allows you to set limits on your daughter's TV viewing and reinforces the idea that TV, like any other activity, should have a purpose.

• *Consult* TV Guide, *the television section of your local newspaper,* as well as magazines that might review upcoming TV programs. Use a highlighter to mark those shows that might be of interest to your child. Cable has opened up new vistas with entire services devoted to specific subjects. You might get your child turned on to a new hobby or reignite interest in an old one through a TV show.

• *Whenever possible, watch with your child.* Television offers opportunities to discuss the difficult topics you need to cover with your middler. Occasionally it might even be worthwhile to allow your child to see something you know will be controversial just so you can begin a discussion. Give your opinion and allow your child to have his say.

• *Make use of your videocassette recorder.* Your daughter may have a favorite program that is on during the week when you limit her viewing. Allow her to videotape it to view with you on the weekend. You may also use your VCR to preview shows that you suspect may be unsuitable. If you decide to let your child watch anyway, you will at least be prepared.

• *Don't be so quick to fast forward through all the TV advertisements, either.* There are some valuable lessons for your middler to learn. "I have allowed my son to purchase items advertised and then have him return them after he realizes the falsehood of the advertising," said the mother of a twelve-year-old from Orlando, Florida.

• *Buy a food product that you saw advertised.* Have your child decide, did it taste as good as it looked on TV? Was she disappointed? Would she have urged you to buy the product if it hadn't been advertised in that manner? Talk about how advertisers show these products in the best light and may not be truthful. In this way, you are honing her media literacy skill.

• *Middlers are notorious for their brand consciousness, and studying TV commercials will give you a chance to air your views on the subject.* Discuss how some companies take advantage of the preadolescent's desire to fit in by wearing the right shoes or jeans. What does she think? Draw her out.

Watching TV can be an isolating experience, but it doesn't have to be. Used properly, it can be an educational tool for your child as well as a vehicle for initiating some pretty interesting discussions.

POPULAR MUSIC—CDs, TAPES, AND MUSIC VIDEOS

Popular music reflects the tenor of the times as seen through youthful eyes. Those sentiments rarely sit well with an adult audience. Back in the 1960s, most parents found song lyrics, which condemned the Vietnam War and extolled the virtues of drugs and open sex, appalling. The themes may have seemed revolutionary, but the lyrics themselves were sanitized. Four-letter words were never used, and references to sex were implied rather than explicit. The songs, while they preached rebellion, mostly advocated peaceful resistance. "If you're going to San Francisco, be sure to wear a flower in your hair." Brotherhood, ethnic equity, and equal rights for women were all important subplots to this youthful drama.

Times have changed. Rebellion is still a theme, but one without a specific target, like a war. Rather, the feeling imparted by these bands that the press has dubbed "alternative rock" is that "life's not fair." Obviously, that sentiment is going to find a middler audience eager to listen. Targets include divorce, economic dislocation, environmental degradation—all topics on the minds of middlers. Often the themes take a dark turn, talking about suicide, murder, rape, and urban violence.

The lyrics that try to express these feelings may, in many an adult's opinion, lack the eloquence of those produced by a Paul Simon or a John Lennon. Substituting for this lack of creativity are words whose only purpose appears to be to shock. Unfortunately, the mind-numbing phenomenon sets in quickly. After listening to four-letter words repeated over and over again, these curses lose their ability to startle us. Imagine what this process does to our children, many of whom have never heard these words before. Song lyrics are quickly memorized and internalized. Should they conclude that because these words are used in songs, it's okay for them to use them, too? No wonder our children's language has suffered so.

The good news is that women have become a force in the world of alternative rock, taking to the stage to belt out lyrics that have a feminist edge to them. The bad news is that the language and messages coming from these women rockers are apt to be as coarse as anything coming from the men.

Rap music has an even harsher edge. Taking the high road, some have viewed rappers as urban poets telling it like it is, often from their vantage point of the disenfranchised. Critics, on the other hand, have seized on the rapper's advocacy of violence and put-down of other groups, particularly women.

Pluses. Music, is, after all, music. We might not agree with our children's choices, but their tastes will evolve. What starts out as a love affair with a popular band may lead to flirtations with Bach, Beethoven, and Brahms. Your middler may decide he wants to play a musical instrument, even if it's the electric guitar and not the piano. Studies have shown that learning to play a musical instrument sharpens intellect. In addition, your child will be developing a love and interest in music, something that can bring him pleasure and enjoyment throughout his lifetime.

Minuses. Along with sports figures, movie and TV stars, musicians frequently top the list of most admired when young people are polled. Perhaps more than any other group, rock stars influence youthful fashions, including affectations such as nose rings and tattoos. While we might be able to put up with our children listening to rock musicians and rappers, we are apt to become concerned when they start to worship them. We can't ignore the fact that many rock musicians are open about their abuse of alcohol and drugs. Add to the mix the fact that well-known rappers are frequently in the headlines for committing crimes such as assault and rape and you have every parent's nightmare. If we are looking for role models for our children, these are hardly the ones we would select.

Controls. Tipper Gore in her book, *Raising PG Kids in an X-Rated Society,* was the first public figure to focus attention on rock's lyrics. In 1990, the Recording Industry Association of America agreed to create a uniform parental advisory logo, a one-inch by five-eighths-inch, black-and-white rectangle that says, "Parental Advisory—Explicit Content."

Who decides which recordings receive a parental advisory label? There is no overall rating organization. Rather, with each recording, the record company consults with the artist in question and decides whether a warning label should be affixed. Needless to say, under such a loose system, many releases that parents might and do object to slip through.

With movies, the use of certain words and themes qualify a film for an R rating. Not so with CDs. As the father earlier in this chapter discovered, drug use, sexual references, and four-letter words do not automatically bring a parental advisory label. Also, there is no law preventing a twelve-year-old from buying a CD with a warning label on it. Record stores will issue refunds, however, if a parent wants to return a CD because it was found to be inappropriate.

What you can do. Most parents remain oblivious to what their middlers are listening to. "I guess I don't worry much about CDs," said one mother, "since my children listen to music in their rooms and I don't listen to their music when I want to listen to music. I really don't know much about it."

Not surprising. Our middlers walk around with their Walkmans and portable CD players plugged into their ears. Listening to music becomes, from their view, a very personal thing, something parents are rarely let in on. Even parents who sometimes accompany their children to rock concerts opt to sit in "parent rooms," where they can avoid listening to the music.

Well, it's time to pull the plug, turn off your own music, and turn on your daughter's. Welcome to Hard Rock 101.

Coax your middler from his room and encourage him to play some of his CDs for you in the family room. Listen with him as you would watch TV with him. Make comments without being judgmental.

Take the assignment that middle school principal gave to his teachers and watch MTV. Even though MTV targets the eighteen- to twenty-five-year-old, many middlers do watch, particularly in households where there are older teenagers. "MTV is not designed for younger children," said Dr. Helen Boehm, a psychologist and senior vice president for public responsibility and network standards, MTV Networks, who screens material for Viacom-owned MTV, VH1, and Nickelodeon. Videos, interview shows, entertainment specials, even cartoons (Beavis and Butthead, MTV cartoon characters with attitude and bad language) are all written to appeal to that eighteen- to twenty-five-age group. (VH1, another music video cable service, aims for the twenty-five-plus audience and thus features tamer material.)

While you may be shocked at what you see on MTV, the music videos are screened. "We review each video for appropriateness and the story it's telling," said Dr. Boehm. Changes are frequently made, she said, if the material is "too out there." Nudity is not allowed, although provocative clothing abounds. If a recording contains an obscene word, it will not be heard when the song plays on MTV.

Once you are better versed in the current rock scene, you can begin to set some guidelines. Because rock stations play all the current hits (more on radio later), you may not be able to keep your middler from listening to everything you find objectionable. You can set some rules with regard to purchasing recordings, however. This decision will be a personal one, based on your own comfort level. If four-letter words push your button, then don't permit your child to purchase CDs that contain these words. Since these words may be included on CDs without warning labels, how can you check lyrics ahead of time? Some of the major record chains have listening stations where you can preview songs. Oftentimes a CD will include printed lyrics. Sales assistants, particularly those who are young, can be helpful. Ask whether the CD you are thinking of purchasing would be appropriate for a preadolescent. Does it contain obscene words or lyrics? Most times a young sales associate will be able to tell you or help you find out.

Major retailers like Wal-Mart's and Kmart will not sell CDs that carry the parental advisory warning. These chains wield such clout (in 1995, Wal-Mart sold 52 million of the 615 million CDs sold nationwide) that the recording company or the artist will agree to release a CD that has been "sanitized," with certain songs dropped, offensive words edited out, and cover art airbrushed to achieve respectability. If all else fails and you get the CD home only to discover it violates your rules, take it back.

You may find that if you refuse to purchase CDs with four-letter words or obscene lyrics that you are seriously narrowing your middler's choice of popular rock music. And since he will probably be listening to these songs on the radio, you need to confront the issue head-on. Talk about the bad language and the images that you find offensive. Artists frequently push the limits, but what is acceptable on stage may be unacceptable in real life. State your disapproval often enough and you will create a recording of your own. When your son listens to these recordings he will keep your opinions in mind, too.

Try to make a distinction between an entertainer's music and personal life. It's possible to enjoy a rock musician's recordings but not endorse his lifestyle. Here, again, are some opportunities for you to discuss your stand on alcohol, drugs, and sex. According to one study done at Central Michigan University, regardless of how much MTV teens watch, those who have close family ties and can talk to their parents about problems are no more apt to have early sex than their peers who are also close to their families and don't watch music videos.

The overall situation isn't so bleak. There are always some popular musicians out there that even a parent could tolerate. Who knows? You might even find a group you like.

MOVIES

As with any artistic medium, film has consistently evolved, with each new generation of filmmakers putting its own stamp on its celluloid creations. In the 1940s, we had musicals, the 1950s, family films, the 1960s, message movies, the 1970s, disaster flicks. Since 1980, as the cost of making movies has escalated, producers have tried to outdo the competition by creating megahits capable of pulling in large numbers of people.

In this high-stakes race, filmmakers have chosen to go with the formula least likely to fail—action films filled with stunts, special effects, and violence. What sells once is awarded with a sequel. So we have strings of films where heroes carry lethal weapons and die hard. Because these movies are advertised heavily on TV and frequently enjoy copromotions with fast-food restaurants, they are hard for middlers to ignore.

Pluses. Americans have an ongoing love affair with the movies, and our children, too, have fallen hard for this medium. Who can blame them? Movies are the ultimate escapist entertainment. We can laugh and cry, get angry or scared, knowing that it's all make-believe. When the lights go on, it's over.

Minuses. Middlers, on the cusp of adulthood, are apt to regard any movie rated G or PG as too young for their tastes. They are apt to be attracted to PG-13 and R-rated films instead. While most of the PG-13 movies are okay for this age group, the R-rated movies really are not. Yet these are the films that they will be clamoring to see. Peer pressure plays a major role. Let one middler see an R-rated movie, and his friends will feel they must see it, too. Thus starts the, "But Mike's parents let him see it. Why can't I?"

Middlers are impressionable and in R-rated movies they are apt to hear and see much that we object to. Does it have an effect? The research says it does. The effects are twofold: imitation (young boys, in particular, have been found to become more aggressive after watching a violent movie) and desensitization (accepting violence as commonplace, our threshold for what we find shocking continues to rise).

Controls. The first film to create controversy over its language was *Who's Afraid of Virginia Woolf,* released in 1966. The offending terms were "screw" and "hump the hostess." Officials from the Motion Picture Association of America (MPAA) reviewed the film and decided to delete "screw," but keep "hump the hostess."

MPAA officials soon realized, however, that *Virginia Woolf* was just the beginning. A few months later, the film *Blow Up* represented another first in movies—nudity. The Production Code Administration in California declined to approve the movie and MPAA backed that decision. But the film company distributed the film anyway.

In April 1968, the U.S. Supreme Court upheld the constitutional power of states and cities to prevent the exposure of children to books and films that could not be denied to adults. MPAA realized that a system was needed to rate movies according to their suitability for children.

That rating system has been revised several times. The categories now are:

G: General Audiences—All ages admitted.

This is a film where nothing in theme, language, nudity, sex, or violence should be found offensive to parents of younger children.

PG: Parental Guidance Suggested—Some material may not be suitable for children.

This rating is an alert for parents to take a closer look. While there is no drug use in the content of a PG film, there may be profanity, some violence, or brief nudity.

PG-13: Parents strongly cautioned. Some material may be inappropriate for children under thirteen.

This warning is a stern one alerting parents to the fact that the movie in question may contain strong language, violence, and nudity. More than one expletive automatically places the movie in the R category, as does rough or persistent violence, and sexually oriented nudity. A PG-13 movie may, however, show drug use content.

R: Restricted. Under seventeen requires accompanying parent or adult guardian.

R-rated movies contain adult material—hard language, violence, nudity within sensual scenes, drug abuse.

NC-17: No children under seventeen admitted.

A film given this rating is for adults only.

Who rates movies? MPAA has a full-time Rating Board of eight to eleven members located in Los Angeles. The Board views each film before its release and decides what most parents would feel the film's designation should be. Each member votes and the majority rules.

While many of the decisions are subjective (What constitutes too much violence? When does a love scene cross the line?), the Rating Board does have certain guidelines to follow, how many expletives to permit before a movie becomes R-rated, for example.

What you can do. The rating system has been established for parents. But, as Jack Valenti, MPAA's president and chief executive officer, said: "If parents don't care, or if they are languid in guiding their children's movie-going, the rating system becomes useless."

In our survey, a majority of parents (52 percent) said that they prohibit their middlers from seeing R-rated films. Another 19 percent said they made the decision based on the film, while 8 percent said they would allow such viewing if they went with the child or screened the movie beforehand. If you don't have time to see the movie in advance, there are other methods you can use to decide whether it is one you will permit your child to see.

- *Check movie reviews.* Most newspaper reviews will include a note at the end, evaluating the content. This is one from the *New York Times:* "*Dragonheart* is rated PG-13 (Parents strongly cautioned). It includes mild violence and has an ending that could sadden dragon-loving children." Magazines, particularly those focused on parenting issues, will evaluate upcoming films. Also, the Catholic Communication Campaign runs a movie review line (1-800-311-4CCC) that rates current films, from A-1 (general audiences) to O (morally offensive). This Catholic service is frequently tougher than the MPAA, thus offering parents another point of view.

Several sites on-line now include movie reviews. Check the entertainment listings and also the parenting areas of America Online and CompuServe.

- *Talk with other parents.* You may find out your daughter was exaggerating when she said "everyone" in her class had seen the latest R-rated film. Discussing movie-going with other parents will give you the opportunity to share views and perhaps ban together when there is a film you all rate with a thumbs-down.

What movies you allow your child to see is a personal decision, but one that should be made with some thought. Allowing your child to see anything that arrives at the cineplex won't work. Neither will banning him from all PG-13 or R-rated films. Evaluating each film on its merits is the best way to go.

VIDEOCASSETTES

The videocassette recorder is the answer to a parent's wish. Using a VCR, we can control when, what, and how long our children watch TV.

Pluses. It's possible to satisfy your child's desire to watch a certain program by selecting an appropriate videocassette. We might not approve of MTV, for example, but we can purchase videocassettes of rock groups that meet with our approval. We can even rent them first to prescreen.

In addition to music, however, there is a wide variety of tapes available for middlers. How-to, history, comedy, and nature are some of the selections.

Minuses. Although the Video Software Dealers Association, the major trade association for video retailers in the United States, strongly endorses the observance of the rating code by individual retailers, there is no law preventing someone under seventeen from renting an R-rated film.

Controls. Videocassettes of movies are also rated by MPAA. Oftentimes film companies will release the videos of movies and put back in parts that were considered too violent or sexually explicit for theaters. One example is Oliver Stone's *Natural Born Killers,* which tells the story of a modern-day Bonnie and Clyde on a killing spree. In order to earn an R-rating for the movie, Mr. Stone had to make 150 cuts to expunge material the Rating Board found unacceptable. Without those cuts the film would have received an NC-17 rating, a label filmmakers view as the kiss of death because it reduces the potential audience. Some newspapers refuse to run ads for NC-17 films. In the video version, the cuts were restored.

What you can do. Some parents feel that an R-rated film is less objectionable when it comes to video. For one thing, it's on a smaller screen. A parent who is watching along with a middler can fast forward through objectionable parts or, if the film becomes too intense, turn it off. Parents do need to exercise some judgment when it comes to renting tapes, however. By the time a film has landed on video, enough people should have seen it for you to find another parent who can assess its suitability.

As with CDs, major chains that sell videos (Wal-Mart's and Kmart) or rent them (Blockbuster) won't carry videos that are rated NC-17 and have had studios reedit objectionable films before agreeing to stock them.

RADIO

Long before cable TV came along, radio had already perfected "narrowcasting," delivering special services to targeted audiences. For this reason, most radio stations have a pretty good handle on their demographics. Rock and hard rock stations are probably first on your middler's dial. Don't discount talk radio, however. Fifteen years ago, there were only eighty-two all-talk radio stations. Now there are over 1,300.

Pluses. Radio continues to enjoy popularity because it is a versatile medium. It's possible to listen to radio while doing something else, driving a car, for example.

Minuses. In radio, the battle is to keep listeners from pushing that button for another station. Besides playing current hits, disc jockeys aim to keep a good banter going between themselves and their audience. The trend seems to have a man and a women cohosting and frequently the banter is heavily laced with sexual innuendo. Some of this might fly over your middler's head. Some of it won't.

Talk radio, like talk TV, covers controversial topics. Conservative talk show hosts have been known to ridicule various ethnic groups. Other radio hosts are notorious for their outrageous comments and language. Talk radio has produced many expert advice programs, everything from career counseling to car repair. However, the ones that will probably get your middler's attention are those that offer advice on sex.

Radio cannot be discounted as a constant presence in many a middler's life. In our survey, a large percentage said they listened to the radio in their room and often played it while doing homework.

With the advent of earphones, your middler can listen to radio without your knowing exactly what he is listening to. You might think he's listening to music before he goes to sleep, when he might be tuned into a late-night talk show on sex.

Controls. As a broadcast medium, radio is regulated by the FCC. The same rules that apply to television, apply to radio.

What you can do. The next time you drive your middler somewhere, listen to his radio station. It's a good opportunity to draw him out about what he listens to and what he thinks about it. You can voice your own opinions as you go along.

One mother found out her daughter was listening to a late-night radio show that offered sexual advice (in somewhat graphic terms) to callers. She asked to listen with her daughter and used the occasion to get into a good discussion about sex. This mother managed to convey the message that she was available to answer questions from her daughter, too.

COMPUTERS

Of some thirty-four million U.S. households with computers in 1995, more than twelve million have modems and more than 7.5 million are connected to the Internet, commercial on-line services, or both. Growth has been phenomenal. In 1988, only 16.2 million households had computers, 1.4 of those had modems, and 0.9 million were on-line. In 1994, on-line services had five million subscribers. So in one year, the number of subscribers increased dramatically. And no one believes a slowdown is in sight. One inducement is that the services offered on-line continue to grow, enhancing the appeal of "hooking up." In addition, technological advances will make the receiving of information seem like entertainment. For example, companies are rushing to transform the TV set into a wide-screen family computer.

Many parents believe that their children will need to be computer literate to survive in the working world of the next century. Ironically, only one in five adult Americans considers himself or herself computer literate. In fact, this generation of parents must play catch-up with their children if they are to exert any influence over their children's experience with computers.

Pluses. Computers have changed the way our middlers are learning. Doing research for a paper, they can crawl through the World Wide Web, finding sources that would never turn up in the local library. Approached in this manner, research becomes fun and exciting. They can E-mail pen pals on the other side of the world. They can enter "chat rooms" and share ideas with middlers around the country. Middlers with an entrepreneurial streak can start their own forums or web sites.

Minuses. There have been instances where middlers have been the targets of abuse on-line. In one instance, an individual entered a "Kids Only" chat room on America Online and sent E-mail with obscene material attached to several of the children who had been in attendance. America Online dealt swiftly with the offender, uncovering the identity and terminating the account. Yet it upset many parents who worry about the individuals their children are meeting in cyberspace.

One mother discovered that her daughter was having "cybersex" with someone on-line, sending and receiving lewd messages. She posted a notice on-line asking other parents if she should be concerned. Other parents responded that, yes, she should be. (One teen magazine carried an article about a fifteen-year-old girl who ran away to be with someone she had met on-line. He raped and robbed her and dumped her in a parking lot. Such stories fuel parental fears.)

Controls. So far, attempts to prohibit transmitting obscene material electronically have failed on the grounds that they violate the First Amendment's guarantee of free speech. Just as pornographic magazines find a place on the newsstand, many people believe pornographic materials will find a place in cyberspace.

However, this area continues to evolve. One alternative might be various screening devices, software that can prevent obscene material from reaching children.

What you can do. If you are going to allow your child to "surf the net," you need to suit up and swim along, too. Don't be intimidated.

It's not as difficult as it sounds. Best bet is to start with one of the on-line services such as America Online or CompuServe, which are easy and fun to use. Each allows access to the Internet and World Wide Web, where navigation becomes a little bit trickier. Enlist your middler as a tour guide. Ask him to take you along to sites that he visits. He won't be able to resist your request, and you will learn a lot about what he does when you're not around.

• *Set some ground rules for being on-line.* Cyberspace can be addictive. One survey at the State University of Buffalo found 17 percent of Internet users who responded logged forty hours or more per week on-line. Eighty-nine percent said it interfered with their lives. Make sure it doesn't interfere with your middler's life. Set a timer when he goes on-line. When his time is up, he should log off.

• *Suggest some sites your middler might want to visit.* Don't assume that because she considers herself computer savvy she will have investigated everything cyberspace has to offer. There are many books on the market that list what is available on-line. Knowing your middler's interests, you may be able to point her in the right direction. (And gain some points with her in the process!)

• *Get to know who your child is meeting on-line.* Ask your son where he likes to "hang out" on-line. Visit with him to make sure these places are okay for him. Make sure he understands never to give out his real name, address, or phone number to anyone he meets on-line.

• *Give your middler some privacy.* While your middler may enjoy showing you around once or twice, he's not going to want to have a parent with him every time he's on-line. Tell him you trust him to abide by your rules, then leave him alone.

• *Know how to use the parental control devices that come with on-line services.* Some of these make it possible for your child to just visit chat rooms without participating.

• *Prepare your child to deal with those who make her uncomfortable.* A statement such as, "What you are telling me is against America Online's rules and I'm going to report you," may be enough to scare the offender off. Remember that local laws, which protect individuals who feel threatened or harassed, may be invoked against a perpetrator your child may meet in cyberspace. Don't hesitate to notify the authorities.

• *Go to "keyword" and type in "parenting" to find on-line sites where you can share your thoughts and concerns with other parents.* You may even E-mail your opinion to executives at the major on-line services.

While our children may be ahead of us in the cyber-skills department, they still need our guidance as they set off on their journey into cyberspace. We need to educate ourselves enough so that we know the possible danger zones in order to help our children navigate around them.

VIDEO AND COMPUTER GAMES

Video games have evolved from *Pong* and *Pac-Man* to interactive movies where real film stars grace the small screen. Computer games are just as sophisticated. Hand-held video games like *Gameboy* and Sega's *Nomad,* allow fans to tote the games wherever they go. Together, the games have proved to be big moneymakers for software producers. The first *Mortal Combat* brought in nearly $150 million when it first went on sale, more than most major motion pictures make in ticket sales.

Pluses. Besides fun, are there any pluses for video and computer games? Proponents are fond of saying that playing video games helps a child increase his hand-to-eye coordination. There have even been some studies backing up that claim.

Some of the games can be educational. *SIM CITY,* for example, challenges a child to build his own city. Build too many public facilities, taxes go up, and people begin to move out. Without a tax base, how can he keep his *SIM CITY* going? The dilemmas presented are real life and call for thoughtful solutions. Other games in the SIM line include *SIM ANT,* where you develop a species, and *SIM TOWER,* where you build a building.

With *Civilization* the goal is to build a civilization from the beginning. The player must find ways for his people to survive and coexist with others, all the while moving through history to become more civilized.

Minuses. If middlers were satisfied playing the educational games, parents would merely have to worry about restricting game time. But what worries parents more is the violent and sexually suggestive nature of many of the games. As the games have improved in terms of graphics and sound, this violence only becomes more alarming. Parents of daughters have had to contend with an absence of games that appeal to girls.

Controls. Who rates the games? Two rating boards—the Entertainment Software Review Board and Recreational Software Advisory Council—review and rate video and computer games. ESRB uses a team of three reviewers (pulled from a pool of 100 volunteers nationwide) to watch and score the games. RSAC, on the other hand, has the manufacturers of the games fill out a detailed questionnaire.

ESRB's reviewers, who range in age from twenty to sixty, undergo an orientation where they look at more than 100 games to familiarize themselves with the product. Each game is reviewed by three people, and their reports are returned to an ESRB staffer who generates a consensus report that will determine the final rating.

How do the ratings work? ESRB's system uses two devices, an age-appropriate icon and a descriptive blurb, to help you evaluate the game's content. The age icons include: EC (early childhood), KA (kindergarten to adult), T (teens), M (mature audience, 17 and over), and AO (adults only). The descriptive phrases (animated violence, animated blood and gore, realistic blood and gore, strong sexual material, mild language, or comic mischief, for example) alert you to the aspects of the game that you might find objectionable. Finally, you may study the illustrations on the package that oftentimes show scenes from the game. If the pictures are too violent for your taste, then the game probably will be, too.

RSAC's system uses three descriptors evaluating on a scale of one (for low) to four (for high) levels of violence, nudity/sex, and language. These descriptors are accompanied by terms such as, "Destruction of living things," describing what kind of violence, for example, "revealing attire," for nudity/sex, and "mild expletives," for language.

What you can do. There is no law that prohibits a video or computer store from selling a game meant for a mature audience to someone under seventeen. But one video game store manager probably spoke for many of his colleagues when he said he tries to discourage such sales. "If I don't, I know a parent will bring it back the next day," he said.

Look at the ratings on the package. You can evaluate how much violence (and what type of violence) is in the game based on the descriptors on the package. If the game is rated for an adult audience, it is probably one to steer clear of. Some stores demonstrate the more popular games on monitors. Make use of this option to prescreen the game.

Several magazines *(Games Players* is one) regularly review the games and will give details about the content. Pick up a recent copy before you go shopping for games.

You may still have a battle on your hands with your middler. "My son, thirteen, is heavily into video games, and most of the ones he is attracted to are the violent, explicit ones, which I am opposed to," said one mother. "We have this constant struggle back and forth over which games he can have. It has become a 'war zone' and I am very uncomfortable. I feel he is wearing me down and that our relationship has suffered."

This mother might try to bargain with her son. Perhaps there are some games that are less objectionable to her that would also appeal to him. Those games with cartoon violence, for example, might be a compromise. If she is opposed to having him buy a violent game, she might allow him to rent one for an evening. Then she could sit with him while he played and point out some of the things she found offensive. She also might gain some insight into her son's thinking.

Middlers and the Media

For better and worse, middlers are inextricably linked to the electronic media. While they are dazzled by the hardware, they need us, their parents, to help them understand the best ways to use these various devices in ways that will enhance their enjoyment and education.

Parental involvement is key. We can take solace in the words of Robert Sylwester, a professor of education at the University of Oregon, whose research has focused on the effects of the electronic media on a developing brain. He found that it's not what electronic media brings to a developing mind that's important but what the developing mind brings to the electronic media. "Children who mature in a secure home with parents who explore all of the dimensions of humanity in a nonhurried, accepting atmosphere can probably handle most electronic media without damaging their dual memory and response systems," said Dr. Sylwester. "They'll tend to delay their responses, to look deeper than the surface of things."

"Further," he added, "they'll probably also prefer to spend more of their time in direct interactions with real people. They will thus develop the sense of balance that permits them to be part of the real and electronic worlds—but also to stand apart from them."

Strategies: Raising a Media Savvy Middler

Here are five steps that you can follow, no matter the medium, as you attempt to make parenting decisions.

STEP ONE: POSTPONE

The longer you can hold off exposing your child to violent and sexually suggestive material, the better off he will be. Make exceptions too early, and you risk opening the floodgates.

STEP TWO: PICK AND CHOOSE

Of course you can't hold off forever. But once you begin to relax your rules, don't stop evaluating every situation individually. All R-rated movies are not created equal, for example. Consider these two: *The Birdcage* and *Silence of the Lambs*. Both were considered inappropriate for children under seventeen. Yet, *The Birdcage* contained very little questionable material, while, because of the subject matter, virtually every frame of *Silence of the Lambs* was unsuitable for children.

STEP THREE: SET LIMITS

Try to introduce a little structure with regard to the media. Specify how much TV your child is allowed to watch and when. Call for a quiet hour in the evening when the CD player and the radio are turned off.

Step Four: Participate

Watch TV and movies with your child, particularly if the presentation is one that you anticipate may have some objectionable scenes. Listen to CDs and the radio. Observe as your child plays computer games or goes on-line.

Step Five: Discuss

Seize every opportunity possible to discuss what you see and hear with your child. Talk about the violence you see on TV or lyrics to a popular song that demean a particular ethnic group or women. Voice your opinion and provide your child with time to respond. Share your thoughts with other parents so that, when the situation warrants action, you may present a united front.

Nine

Lions, Tigers, and Bears

Protecting Your Middler from Tobacco, Alcohol, and Drugs

"I think about death and violence and drugs and this big thing 'the real world,' that adults talk about. What is it anyway?"

(Eighth-grader from New York)

Few things are as fun and thrilling for children as viewing lions, tigers, and bears, whether these wild animals are pacing in cages at the zoo or roaming free in natural settings. Oftentimes these beasts appear tame, even cuddly. That benign image, reinforced by memories of animated characters like Simba, Tony the Tiger, or Winnie-the-Pooh, may cause our children to downplay any threat to their safety. Certainly, they think, it's possible to get close or even risk touching one of these animals without being injured. We know that's not the case and rush to swoop them out of harm's way.

In some ways the real world our middlers are fighting to join is like a large wildlife theme park filled with excitement and peril. As they get older, they want to be on their own. We can no longer be there to rescue them in the nick of time from a sharp claw or snapping jaw. We must send them on their way, hoping they will steer clear of any hazards.

These dangers our children face—tobacco, alcohol, drugs, AIDS (discussed in the next chapter)—are as deadly as ferocious animals. Once again, however, many young people minimize the risk. Just as the beasts have been domesticated by the media, smoking, drinking, and drugs have been glamorized. Cigarette ads show attractive and youthful men and women frolicking on a beach or screaming with delight on a roller coaster. A baseball game is interrupted with a TV commercial for beer, where young people can be seen playing golf, kicking soccer balls, throwing footballs, all activities inconsistent with drinking. Movies treat drug use casually, as part of the everyday scenery.

A survey done by the publication, *Weekly Reader,* reported that as early as fourth grade, 40 percent of students felt pushed by friends to smoke cigarettes, 34 percent felt pressure to drink wine coolers, and 24 percent said their friends encourage them to try crack or cocaine.

Many finally succumb to the pressure. According to the Carnegie Report:

• Among eighth-graders the rate of smoking rose by 30 percent between 1991 and 1994, from roughly 14 to 19 percent.

• Two-thirds of eighth-graders report that they have tried alcohol and a quarter say they are current drinkers. Twenty-eight percent say they have been drunk at least once.

• Marijuana use among eighth-graders more than doubled between 1991 and 1994. One-third of eighth-graders reported using illegal drugs, including inhalants such as airplane glue, hair spray, and nail polish remover.

Smoking, drinking, and drugs used to be problems parents encountered when their children were in high school or left for college. No more. Yankelovich Partners surveyed a nationwide sample of twelve- to thirteen-year-olds and found that 70 percent knew someone their age who smoked, 44 percent knew someone who drank, and 33 percent knew someone who did drugs. The average age of the first use of marijuana has dropped to twelve years old from nineteen years old in 1960, according to PRIDE (National Parents' Resource Institute for Drug Education), a nonprofit organization that develops strategies to prevent drug abuse.

The earlier a child begins to experiment and regularly use tobacco, alcohol, or drugs, the more difficult it will be for that young person to stop. Two-thirds of adolescent smokers say they want to quit smoking, and 70 percent say they would not have started if they could choose again. Prevention is the best course. Never starting is better than having to quit.

In this chapter, we will talk about the substance-abuse epidemic that threatens middlers. Some reports have portrayed parents as powerless. Nothing could be further from the truth. A survey done by the Parents' Resource Institute for Drug Education (PRIDE) found that the more parents talk to their children about drugs, the less likely those young people will be to use drugs. So you are in a position to influence your child, and the years from ten to fifteen are critical ones.

To a middler, "just say no," will be merely a catchphrase unless you can back up your stand with the facts. We will give you the information you need as well as strategies for passing that knowledge along to your child. Because peer pressure figures in substance abuse, we will help you help your child to walk away without losing face.

We can't minimize the dangers, but we also want to point out that there are many middlers out there, not only staying clean but also actively campaigning against substance abuse. Some, for example, are working to change the way tobacco and alcohol products are advertised and marketed to appeal to a youthful audience.

Tasting the Forbidden Fruits

It would be difficult to find a middler who doesn't know the risks involved with using tobacco, alcohol, or drugs. In a health class, your son has seen the photos of blackened lungs taken from a lifetime smoker who died a long, agonizing death from lung cancer. Your daughter may know that there are more cancer-causing agents in marijuana smoke than in cigarette smoke. They both have heard that alcohol is responsible for thousands (30,000 to get specific) unintentional injury deaths each year.

So, in the face of all this negative information, why would a middler try smoking, drinking, or drugs? The reasons include:

Peer pressure. In one survey, fourth-, fifth-, and sixth-graders said they would begin drinking to fit in with other youths. So your son's friendships do matter. "We are trying to teach him how important it is to choose the right friends carefully," said one mother who responded to our survey. "Although that isn't a safeguard, there is safety in numbers. If you're not alone in your decision to say no, it's a lot easier to walk away. When he does make a decision that we question, I always pose, 'What if it had been drugs? Would you have gone along or said no?' "

Curiosity. Middlers are, after all, bursting with curiosity about the world and eager for new experiences. It's not unusual for your daughter to wonder what it feels like to smoke or get high.

Advertising. While companies that produce tobacco and alcoholic products deny that their advertisements target teenagers, young people are influenced by this media onslaught. Middlers, in particular, are not sophisticated enough to separate hyperbole from fact. Many fall for advertising's promise that smoking and drinking are the keys to fun and popularity.

Invincibility. Middlers think they are indestructible. They minimize whatever risks may be involved with using tobacco, alcohol, or drugs, believing that they will be able to remain in control.

Escape. According to the Partnership For a Drug-Free America, 44 percent of teens in 1995 said that "being high feels good," an increase over the 36 percent reported in 1993. Unfortunately, young people who are struggling with identity issues, difficult home situations, or school problems may use alcohol or drugs as a way to ease their depression and make their pain go away, even if just temporarily.

Genetic predisposition. Children of alcoholics (COAs) are at high risk for alcohol and other drug problems. Often these children live in a stressful home environment where an adult is battling a substance-abuse problem.

Some middlers will resist the temptation to taste the forbidden fruit. Others will satisfy their curiosity about smoking, drinking, and drugs and move on. Unfortunately, a small group will fall into a pattern of regular use.

You are the best role model for your child. Teenagers whose parents smoke are twice as likely to start smoking as teenagers whose parents are nonsmokers, for example. If you turn to alcohol when you are under stress or depressed, your child is unlikely to listen when you lecture about drinking.

Recognizing the importance of adult role models, middle schools have teacher advocate and advisory programs to provide one-on-one support for middlers. "I gave one of my students with a substance-abuse problem my home phone number and said his calls were always welcomed," reported a teacher from Louisiana. Our survey showed that substance abuse increasingly is a problem teachers must deal with. A full 78 percent said they have had students abusing tobacco, alcohol, or drugs. As a result, middle schools have experienced personnel ready to help. "We have a core team that handles these referrals," said a counselor from New Jersey. "We send the students out to be tested and involve the parents in interventions."

Middle schools in the United States and Canada are doing their part educating middlers about substance abuse. There are classes where the dangers of tobacco, alcohol, and drugs are discussed in great detail. Role-playing, where a student may be forced to defend his decision to say no, helps to arm young people for real-life situations.

Tobacco—The Gateway to Drugs

Three million Americans under the age of eighteen smoke, and 82 percent of the people who smoke began before their eighteenth birthday. The Food and Drug Administration, calling tobacco a "major pediatric addiction," said that one million children take up smoking every year, 3,000 each day, and one-third of those will eventually die from tobacco-related illnesses.

Besides the health factor, there is another compelling reason to keep your middler tobacco-free. Tobacco is a "gateway" drug. Young people who smoke are more likely to go on to try marijuana, alcohol, and other drugs. Eighty percent of teenage cigarette smokers have tried marijuana, compared to 17 percent of nonsmokers. Young smokers are three times more likely to use alcohol and eight times more likely to smoke marijuana.

"I recently found out that my twelve-year-old daughter has started to smoke," said one mother. "I haven't said anything yet because I'm not sure what to say. I managed to find her cigarettes, and she is smoking one of the lightest brands on the market. I assume she's doing it with her friends. There is such a drug problem in this area, I'm seriously considering letting her smoke with us so she won't have to go and do it in an alley where she could be exposed to worse things."

Many parents still don't understand the link between smoking and drugs. As this mother's comments illustrate, cigarettes are often dismissed as somehow being safer than drugs. In fact, cigarettes are addictive and deadly. And smoking won't prevent your middler from trying drugs. Instead, smoking will probably hasten your middler's experimentation with harder substances.

Here are some other facts about tobacco products that might cause the mother quoted above (and you, too) to act quickly to discourage a middler from smoking:

• Forty-two percent of young people who smoke as few as three cigarettes go on to become regular smokers.

• The resting heart rates of young adult smokers are two to three beats per minute faster than nonsmokers.

• Teenage smokers suffer from shortness of breath almost three times as often as teens who don't smoke.

• Smoking at an early age increases the risk of lung cancer.

• Young people who smoke harm their physical performance and endurance. Smokers run slower than nonsmokers.

• A fifteen-year study done by Harvard University found that lung development is impaired in teens who smoke as few as five cigarettes a day.

• Someone who smokes a pack or more of cigarettes each day lives 6.6 years less than someone who never smokes regularly.

• Young people who try to quit smoking suffer the same nicotine withdrawal symptoms as adults who try to quit.

Nicotine—A Psychoactive Drug

Why do smokers find it so difficult to quit? Nicotine, a main chemical ingredient in cigarettes and smokeless tobacco, is highly addictive. Nicotine stimulates the "pleasure centers" in the brain that are responsible for regulating well-being, mood, and memory. Initially, a smoker will feel alert. However, after nicotine levels drop (anywhere from twenty to forty minutes) mood changes occur, and the person will feel irritable, anxious, and uncomfortable. An intense craving for more nicotine sets in, satisfied only by that next cigarette.

Nicotine, found in the tobacco plant, has been around a long time. In fact, ancient hunters would often put nicotine on the tips of arrows to fell an animal. At other times in history, nicotine was used in tribal rituals. Dissolved in water, nicotine is a powerful insecticide. A drop of nicotine (seventy mg) would be enough to kill an adult. The average cigarette contains only ten milligrams, and only about one-tenth of that is inhaled by a smoker. Still, even that small amount of nicotine does damage, raising a person's heart rate, increasing blood pressure, and constricting blood vessels.

The other components of cigarette smoke—tar, ammonia, cyanide, formaldehyde, and carbon monoxide—also wreak havoc on the body's organs and circulatory and central nervous systems. Virtually every part of the body is adversely affected. Smokers risk cancers of the lung, throat, liver, vertebrae, kidneys, bladder, and mouth. In males, smoking can cause impotence and females may damage their reproductive systems.

While a young person in good health may find it hard to envision dying of cancer, some of the more immediate effects of smoking will be harder to ignore. One antismoking ad that has been quite effective shows someone interviewing smokers while wearing a gas mask. Other ads are aimed at young women and show what smoking can do to beauty. For example, smokers have bad breath, stained teeth, smelly hair and clothing, and often suffer from premature wrinkles. And studies have shown that most young people (86 percent) prefer to date those who don't smoke. What could be more convincing than that statistic to a middler worrying about popularity?

Spit Tobacco—A Dangerous Alternative

Many youthful cigarette smokers, particularly males, began by using smokeless tobacco. In fact, research done by the Office of the Inspector General at the Department of Health and Human Services found that the average age of initiation for users was 9.5 years, with 67 percent starting at twelve years old or younger. Twenty-eight percent were five years or younger when they first began!

Smokeless or spit tobacco includes two types, snuff and chewing tobacco. Young people who use snuff place a small amount of shredded or finely ground tobacco, either loose or encased in a paper pouch, between their cheek and gum. Those who chew tobacco place a wad of loose leaf tobacco or a plug of compressed tobacco in their cheek. In both cases, the user sucks on the tobacco and spits out the juices and saliva that result.

Because the tobacco is absorbed into the bloodstream, both products can lead to nicotine addiction. Short-term use of spit tobacco often causes leukoplakia, which are white, wrinkled skin patches inside the mouth. Over time, these patches may become malignant. Long-term use of spit tobacco increases a person's risk for cancer of the mouth and throat. Smokeless tobacco also causes stained teeth, gum disease, bad breath, slow healing of mouth wounds, and a lowered sense of taste and smell.

What accounts for spit tobacco's popularity? Many are under the erroneous impression that smokeless tobacco is less harmful than smoking. A survey by the Department of Health and Human Services found that the majority of young people felt their parents would agree that using spit tobacco was better than smoking or using drugs. One respondent said his grandfather introduced him to spit tobacco, while one father commented: "(Spit tobacco) keeps the kids off hard drugs and they don't use a lot of candy."

Another influence is the number of famous athletes, particularly baseball players, who chew tobacco. Tobacco manufacturers each year hand out millions of dollars' worth of free samples at sporting and entertainment events such as rodeos, auto racing, monster truck shows, and country-western concerts.

Many developed countries—New Zealand, Australia, Hong Kong, Ireland, and Belgium—have banned sales of spit tobacco. But while the Secretary of Health and Human Services has been critical of spit tobacco, there has been no move in this country to curb its use.

Contrary to the belief that chewing tobacco among youths is more prevalent in the South, high spit tobacco use is not confined to any one region. From Maine to California, middlers are chewing and spitting. (There is evidence, however, that Native Americans as a group have the highest rates of use. In one survey in North Dakota, for example, 91 percent of Sioux County's male seventh-graders and 83.3 percent of eighth-graders were using spit tobacco.)

Joe Camel in Marlboro Country

Between 1988 and 1993, the tobacco industry doubled the money it spent to advertise both cigarettes and smokeless tobacco. According to the Federal Trade Commission, cigarette advertising dollars increased from $3.3 billion in 1988 to $6 billion in 1993, while smokeless tobacco advertising went from $68.2 million in 1988 to $119.1 million in 1993.

The tobacco industry argues that its advertisements are not aimed at young people. However, the facts tell a different story.

• Since the Joe Camel cartoon character was introduced in an advertising campaign begun in 1988, Camel's share of the adolescent cigarette market has increased dramatically, from less than 1 percent before 1988, to 8 percent in 1989, to more than 13 percent in 1993.

• One study conducted by the *Journal of the American Medical Association* found that Joe Camel is as recognizable to six-year-olds as Mickey Mouse. Ninety-one percent of six-year-olds polled not only identified Joe Camel but were able to correctly link him with cigarettes. This percentage was the same that was able to name Mickey Mouse.

• About 86 percent of adolescent smokers who buy their own cigarettes buy either Marlboro, Camel, or Newport, the three brands that are most heavily advertised.

It appears that all of these advertisements and promotions pay off. Children and teenagers constitute 90 percent of new smokers. The average teen smoker starts at thirteen and becomes a daily smoker at 14.5. Of current adult smokers, 89 percent started before age eighteen.

Over the past ten years, the number of smokers has decreased in every age-group except for teenagers. Nearly 35 percent of teens seventeen or younger said they had smoked in the last month before a survey done by the Centers for Disease Control in the spring of 1995, up from 30 percent in 1993 and 27.5 percent in 1991. More than 16 percent said they smoked more than twenty cigarettes during the month. The segment that showed the largest increase was black males, which went from about 16 percent in 1993 to 28 percent in 1995.

The adolescent market represents huge revenues for the tobacco industry. Tobacco products sold illegally to minors are worth $1.26 billion and generate $221 million in profits. Is it any wonder that tobacco companies resist efforts to restrict their advertising and marketing activities?

Despite industry opposition, the Food and Drug Administration in 1996 finalized rules aimed at reducing young people's access to tobacco products. Several of these rules merely reiterated regulations that are already in force (prohibiting the sale of "loosies," loose cigarettes, for example). Others will restrict how tobacco products are allowed to be promoted. Tobacco companies will no longer be permitted to use brand names when sponsoring a sporting or other event. Only corporate-name sponsorship will be permitted. This change is an important one because these promotions have helped to sear the image of brand-name cigarettes into the minds of youths. During a Marlboro Grand Prix telecast, citing one instance, the cigarette's logo was seen or mentioned nearly 6,000 times and visible for forty-six out of ninety-four minutes the race was broadcast.

Special promotions that feature free merchandise with cigarette logos will also be outlawed. One survey of 1,200 teens found that 21 percent had a T-shirt or hat with a logo on it, transforming them into walking advertisements for cigarettes.

Companies will no longer be permitted to hand out free samples, although mail-order sales will still be allowed. Billboards advertising tobacco products may not be placed closer than 1,000 feet of schools and playgrounds. Color imagery will be restricted to billboards placed in "adult-only" facilities. These billboards must not be visible from outside and not removable.

Opposition to Controls

These new rules will only be effective if they are rigorously enforced. All states prohibit tobacco sales to anyone under eighteen, and forty-one states license cigarette and smokeless tobacco retailers. But compliance varies widely. According to the National Institute of Drug Abuse, nearly 75 percent of eighth-graders and 90 percent of tenth-graders reported that cigarettes are "fairly easy" or "very easy" for them to get. More than 75 percent of the underage students who bought cigarettes in the month before they were surveyed said they had not been asked to show proof of age.

Critics claim the FDA rules did not go far enough. What are other ways that would make it more difficult for children to buy cigarettes? They include:

Keep cigarettes behind the counter. While the FDA rules block self-service displays, many stores keep cigarettes within easy reach of minors who may snatch up a pack, plunk down their money, and be out the door before store personnel has a chance to react.

Ban cigarette vending machines. The FDA failed to outlaw vending machines. Most state laws now require that vending machines be placed in areas that are off-limits to children, in adult bars, for instance. Yet children succeed in purchasing cigarettes from vending machines placed in "adult-only" areas three-quarters of the time. The only way to stop children from buying cigarettes from vending machines is to get rid of vending machines.

Police the sale of "loosies." Although it is against federal law to sell cigarettes that do not come in a sealed package with a warning label, many stores flout this rule. Cigarettes are taken out of their packs, placed in cups or trays, and sold individually. A study of stores in southern California found that almost half sold "loosies," as they are called, and young people were apt to buy them twice as often as adults.

Post signs warning that selling tobacco products to youths is illegal. Research has shown that, in order to be effective, these signs must be visible to the clerks. Young people are apt to disregard the signs or view them as a challenge.

Ban cigarette ads in stores. Tobacco companies offer financial incentives to stores to display their advertisements in prominent spots. The effectiveness of warning signs is oftentimes negated by the prominence of advertisements that appeal to young people. Retailers who are conscientious about not selling to young people will agree to remove these promotions.

Raise cigarette taxes. Estimates say consumption among teens would drop 12 to 14 percent if taxes were raised. The proceeds could then be used for antitobacco advertising and enforcement.

While the above options appear to be those that should be taken up by antitobacco lobbyists, the medical community, and health advocates, increasingly these activities are being performed by young people themselves with the help of their parents. The Centers for Disease Control have a program called "Stop the Sale—Prevent the Addiction," which encourages community activism. Young people, with adult supervision, enter stores and attempt to buy cigarettes. Later, adults return to the stores that sold the cigarettes and talk with the owners, managers, and clerks about the law. The approach is nonconfrontational, aiming to educate and enlist the support of the stores, rather than seeing them prosecuted. Stores that react positively often receive good publicity. Clerks who refuse to sell to minors have been awarded with gift certificates from grateful parent groups.

For more information on starting such a project in your own community, contact the Centers for Disease Control and Prevention (CDC), Atlanta, GA 30341–3724.

What are some things you can do at home to discourage your child from smoking?

State your disapproval often and loudly. Research shows that parents who state their disapproval are more likely to have children who avoid the habit. Be specific. Point out that in addition to the health and safety factors, smoking causes bad breath, stained teeth, smelly clothing, and stained fingers. It may affect athletic performance.

Warn of the consequences. Use the statistics you have found in this chapter to help your middler understand that nicotine addiction has serious side effects. One mother went a step further, having her child help out in the cancer ward of a hospital where she saw graphic evidence of the devastating effects of long-term smoking.

Don't feel you can't preach if you smoke. There are many things that adults do that children are not allowed to do. Using tobacco products is one such activity. Of course, it's best if you don't smoke (or offer to quit with your middler), but if you do smoke and intend to keep doing so, you can still discourage your children.

Ban smoking in your house and car. Allowing your child (or your child's friends) to smoke in your presence, even if you have good intentions, will weaken your position. It is illegal for someone under-age to possess tobacco products. Don't be an accessory to a crime. Show your middler that you take this law seriously and you expect him to obey it, too.

Don't buy your middler cigarettes. As crazy as this sounds, one mother admitted that she did this just so her son wouldn't get caught stealing. (She did say, however, that she made her son pay for his cigarettes.) Would you buy an alcoholic liquor? Tobacco products are addictive. Don't help your middler get hooked.

React quickly and strongly when you discover your middler has been smoking. Tell your middler you won't tolerate her smoking and if she is caught again she will be disciplined. (Check the guidelines in Chapter Four to decide on an appropriate punishment.) The PRIDE survey found that 50 percent of the children surveyed were not disciplined routinely when they broke parental rules relating to smoking, drinking, and drugs. Don't be lax. Follow through.

Offer to help him quit. "Help! We caught our fifteen-year-old daughter smoking. How can we best help her to quit? She claims that she is not addicted. But I can't be sure of that." Two-thirds of young people say they would quit if they could. Your child could honestly want to stop but needs help to succeed. Offer to pay for cessation classes, nicotine patches, or whatever will work.

Alcohol—A Younger Generation's Drug of Choice

Back in the 1930s, young men typically waited until they were seventeen before taking their first drink. Young women held off even longer, finally indulging at the age of nineteen.

The age of initiation has been drifting steadily downward ever since then. Now 50 percent of adolescents say they had their first drink between the ages of thirteen and fifteen, while 30 percent of first timers say they were between nine and twelve when they began to drink.

If that development isn't shocking enough, try this: the average binge drinker (bingeing being defined as having five or more drinks in a row) is sixteen and was twelve when he or she began drinking. And binge drinking isn't strictly a macho event. Although 59 percent of binge drinkers are male, 41 percent are female.

The reasons that young people drink aren't all that different from the reasons adults drink. According to *Fateful Choices,* a report from the Carnegie Council on Adolescent Development, of the 10.6 million students who drink, 41 percent say they drink when they are upset about something, 25 percent say they drink when they are bored, and 31 percent say they drink alone. In surveys, reports, and newspaper articles, adolescents echo the same sentiments: alcohol helps them relax and overcome shyness in social situations.

If young people possess adult attitudes about drinking, they remain woefully naive about alcohol's potency and potential for destruction. The Department of Health and Human Services administered an IQ test on alcohol and drinking to adolescents and found that these young people were surprisingly uninformed about what they were consuming. Most did not know how much alcohol was in what they were drinking. For example:

• When given a list of various beverages, two out of three students could not distinguish between alcoholic and nonalcoholic ones.

• Almost 80 percent of the students did not know that "a shot" of liquor contains the same amount of alcohol as a can of beer.

• Almost 55 percent did not know that beer and wine have about the same alcohol content.

Another survey found that 1.6 million youths did not know it was against the law for them to buy alcoholic goods and 2.6 million didn't know it was possible to die from drinking too much.

Our survey found more than one middle schooler was flirting with disaster. "I got drunk at a party and passed out with some chick," said a male student, fourteen, from Minnesota. It's possible that this young man began drinking at that party to lose his shyness. Yet alcohol can also cloud a person's judgment and thinking. One wonders what happened before he passed out with that young woman. Unprotected sex perhaps? Chances are the next morning, both individuals, besides feeling hung over, were feeling embarrassed, guilty, and apprehensive. Some party.

Days of Wine Coolers and Four Roses

A middler watching an average amount of TV will see 2,500 wine and beer commercials each year. Is it a coincidence that wine and beer are the most popular alcoholic drinks among young people? Many parents don't think so, pointing out that adolescents drink 35 percent of all wine coolers sold in the United States each year and 1.1 billion cans of beer. Also telling is the fact that in 1994–95, when the industry stopped heavily promoting wine coolers, consumption among middle schoolers actually dropped.

While the companies that produce alcoholic beverages will deny that these products are marketed to young people, the appeal to youthful sensibilities is obvious. Commercials for beer frequently feature actors or well-known athletes who are tanned, fit, and attractive. The message may not be stated outright, but the implication is there: These are the kinds of people who drink. Wouldn't you like to be like them? To a middler, worried about being liked and fitting in, the invitation is a hard one to turn down.

Young people who start drinking often do so after trying a sweet-tasting alcoholic beverage. For many, the drink of preference has been the wine cooler, which may contain anywhere from 1.5 to 6 percent alcohol by volume. These drinks, which come in flavors apt to appeal to a youthful palate, have been heavily advertised and promoted by spirits companies.

The success of wine coolers has led the industry to introduce other beverages irresistible to the sweet tooth. These drinks, however, pack a more powerful punch. Mixed drink coolers, for example, contain 4 percent alcohol, while fortified wines (Cisco, Thunderbird, and Night Train, all marketed in a variety of fruit flavors) contain 20 percent alcohol by content. Cisco, whose taste has been compared to Kool-Aid, is particularly popular among young people, but in the Department of Health and Human Services survey, 36 percent did not know that this product was a fortified wine and contained 20 percent alcohol. Of course, the manner in which these beverages are labeled and marketed does not help to clear up any confusion. The Cisco label bears the statement, "This is not a wine cooler," leading one to conclude that it is, therefore, not an alcoholic drink.

Beers, too, are confusing as to their alcoholic content. Regular beers contain 4 to 4.8 percent alcohol by content, while lite beers contain about 3 percent. Malt liquor, which is packaged like beer, contains twice as much alcohol as regular beer.

Then again, there are other products that have turned up in the marketplace that would seem to appeal more to young people than adults. These include alcohol-laced gelatin desserts and ready-made cocktails packaged in test tubes. The gelatin dessert, which many young people have already been concocting on their own, can be particularly dangerous. Because it is potent and easy to consume, the chance for overdosing is great.

Young People at Risk

An adolescent alcoholic should be an anomaly. Unfortunately, that's not the case. An estimated 20 to 30 percent of teenagers who drink are already alcoholics or well on their way to becoming so. While it may take an adult ten or fifteen years to become an alcoholic, the adolescent can accomplish this feat in a shorter time frame, anywhere from six months to three years.

As with cigarette smoking, once a young person becomes addicted, it will be more difficult to stop. Your goal should be to hold off the time at which your child becomes a drinker. That's quite a task, because one out of three boys and one out of five girls classify themselves as drinkers by age thirteen.

Particularly vulnerable are the children of alcoholics (COAs). This genetic factor is so strong, that COAs who are adopted by nonalcoholics are still in danger of becoming alcoholics. One out of five young adults with an alcoholic parent has become addicted to drugs.

For parents who are not alcoholic, the issue of drinking isn't so clear-cut. Many adults are able to drink socially and enjoy doing so without becoming addicted. How can we discourage our children from doing something that we do? Isn't that hypocritical?

Not at all. It is far riskier for a young person to drink for the following reasons:

Drinking is illegal. Unless you are twenty-one years of age, it is against the law to buy, possess, or consume alcoholic beverages.

Drinking clouds judgment, control, and coordination. A young person who has been drinking is apt to take risks, some of which could have deadly consequences.

Drinking is especially risky for females. Females have far smaller quantities of a protective gastric enzyme in their stomachs. Without this ability to break down alcohol quickly, females absorb about 30 percent more alcohol into their bloodstream than men do. So two ounces of liquor would have the same effect on a young woman as four ounces of liquor would have on a young man. A young woman who drinks places herself at risk.

Drinking intensifies feelings. The old adage about drowning your sorrows in drink simply isn't true. Getting drunk may eventually render a young person senseless, but when the effect wears off, the depression will return and probably be even worse.

You can help your child develop a responsible attitude toward alcohol so that when he does drink he will not be an abuser. A lot depends on your own approach to drinking. Cultures that teach children the appropriateness of drinking tend to have lower rates of alcoholism than those that forbid children to drink altogether. Teach your child the who, how, when, where, and why's of drinking:

Who. Don't drink when you are alone. Drinking is a social activity, done with family and friends.

How much. Don't drink to get drunk. Many young people use alcohol as a "head drug," that is with the aim of getting drunk. If you preach and practice moderation, you can counter this attitude.

When. Set an example and never drink when you plan to get behind the wheel. Driving under the influence has become the leading cause of death for young adults, aged fifteen to twenty-four. While middlers are too young to drive, they are still at risk of being passengers in cars where the driver has been drinking. Tell your middler never to ride with someone under these circumstances. Make it clear he can call you for a ride home, no questions asked.

Where. There are places where drinking is acceptable. In general, these times would include social events and during meals at home or in restaurants. Responsible drinkers don't drink at work, at school, or while performing in an athletic event, for example.

Why. Don't drink because you are depressed or angry. Instead, go for a run or read a book. Let your child see that you know alcohol will not solve your problems but only make them worse.

As with tobacco, you as the parent, are in a powerful position to influence your child on alcohol. Know your own strengths and weaknesses and be prepared to deal with them so that you can be a positive role model. Talk about the issues without lecturing. Listen, too, so that she can feel comfortable confiding in you. Establish limits and be prepared to hand out punishment if warranted. Be understanding, too. Most young people will take a drink at some point just to experiment. That doesn't necessarily mean your child will develop a drinking problem.

Drugs—A Cornucopia of Choice

The average American child is exposed to drugs at least once by age 12.5 and one-third of eighth-graders have used an illicit drug. In fact, American adolescents see drugs as their biggest worry. A 1995 study from the Center on Addiction and Substance Abuse at Columbia University found that 32 percent of the young people surveyed named drugs as their greatest problem, ahead of crime in school.

Drugs are ubiquitous; the pressure to use them, overwhelming. Yet many parents are into denial. The Partnership For a Drug-Free America found that parents consistently underestimate their children's drug use. While only 14 percent of the parents interviewed thought their children had experimented with drugs, 38 percent of the children said they had tried drugs. Similarly, 34 percent of parents thought their children had been offered drugs, while 52 percent of the children reported such an offer had been made to them. Pointing up the lack of communication, 95 percent of parents said they had spoken to their children about drugs, while only 77 percent of the children said they and their parents had such discussions.

Clearly, parents need to have more conversations about drugs with

How Can I Tell If My Child Is Using Drugs? Warning Signs:

1. *Child's personality undergoes a change.* He becomes more irritable, less affectionate, hostile, depressed. He may exhibit a lack of motivation and boredom.

2. *Child shirks responsibilities.* She won't do chores, homework, and will forget family celebrations.

3. *Child changes friends, style of dressing, and interests.* At the same time, she may become secretive and defensive about these new liaisons.

4. *Child becomes difficult to talk with.* Communication stops. He refuses to discuss his friends, routine, school, and may become defensive when discussing drug issues.

5. *Child shows physical and/or mental deterioration.* He may have trouble concentrating, become forgetful, and show signs of disordered thinking. Marijuana use may trigger an intense craving for sweets. He may lose weight.

6. *Child steals.* Cash or valuables may mysteriously disappear. When questioned, she will lie.

(Based on information from the Center for Substance Abuse Prevention, Centers for Disease Control and Prevention.)

their children. But before the talking begins, parents need to educate themselves about the types of drugs available and the dangers they pose.

MARIJUANA

The main mood-altering substance found in marijuana is THC (delta-9-tetrahydrocannabinol). During the 1960s, when the drug was enjoying its first wave of popularity, the THC level averaged 0.2 percent. The marijuana now available contains THC levels of at least 5 percent, twenty-five times more powerful. Besides THC, marijuana contains more than 400 other chemicals that can be health hazards. In fact, there are more known cancer-causing agents in marijuana smoke than in cigarette smoke. Marijuana smokers try to hold the smoke in their lungs longer, making one marijuana cigarette as damaging as four tobacco ones. In addition, some of the marijuana sold on the streets is mixed with other drugs. "Primos," for example, are laced with cocaine, while "illies," with formaldehyde. The result? Fifty percent more twelve- to seventeen-year-olds are becoming ill after smoking pot and ending up in emergency rooms.

Marijuana's impact is both quick-acting and long-lasting. The drug produces an immediate "high," which can last for several hours after use, impairing mental functions, judgment, attention spans, and decision-reaction times. THC rapidly settles in the fatty tissues of the body, particularly the brain, where it may remain for as long as four weeks, adversely affecting brain activity.

Besides the brain, marijuana affects the heart, lungs, sexual organs, and immune system. Pediatricians are particularly concerned about middlers using marijuana for the following reasons:

Middlers are actively engaged in sports. Because marijuana use distorts the senses, middlers risk athletic injuries if they pursue sports while high.

Middlers are searching for their identities. The years from ten to fifteen are ones when your middler should be making friends, meeting challenges, and growing independent. Because heavy marijuana use can make a child withdrawn and less motivated, it can interfere with this process.

Middlers are beginning to think, function, and act like adults. Marijuana's propensity to impede learning and memory will thwart this process.

Middlers are discovering themselves as sexual beings. Marijuana use will add to their confusion. Also, a middler who is high is apt to take chances, risking an unplanned pregnancy or a sexually transmitted disease.

Middlers who experiment with marijuana may move on to harder drugs. One study found that 98 percent of cocaine and heroin users started with marijuana.

Marijuana paraphernalia has glamorized this drug. Hats, rings, T-shirts, and other items sport the leafy green emblem lending a certain cachet to the drug. Adidas even produced a shoe called the Hemp, partially made from the marijuana plant. In addition, TV shows *(Roseanne)* and movies *(How to Make an American Quilt)* that show people smoking pot without adverse side effects minimize the dangers. To a media-conscious middler, the temptation to find out what all the fuss is about may be irresistible.

Some middlers may flirt with marijuana but never make a long-term commitment. Yet parents who are not vigilant may not be aware of a child's experimentation and may miss the opportunity to discuss the subject and head off possible addiction.

Medical experts identify the three stages of use as:

Experimentation. A young person out to experiment just wants to have fun, often at the urging of peers. During this stage, use is confined to weekends, often at a party or someone else's home.

Actively seeking. At this point, the child has made a decision to use marijuana on a more regular basis. No longer confined to the weekends, he may start smoking midweek, often to bring back the good feelings the drug imparts. Soon, behavioral changes occur and schoolwork may begin to slip.

Preoccupation. This is the danger zone. Use becomes heavy and costly. Even though marijuana is relatively cheap, trying to finance such a habit requires effort. Doing so often means the young person will resort to stealing or dealing (selling to others to get drugs for free). These activities place your child in serious jeopardy.

No parent wants to turn into an agent for the Drug Enforcement Administration, rifling through a son's drawers or raiding a daughter's diary in order to make sure the child is drug-free. With the middler's penchant for privacy, such invasions are apt to destroy the atmosphere of trust that you have worked so hard to create. Still, how does a parent keep informed without becoming intrusive? Here are some ideas:

Get to know your son's friends. Because peer pressure to experiment is so overpowering, knowing that your son's friends steer clear of illegal substances will give you peace of mind. Watch for any new friends who may arrive on the scene.

Get to know other parents. Talking to other parents is a great way to find out what is going on among your daughter's friends. Manhattan-based Parents in Action has maximized this approach and become a role model for parent groups nationwide. Founded in 1980 by a group of parents concerned about substance abuse, this nonprofit organization trains parent volunteers as facilitators to lead discussions in schools. Parents are encouraged to talk about issues of concern to them, and participants leave such get-togethers knowing more about one another and their children.

Keep track of your son's whereabouts. Middlers crave independence. That's fine, but impress on your son that you want to know where he is, what he is doing, and with whom. Have him call in every few hours, especially if he moves to a new location. Don't permit a last-minute change of plans unless you can check out the activity.

Be firm that drug use will not be tolerated. Don't accept arguments like, "Everybody's doing it," "You did it once," or "Marijuana's no big deal." Marijuana is dangerous and illegal.

Talk about drugs in a nonconfrontational manner. Use the occasion of a movie or TV show where drug use is shown to get into a discussion. "We talk about others who are involved in substance abuse and what's happening with them, how it has destroyed lives, families," said one mother in our survey. Initiate a talk by asking your child what he is learning about in a health class.

Don't think, "Not my kid!" Many parents, even when faced with evidence that their child is using drugs, refuse to acknowledge that there is a problem. Denying what is happening won't make the situation go away. In fact, delaying to act will probably make things worse.

Give your child ways to say no to peers. Many children feel confident enough to say no without offering an explanation. But if your son needs one, here are some he can use:

"My parents will kill me."

"It will stunt my growth and I want to try out for the NBA."

"My coach says it will hurt my game."

"I can't. I'm doing something else that night."

"I'd rather go to a movie."

Make sure your child knows never to accept an unknown substance, even from a friend. If he is invited to a party, he should find out whose parents will be there and should call you before agreeing to go. At the first sign of drug use, he should call for a ride home.

HARD DRUGS—COCAINE AND HEROIN

Only a small percentage of middlers will experiment with harder drugs such as cocaine or heroin. The young people most at risk are those who regularly smoke marijuana. Environment plays a major part, too. One can't discount the pressures of living in neighborhoods where the lure for making easy money selling drugs seems like the only Horatio Alger route out of poverty.

All parents must remain alert, however. Impressionable youths are influenced by pop culture. Cocaine and heroin abuse are rampant in the rock music industry. Models, pale and thin with black-rimmed raccoon eyes, have created what has been called heroin-addict esthetic or junkie chic. As long as middlers idolize musicians and models, parents will worry about the influence.

Cocaine comes to the school yard from the foothills of the Andes Mountains, where the coca bush grows. The leaves of this plant are gathered and then soaked in a chemical mixture. This produces a cocaine salt that is then dried and crushed into a bitter, snowy, white powder.

Applying modern marketing methods, drug dealers have lowered the price for cocaine in order to increase sales. That strategy has been successful. Previously the drug of choice for an affluent segment of society, cocaine is now within reach of the masses. The drug, viewed as a symbol of status and success, often is appealing to young people.

Freebase cocaine is a hardened powder that is smoked in pipes. Crack is the street name given to a form of freebase cocaine that comes in the shape of small lumps or shavings. Called crack because of the crackling sound it makes when smoked, the drug is cheap, usually between $5 and $10 for one or two doses and easily transportable, usually sold in small vials, folding paper, or tinfoil.

Whether snorted through the nose, smoked, or injected, cocaine is a highly addictive drug that can kill. The user can never predict whether the next dose will prove to be fatal. The drug speeds up the heart rate while also constricting blood vessels, limiting the amount of blood reaching the brain. The result may be seizures, cardiac arrest, respiratory arrest, or stroke.

Heroin, a depressant derived from the opium poppy, can be lethal. Highly addictive (users almost immediately crave increasingly strong doses to produce the same high), heroin usually is injected. But the purity of the heroin now being produced means that it can be snorted or smoked, thus increasing the drug's appeal among users who are scared of using a needle. A survey of eighth-graders in 1995 found that 2.3 percent had tried heroin, double the rate from 1991. The number of rock stars and celebrities who have struggled and died from heroin addiction has, ironically, increased the appeal of the drug.

Antidrug crusaders are worried that young people do not fully grasp the dangers involved in experimenting with cocaine and heroin. Parents need to make sure their children understand that addiction to these substances happens quickly, lasts a long time, and can kill.

Inhalants

Inhalants are the fastest-growing form of substance abuse and the third most abused substances overall after alcohol and tobacco. Because inhalants are essentially everyday household products, readily available in any home, they are well within the reach of middlers. The high is produced by "huffing" the vapors. Twenty percent of seventh-graders—more than five million teens—have tried inhalants.

Inhalants include:

Adhesives—airplane glue, rubber cement, PVC cement
Aerosols—spray paint, hair spray, deodorant, air freshner, analgesic spray, asthma spray
Solvents and gases—nail polish remover, paint remover, paint thinner, typing correction fluid, natural gas, cigarette lighter fluid, gasoline
Cleaning agents—dry-cleaning fluid, spot remover, degreaser
Dessert sprays—whipped cream

The signs of inhalant abuse include red, runny eyes or nose, chemical breath, sores around the mouth, loss of appetite, anxiety, irritability, and paint stains on body or clothing.

Continual abuse of inhalants has been known to cause severe anemia, liver damage, brain damage, and sudden sniffing death (SSD). The method of inhaling the vapors from a paper bag to induce a more intense high also increases the possibility of suffocation.

Keep Your Middler Substance Free

The odds may seem insurmountable, fighting to keep your middler drug free when he is being pressured by peers and influenced by cultural forces that not only condone but also appear to celebrate deviant behavior. Don't underestimate, however, the power you wield as a parent. Start early to talk with your child about these substances. The more you talk, the more effect you will have over the choices he makes. Be a positive role model and steer your child toward other adults whose values you would like to see him emulate. Stay informed about your child's life—where he is, who he is with, what he is doing. Don't sit back and be complacent. If you suspect there is a problem, you're probably right. Act quickly before things get out of hand.

Strategies: Making Your Middler More Resilient

Researchers have spent lots of time trying to discover why some children become drug addicts or alcoholics. An equally compelling question is, what keeps the child in a drug-infested neighborhood, or in an abusive family, drug free? Educational experts now believe that resiliency, the ability to recover quickly in the face of adversity, is the key characteristic that equips a young person to flourish despite seemingly insurmountable odds. How does a parent develop this quality in a son or daughter? The answer, both simple and complex, is good parenting. Specifically:

By offering care and support. Nothing can substitute for a loving home, a place where your middler knows he is safe, secure, and well taken care of.

By having high expectations. Middlers want to please their parents. Set limits and enforce those rules. Let your son know you expect the best from him and he will deliver.

By participation. Being involved with your child in a variety of activities is important. You should be spending time together as a family, at school, and in the community.

Enlist other caring adults. If you are a single, overworked, time-pressured parent, seek out a coach, teacher, relative, or family friend who can establish a secure bond that will help fortify your middler's self-esteem.

Look at the light side. A child who is able to laugh at himself and see the humor in impossible situations is a child who will rise above adversity without turning to alcohol or drugs.

Ten

The Tunnel of Love
Sexuality and Your Middler

*"The biggest secret I've kept from my parents is that I
am having sex."*

(Thirteen-year-old Hawaiian island girl)

To ride the Tunnel of Love you have to be a certain height (not a
certain age). And so some children who are tall for their age wind up
in over their heads. The tram, whisking one and all, descends into
dark, cavernous territory, punctuated with scary surprises. You can feel
your heart pounding, your pulse racing, and your adrenaline pump-
ing. There's this uncontrollable urge to scream. You try to reason with
yourself and control your impulses, but you can't. You shriek and feel
this incredible rush. Quicker than you anticipated, you reach the
climax—the scariest blast. Then abruptly the tram rolls to a stop,
leaving you breathless and yet wanting to board again.

Sounds a lot like sex, doesn't it? You may not be ready to embrace
your daughter's burgeoning sexuality or your son's mounting erotic
desire, but ready or not, here it comes. The age of first intercourse is
getting younger and younger: 43 percent of fourteen- to seventeen-
year-olds admitted they had sexual intercourse in a recent study. By
age fourteen, more than half of all boys have fondled a girl's breasts
and a quarter have touched a girl's vulva. By eighteen, three-quarters
of all young people have engaged in heavy petting and one-quarter
have experience with fellatio and cunnilingus.

It is during preadolescence when Daddy's Little Girl is going to fall
in love for the first time, this time around complete with sexual feel-

ings. And Mama's Boy, he's about to become preoccupied with sowing those proverbial wild oats.

As a parent you are responsible for orchestrating the sexual awakening of your middler. You have to nurture your son and your daughter as each finds his and her sexual identity. You have to teach sexual ethics and restraint. And you must avoid preachy platitudes or your middler will surely tune you out. This is a daunting job.

You already know the odds are stacked against you, given the eroticized culture in which we live. MTV, sexually explicit movies, subliminally sexy commercials—young people are being seduced at every turn even before a bona fide sexual proposition pops up. The risk of your child making the wrong lustful move is reason to shudder. Every thirteen seconds a teen in the United States contracts a sexually transmitted disease. Every thirty seconds a teen gets pregnant. Contracting AIDS looms on every romantic horizon. The number of teens who test positive with HIV—the virus that causes AIDS—doubles every fourteen months. Despite these dreadful realities, you as a parent still want your middler to grow up, find love, get married, and enjoy a fulfilling sexual relationship. Most will, but not necessarily in that order.

In this chapter, we are going to explore the sexual terrain upon which your young adolescent is embarking. Middlers will tell you their secret sexual fantasies. We will delve into the middler's book of love to see what kinds of relationships are being formed. Parents will confess their fears. After interviewing the most progressive and knowledgeable sex education trainers in the country, we will bring you their best advice. Helping your daughter—and your son, too—achieve intimate and satisfying romantic attachments is perhaps the most important lesson you will ever teach.

The Sexual Awakening

From birth we are sexual creatures. Chances are you have heard or read that already. However, it is during the years from ten to fifteen, with the help (or hindrance) of hormones, that sexual feelings change and intensify. Every middler is in the process of discovering that sexual self with its twinges of lust and pangs of love. Exploring these personal passions stirs curiosity and involves experimentation. Your middler is grappling with self-knowledge, attitudes, and values. Sexual issues encompass thoughts and feelings, and in the larger and trickier context: sexual identity, gender roles, and relationships.

Is is really true that thirteen-year-olds are contemplating *to sleep or not to sleep with boyfriends?* The spin-the-bottle innocence that parents may recall when they think of their preadolescence is obsolete. At what age did you pop that sexual question? When did you say yes to the erotic proposition? At eighteen? Or when you were engaged to be married? The age of consent is much younger than it was in the 1960s and 1970s.

Parents who were free-love advocates of the sexual revolution of the 1960s are reeling at how fast today's youth run "sexual bases" from first to home run. Paradise by the dashboard lights, indeed.

One single mother electronically huffed, "My twelve-year-old daughter is obsessed with sex. She wants to know what it feels like. To my knowledge she is still a virgin. She has told me that she got a tingling feeling in her vagina around certain boys. We talk openly about sex. A lot of her thirteen-year-old friends are already sexually active. I don't know whether to trust her, put her on the pill, or what! Where do I go from here?"

It's one thing to broach the facts-of-life "plumbing" of penises and vaginas, or the reproductive themes of fallopian tubes and sperm. It's quite another matter when we, as parents, have to face the real live human sexual response of our children!

Are you up to the challenge? Let's be honest here. Sexuality is perhaps the most uncomfortable subject a parent faces during child rearing. The whole subject is too intimate, too primal, too riddled with insecurity and taboo. It's little consolation, but your middler is equally embarrassed. Children cannot imagine their parents having sex. Parents don't want to imagine their children having sex. Despite this mutually held mental block, you must rise to the occasion of your middler's sexual dawning. They desperately need information and guidance. Otherwise peers will be filling in with inaccurate and risky advice.

Start with accepting that sexual awakening and desire is a normal and healthy part of young adolescent development. Naturally, parents want to supply answers congruent with their family values and religious beliefs. However, your middler, and not you, is directing this erotic play. You probably will not know exactly when your son begins his sexual explorations or which boy your daughter will entice with that first soulful kiss. The *private* in their private lives definitely takes on a new disquieting feature. The sexual decisions your child makes will be a combination of her readiness, his impulse, and your values.

Learning about sexuality and *becoming comfortable* with one's own is a process that middlers do not experience alone or in a vacuum. Young adolescent boys and girls need one another to define themselves, and parents, more than ever, to help them understand this sexual transition from child to man and woman.

"Going Out," "Going With," "Gone"

It starts as early as fifth grade, this who's "going out" with whom endless conversation. Nervous parents craning their necks to get within earshot of giggling conversations soon learn that "going out" in middler-speak doesn't really mean going anywhere. These ten- and eleven-year-olds are not dating. "Going out" means simply hanging out together, pairing off in the hallway, playground, or cafeteria. And yet as the hormones escalate, the chemistry becomes more compelling. "Going out" evolves into "going with" so-and-so to the movies and then the junior prom. Along the way many dating young people fall in love, as in "gone," romantically speaking.

Being attracted to someone and having those signals reciprocated, forming that romantic bond is a wonderful and intense experience. Ah, that first time, that first love—our middlers are entering magical and memorable territory. Caring for and sharing intimacies with another delivers great pleasure. Relationships of this dimension are a giant step for middlers. Infatuations can transform the hectic and harried middler existence into heaven.

"My twelve-year-old daughter told me in passing that her life was 'perfect,' " a forty-six-year-old Florida mom recounted. "Now she'd always been a good student, a fine athlete, and satisfied with her friends. I suspected the added luster kicked in because she had fallen for an eighth-grade boy and this was her first crush. Apparently he was smitten, too. Oh, to be young, and in love, and to feel that life was perfect. How I envied her!"

Such brushes with young love provide superb opportunity for emotional growth. Empathy. Disclosure. Sensitivity. Sacrifice. Romantic muscles begin to flex and to get a good workout. These budding romances act as necessary rehearsals for mature love and marriage.

Unfortunately, some young love affairs can be emotionally toxic. A 1995 headline, EIGHTH-GRADE SWEETHEARTS IN A LOVE SUICIDE, told a Miami story having all the elements of Shakespearean tragedy. Two strident lovers, immigrants—the fourteen-year-old boy was from Mexico and the thirteen-year-old girl was from Nicaragua. Both were honor students, living in the United States since early childhood. Disapproving parents, who thought their daughter was too young, forbade her from seeing her beloved. The two penned suicide notes professing "can't live without each other" sentiments and dove together into a canal. Neither could swim.

This is an extreme case and rare. However, many young couples veer into troubled waters. Young people don't know this, but almost all early adolescent love affairs, the smooth and rocky ones, the full-blown erotic varieties, and the innocent, are destined to lead to heartbreak. The reason, middler boys and girls are at cross-purposes psychologically. Experts in development explain females seek to define themselves by their attachments. Loving someone makes a girl feel like a woman. Boys, on the other hand, are engaged in the task of separating themselves from mothers, and females who mirror that loving bondage. Leaving someone makes a boy feel like a man. Alas, the courtship dance between adolescents is doomed by who they are and who they are struggling to become.

Given the emotional turbulence of middler romances, a component of sex education should be relationship support, guidance, and training. Little is offered. The National Commission on Adolescent Sexual Health pointed out that research focuses on pregnancy or contraceptive use, but rarely on the *context* of adolescent relationships. How are middlers supposed to learn how to construct healthy romantic attachments?

When we were young, our parents modeled relationship behavior, but now many middlers *don't* grow up privy to two parents' long-term love affair? Instead they watch marriages fall apart. They bear witness to the fury and vengeance that accompany so many breakups. Divorce is the education half of our young people get.

And yet, the news isn't all bad on the sociology front. Postdivorce adults reenter the world of dating. Their *second-chance-at-love* escapades give middlers a front-row seat to watching the social mechanics.

How an adult judges a potential romantic partner, the way relationships progress, what qualities produce success or deliver unhappiness—these are a few lessons middlers can observe.

Regardless of whether you are happily married, divorced, a single parent, or in a blended family, there are opportunities to teach romantic sense and sensibility. Parents have to get into "relationship talks," dialogues about romantic issues with their sons and daughters. If you don't know how to begin such conversations, here are a few questions designed to get you into the thick of amorous territory.

"What makes you find him so attractive?" (Or "Why do you think your best friend finds that girl so great?") When you ask your child to explain the reasons behind a romantic choice, you are teaching your daughter to analyze, or your son to judge romantic character. Is the attraction just physical as in "I like his smile, her blue eyes"? Do his interests, mountain biking or drama club, factor into your decision to choose him for companionship? Is her popularity a plus, or is her shy nature appealing? Are you impressed by her musical talent or his performance on the football field or track? Being drawn to another person is mystical and magical, but there is more to choosing than mere animal magnetism. Bringing detail and understanding to romantic selection will instruct your middler how to make informed decisions and eventually lead to thoughtful and compatible choices.

"What's your idea of the perfect night out with a date?" Now, your son is never going to admit if it's a Lover's Lane scenario. Given that total honesty is unlikely, you can still elicit useful answers. A dream date might be to the roller rink, movies to see the latest thriller, hiking along the beach or a mountain trial, taking in a hockey game, or going to an amusement park. The point is not so much where your middler goes as how a great date *feels*.

Going out with someone (or in a group) is supposed to be fun. Dating is supposed to mean good times (parties, events), which will be recalled as *the good old days*. When you make this connection between dating and fun, a middler will question a relationship lacking in mutual enjoyment. Your child will be less inclined to stay in a "breaking-up and making-up" relationship that features misery.

When your daughter finds herself getting the third-degree from a jealous boyfriend for attending some school function, or when your son finds himself monopolized by a possessive loner who shuns the crowd, each will wonder: "Why can't he lighten up?" "Why can't she enjoy teenage life?" And finally, "Is this person worth sacrificing happy times for?"

"Why is that boy or that girl so popular?" Popularity is the crowning glory stuff in the world of young adolescents. It can be enlightening for your middler to probe what makes someone likable by consensus. Is a girl sought after because of a bubbling personality, a beautiful body, or because she's "easy"? Is a boy the fantasy of every seventh-grade girl because he's accomplished at something, or because he's a rebel? When your middler dissects a peer's popularity out loud, he will be exploring how achievement or disposition, looks or sexual availability affect one's appeal. She will be drawing conclusions about the effects of working hard, being nice, or being too accommodating. During all this, you will be gleaning what your son thinks of sexually adventurous girls, how your daughter rates the James Dean (or Dylan McKay) type.

Young adolescents are "trying on" a variety of personas the same way they are experimenting with looks. Perusing the popularity of vixens, delinquents, preppy cheerleaders, and jocks will help them sort and process the ramifications, both positive and negative, of certain behaviors and roles. This is not a how-to-become-popular exercise. It is a method for identifying assets, motives, and vulnerabilities, which will give a middler strategies to use in his social quest, warnings to heed, and motivation for developing assets.

"How many ways are there to say 'I love you!'?" Teach your middler to count the ways. Why? You can guess the answer to this one: so a middler doesn't assume the only way to say "I love you" is with sexual intercourse. Sooner or later your daughter is going to hear the "if you really love me then you'll have sex with me" refrain. Prepare your daughter and son by cultivating intimacy skills.

Show them that expressing affection takes many forms. This may be obvious to you, but it is not to your young adolescent. The proof of love (i.e., having sexual intercourse) is the romantic gesture that gets all the media hype. So expand the proving grounds. List other demonstrative options. For example, love is sharing a secret. Giving a gift. Providing applause for a goal accomplished, as well as a shoulder to cry on after a disappointment. Listening. Planning a good time. (For more items get *100 Ways to Make Love Without Having Sex,* a brochure produced by the State of New York Department of Health, based on suggestions written by New York Teens. Available from Planned Parenthood.)

Being fluent in intimacy and creative is critical to young boys and girls at this moment in their lives when communicating emotion is paramount. They are romantic trailblazers zeroing in on the scent of the opposite sex. They are not going to stop nosing around. If parents want to keep explicit sexual displays at bay, then middlers need alternatives to convey their compelling, overwhelming sentiments. They need to digest the fact that love doesn't always mandate sex, nor does sex necessarily demonstrate love.

Sexual decision-making revolves around a lot more than protestations of love. There is a great deal to consider. Use this checklist to teach your child how to examine sexual behavior.

- *Survey personal motives.* "Am I just going along so he won't leave me?"
- *Recognize the pull of outside pressures.* "Isn't everyone else doing IT?"
- *Calculate possible drawbacks.* "Will I feel guilty afterward?"
- *Tabulate social consequences.* "Will he tell his friends?"
- *Assume the responsibility for birth control.* "Do I have a condom ready?" or "Is she on the pill?"
- *Consider ethical and religious considerations.* "Should I wait until I'm older or married?"

"What would you do for love?" How much would you be willing to sacrifice, gamble, or forfeit in the course of a relationship? Ask your young adolescent just what his friends may be doing for love. Does a girl allow her boyfriend to cheat off of her paper during a test? Does a boy share a beer or a cigarette with his steady because he doesn't want to hurt her feelings by criticizing her? Are best friends suddenly left in the dust in favor of beloveds? Does a girl rationalize a slap across the face or being called a "bitch" because she knows deep down "he really loves me"?

Relationships that contain unhealthy elements don't suddenly materialize in adulthood. Patterns of self-destruction, codependency, verbal abuse, and spouse-battering begin in these formative years. So it is critical to teach sons and daughters to recognize self-sabotaging, exploitative, or abusive signals in romances. And then to run.

Sexual Value (and Values) Begins at Home

Many of the experts in the field of sex education told us that parents approach sexuality instruction with their youngsters backward. Mothers and fathers hem and haw over "the birds and the bees talk," when it is conversations about values, not the facts of life, that young people need. Parents jump ahead to the main event. For girls, the focus is usually on virginity and prevention; for boys, oftentimes little more than condom use. Worst case scenarios are basic themes. Mothers try to warn their daughters about date rape. Boys are cautioned about the accidental fate of getting a girl pregnant. Parents battle one another and the local school boards about sex education curricula and condom distribution. The charges fly. While adults are busy labeling each other moral bullies or permissive hedonists, young adolescents are left behind, by themselves, to tackle the confusion and complexity, propriety and etiquette, and the nuances of sex and love.

Will your daughter get a reputation? Will your son act like a sexual predator? Parents want to help their children avoid the fates of promiscuous girls and cavalier, misogynous boys. Mentoring your middler on issues of sexuality means laying a foundation of values.

Expose the double standard. It will hardly surprise you to hear that, sexually speaking, it is still a man's world. Boys are proud of their sexual prowess and conquests. Girls are not. A 1994 poll from the *Journal of Sex Research* cast young girls as more regretful about their sexual experiences than boys. They were less likely to describe forays as pleasurable, more likely to shoulder negative consequences.

Girls more often attached the concept of love to sex, a fusion that bodes trouble. After interviewing 400 teenage girls about their love lives for her book *Going All the Way,* Sharon Thompson found girls who saw intercourse as "the apotheosis of romance," were twice vulnerable. They were more likely to fully engage sexually and less likely to protect themselves against pregnancy and disease.

Girls still labor under the Victorian legacy that good girls don't have sex or carry condoms. The sexual revolution may have given females sexual freedom, but sexual power to say yes without repercussions, that is clearly another matter, still.

The double standard of sexuality cuts both ways. Boys are discriminated against as well. How so? Sex education is basically "girl talk." Mothers do all the talking about sexual matters, and mostly with girls. They start sexual tête-à-têtes with daughters on average two years earlier than conversations with sons, and more frequently. Not only do girls get more talk sooner than boys, but on a wider range of topics. Mothers regularly cover feelings, the nature of love, and communication skills.

Not only are mothers remiss. Timely father-son relationship conversations rarely happen. Fathers are the absentee teachers of mores. To make matters worse, classroom sex education agendas have also shortchanged young adolescent males. Boys have been the missing link in sex education curricula. "Just say no" refusal skills lessons are usually geared for girls. What training are boys being given? Not enough, the experts agree.

You must know how each gender is shortchanged. Middler girls must be given permission to feel good about their erotic potential. Otherwise they will not be able to make sound, healthy relationship decisions now or ever, not to mention enjoy a fulfilling sex life (hopefully after marriage). On the other hand, boys need clear messages about *not* taking advantage of every sexual opportunity. Each gender needs consistent and uniform counseling about how to react to sexual urges. Parents have to liberate their girl's mind-set (not behavior) and restrain their boy's sexual self-image and actions. Both need to hear the message that sex is good, a pleasure that is meant to last a lifetime, but one that demands caution with a capital C.

Teach respect for women. Working moms will be distressed to learn that, according to several different surveys, young men still believe by significant margins that a woman's place is in the home. And her role is to have babies. Young men don't favor the liberated-female variety, even though they do understand that women want careers.

Not only has the women's movement missed its mark, but the sexual revolution had backfired a bit. Think back to when we were young in the backseat of those Chevy Impalas on Lover's Lane. When girls said, "Stop," boys complied (if not altogether enthusiastically). A code of chivalry existed that ensured the safety of most females in isolated situations. Today, boys assume that no really means yes. Or they just override the girl's objection, which is called date rape.

What restrains a boy, restores the gentleman within? Only one thing—having respect for a girl as a human being and this is learned at home. How a father behaves toward his wife, and vice versa, imprints both sons and daughters with values. Does a husband listen to a wife's no? Are her requests met with consideration? Are females shown respect? Or do sexist remarks such as "Hey, look at the boobs on that one!" send mixed messages? Is women's work (in and outside the home) recognized? Are both parents entitled to ambition and recreation?

The equal rights debate is not solely a political matter. The values about women and men that your middlers absorb from the home environment become the instincts they take on dates. Boys who mistreat (and the girls who tolerate such treatment) both learned sexist lessons at their mother's or father's knee.

Define what it is to be a real man and a real woman. Wayne Pawlowski, a licensed social worker and director of training for Planned Parenthood of Metropolitan Washington, D.C., made a profound connection between sex and gender roles. He explained, "Our cultural myth and message says to men: when sex is presented—take it! To do otherwise (which means to choose abstinence) is to sacrifice one's masculinity."

Young adolescent boys can't "just say no" when doing so jeopardizes the identity as a man that they are struggling so hard to establish. There are so few rites of passage in our culture for young boys. First intercourse is the biggie, the foolproof demonstration of manhood. If we ask adolescent boys to forfeit this passage into manhood, with what are we going to replace it? How are they going to know they are real men?

Is there one strategy a parent can employ to show a middler how to be a man? "There is no magic bullet to make a boy feel like a man," says Peter Scales, a research fellow at the Search Institute, youth advisor for two decades on adolescent development and sex education trainer. One way parents, and especially fathers, can help is to model consciously what real men do: they work, they nurture, they help with the domestic chores. Men enjoy looking at, being aroused by, and loving women. They don't oogle, make snide remarks, or abuse.

Young adolescent women have to get a grip on handling their sexuality and maintaining their worth. The message that babies make a woman needs to be questioned. While motherhood may be the zenith and fulfillment of womanhood, it is a role too demanding for the adolescent years. A woman who is still very much a child does not make a good mother.

Seven Illusions About Young Lust

Laying a groundwork of abstract values may be fundamental, but what about the nitty-gritty? How does one prepare a middler for those magic moments when the moon is full, the passions are rising, and the will to stop is waning? Parents need strategies to arm daughters and sons for the clinches. Start your training by saying farewell to the following myths.

1. *Middlers today are more sexually aware and savvy than we were at their age.* Here's a joke from the annals of research on preadolescent sexual behavior. The professor conducting the survey asked, "Are you sexually active?" The female middler responded, "No, I just lie there."

Obviously that young lady was confused about the definition of sexually active. The point is that middlers are concrete thinkers. They are heading into the abstract-thinking territory, but each at her own pace. This means that young adolescents require specific information in plain language.

Terms like "making love," or "having sex" are too vague. In all discussions you have with your middler about sexual behavior, make sure you use exact words. Petting. Rape. Intercourse. Follow up by asking if he knows specific definitions. Middlers may be talking about "tonsil hockey" (French kissing) and "lip-wrestling" (necking), but don't be fooled into thinking that they have a sophisticated grasp of what they say and hear. Don't forget that you are talking to someone who may have heard it all, and even seen it all, but that doesn't necessarily mean he understood it all.

Middlers are still half children. That point is well made by a Kentucky seventh-grade teacher. "A student who I overheard bragging in the hallway about having a condom in his wallet begged me to go to the bookstore. He returned to class with a Scooby Doo notepad. I think this about sums up adolescence."

2. *Not my daughter; not my son.* Some parents can read all the headlines about preadolescent sexual activity. Sexual precocity and promiscuity may be rampant, they concede, but none of this applies to their child. These parents are fooling themselves. Sexual experimentation and exploration are part and parcel of growing up. Almost all adolescents engage in some type of sexual behavior, according to survey results reported by the National Commission on Adolescent Sexual Health. This commission collected extensive data on preteens and older adolescents.

Although each middler dips a toe into steamy waters according to his own timetable, because of physical changes like hormones and emotional maturity, the truth remains that every middler will do some wading into erotic pools during these young adolescent years. And those who aren't dabbling in the erotic zone are contemplating whether to or not.

"Last year, we were concerned," began a Washington mother, "because we overheard a telephone conversation, our thirteen-year-old daughter discussing *touching*. Apparently this was happening with her boyfriend. Our eighth-grader was confiding that she wanted to wait until she was married for sex, but she thought touching was okay, wasn't it? Well, we thought times may have changed, but *too* much *too* young was still *too* heavy of a load. We talked to a counselor, and began some in-depth discussions with our daughter. It turns out she was feeling somewhat rushed and pressured by the boy."

That wasn't your daughter. But, suppose this mom bought the not-my-daughter illusion? She would have missed the opportunity to provide her thirteen-year-old with a dialogue (and a time-out) about a relationship that was getting hot and heavy. Her child was able to express feeling pushed. Afterward, the young adolescent had a clear, reinforced personal platform on which to proceed romantically.

What's the best way to initiate such a dialogue? Don't pry or accuse. Use "I" as in "I am concerned and I feel I have to share my concerns." Or "I feel uncomfortable bringing this up, but I wouldn't be a good parent if I didn't." Acknowledging your struggle and caring draws a child in, as opposed to pushing her away with personal attacks or invasions of privacy.

3. *The media will cancel out my efforts.* Yes, sexier television programs, R-rated movies, and racy music videos do glorify sex and influence middlers. Parents feeling powerless may be tempted to throw in the monitoring towel. Don't. Why? The world that middlers see onscreen is not the one in which they are living, dating, and loving.

Middlers need a reality check. According to a 1996 study by the Henry Kaiser Family Foundation, 53 percent of 1,500 teens (twelve- to eighteen-year-olds) admitted they get their information about sex and birth control from TV and movies. Hollywood portrayals affect 75 percent.

What they see is first dates that end in intercourse and girls who never say "no." Lusty adventures prevail with sexual responsibility absent. In a study of teen's favorite programs, one in four interactions conveyed sexual messages. Yet only two of the ten shows analyzed over three weeks wrote consequences into the script. Onscreen couples don't use condoms, don't get sexually transmitted diseases or AIDS, or risk unwanted pregnancy. "The Beautiful and the Willing" could be the title of much TV fare, when in real terms young adolescents are a documentary: "The Ordinary and the Vulnerable." Rather than be discouraged, parents need to double their efforts so that young people can get sexuality into realistic perspective. Tuning in may mean getting turned on for young people, but their decisions depend on a parent's critique.

4. *Talking about sex gives permission.* Or talking about it puts the idea to have sex in a middler's head. Mothers and fathers needn't worry about putting illicit thoughts in the minds of young adolescents. Why? Because X-rated ideas are already there!

All kidding aside, there are parents who sincerely agonize over sex education curricula in school. Although 90 percent of parents want some sex-oriented training, the remaining and often vocal 10 percent don't because they fear explicit talk will arouse and energize the listeners and expedite sexual ventures. We asked experts to address these fears and this is what we learned.

To date thirty-five studies conducted across the country have examined the impact on youth of sex education programs. There is absolutely no "cause-and-effect" evidence suggesting educating young adolescents about sex absolutely triggers sexual activity. In fact, exposure to education probably influences young adolescents to continue to delay sex. Older teens, fifteen and up, may not delay their sexual activity but will use protective measures more often, and more effectively, which means "graduating" from withdrawal as a preventive strategy to condom use and oral pill contraceptives. Sex education is not suggestive. It is valuable and urgent. On that point the experts were unanimous.

Talking about sex *does* give kids permission, *permission to talk* about sex. The middler's job is to explore erotic feelings and possibilities. The parent's job is to let them explore. Discussions enable them to *explore mentally.* Don't ever tell a young adolescent, "You're too young to talk about this" or "You shouldn't be thinking about that!" By encouraging your son or your daughter to talk openly about sensitive sexual issues, you are enabling them to process facts and attitudes, and even more importantly, to think about things ahead of time. Then when she is in a sexually charged situation, she will not be thinking about what to do for the first time and in the heat of the moment!

Be careful not to jump to conclusions. Your son asks, "Is masturbation harmful?" Or your daughter says, "My friend says French kissing can give you AIDS." Bringing issues up does not mean young adolescents are *doing* what they are asking about. Sometimes it really is a friend, not a convoluted disguise. At such moments your middler is giving you cues that he is ready to talk. And listen.

Unlike some. "My daughter, age twelve, refuses to talk about anything sexual," lamented a New York mom who repeated what many parents encounter. "Every time I try to get into a conversation about kissing or sexual attraction, she balks, decreeing 'that's disgusting'! How can I get through? I don't want to traumatize her, nor do I want her to get her facts from the grapevine."

If you think a middler is ready but unwilling to broach these touchy subjects, several parents suggested the right book can work miracles on the sexually squeamish. "I bought *It's Perfectly Normal—A Book About Changing Bodies, Growing Up, Sex and Health* by Robie Harris and gave it to my twelve-year-old on her birthday," offered a Connecticut mom. "At her sleepover party that night, the girls locked themselves in my daughter's room and pored over those pages. And pictures. Every so often my child came out to ask a question."

Or take a roundabout route. Ask your daughter about how her peers are making decisions about French kissing, for example. Inquire about what kinds of behaviors (start with dating) your son's friends are into. Get his judgment call. The goal is to talk so that you can inject your values.

Strike before the irons are too hot. Once young adolescents become sexually active, they stop sharing details. Girls, especially, think you as a parent will think less of them for engaging in any sexual expression. Both boys and girls think sexual exploits will ruin your relationship and get them into deep trouble. Their reluctance can be compounded by yours. Parents often instinctively know when sex is in the air, but feel tentative about getting into a talk. Your avoidance puts another brick in a wall that should not be going up. Not now when sexually active relationships can be fatal attractions.

5. *Preaching abstinence is wasting your breath.* Today's generation of middlers are living in a world when boys and girls begin puberty earlier (by a year or so) and marry later (twenty-five on average for women, twenty-six for men). Can sex realistically be postponed for all those intervening years, from pubescent stirrings to late-twenty-something wedding nights? In the light of these statistics, isn't it useless to try the "just say no" strategy? No.

Abstinence is the advice and policy of choice endorsed by all sex education experts. Yet, if abstinence is to succeed, it needs to be defined and presented positively. First, what exactly does abstinence mean? Spell your definition out plainly. Abstaining means refraining from sexual intercourse. It does not mean you cannot be affectionate or intimate with someone you love. This affords young people room for breathing, even a bit of heavy breathing.

Next, make a logical case for postponing sexual intercourse. This is not hard to do. List the drawbacks. An unplanned pregnancy is a risk and a huge responsibility if it happens. This point should be made clear to boys, the potential fathers, as well as to the potential mothers.

Sex is not as safe as it once was. Explain sexually transmitted diseases such as chlamydia, the most common STD, and genital herpes.

Tell middlers that adolescents have the highest rate of chlamydia and, if untreated, it can lead to sterility and infertility. Let young girls know that because their cervixes are underdeveloped during these years, they are more susceptible to STDs and infections. And they have fewer protective antibodies than older women.

Then there's HIV, the virus that becomes full-blown AIDS, for which there is no cure. Young people need to be told that not only homosexuals are at risk for contracting HIV. Heterosexuals, especially women and minorities, are the new story, a fast-growing category of victims. In 1993, 75 percent of new cases had female faces of color. For casualties reported among children under thirteen years of age, 84 percent were minorities. Using condoms can reduce the risk, but the only 100 percent sure way of escaping the risk of HIV is abstinence.

Emphasize that lots of young adolescents are abstaining. The media only makes it look like everyone is doing it!

Aside from the risk of fatal and serious infection, underscore the emotional consequences of rushing into sexual behavior. Remind your middler that anticipating consequences is not his strong suit. Point up to your daughter that her habit of "living in the now" won't protect her from suffering the fallout of poor sexual decisions. Young adolescents are just learning about all the intense emotions and issues that surround love and lust. Jealousy. Insecurity. Heartbreak. Reputation. Rumor. A romance with premature sex is a time bomb, destined to explode and leave a young adolescent's heart and social life in smithereens. If you lay this all out, it will make sense to many young ears. Advise them to wait until at least high school, when they have acquired more reasoning ability and social skill to contemplate heavier sexual complicity.

Abstinence is a choice. Once middlers see it in terms of gains rather than sacrifices, many can endorse it more wholeheartedly than you anticipated.

6. *There is no antidote to breathless, impulsive decision-making.* "Even though my child knows right from wrong, my biggest fear," confessed a New Jersey mother, "is that her choices will be the wrong ones. I am not talking about the little decisions, but the sexual ones leading to events with lasting repercussions. She may know full well about the consequences of unprotected sex, but I'm afraid feelings will carry her

away." This woman is not alone. She may be justified and right to worry, but wrong in assuming that a young adolescent cannot make sound decisions in the romantic clinches.

Middlers can and do make bad decisions. "The biggest secret I've kept from my parents is about my friend," confided an Oklahoma seventh-grader. "She told her mom she was spending the night at my house, but she went to a hotel with a bunch of boys." We don't learn what happened next, but probably you are shuddering at the risks of that idiotic move. This young girl was never schooled in responsible decision-making.

Young adolescents are capable of making sensible judgments once we teach them how. There are strategies and skills that can be imparted (and often are in sex education class).

According to sex counselors, it is normal for young adolescents to want sexual experiences—from French kissing to petting—as they grow through these years. Parents have to convey a message that says such desires are natural and fine, but having an impulse is not reason enough to satisfy it.

Explain the sexual progression of intimacy. Remember "first base," "second base"? Our children need an understanding that erotic expression escalates from kissing all the way to intercourse. Providing an erotic map empowers them to be able to take one step, then another, with the clarity of the possibilities ahead. In this way they will be able to stop at one "erotic destination" any time, rather than assume that kissing or petting inevitably leads to intercourse.

Planning is a skill to be practiced. You will not be there in the dark with the two young lovers, but you can train your middler to anticipate sexual dilemmas. The time to decide whether to say yes or no to a kiss or more is before the date, not when lips are glued together and bodies entangled. If the romance is heating up, instruct your middler to avoid isolated places where erotic temptation goes unchecked. Let her know using drugs or alcohol will complicate everyone's ability to say no or take no for an answer.

Practice arguments together for making the case against hot and heavy behaviors. Middlers crave peer approval. So help your daughter find a way to assert herself without alienating her boyfriend. These statements fit that requirement:

"I'm not ready."

"I know it feels right for you, and I do care about you, but it doesn't feel right for me."

"I'm not making any decision that I don't feel comfortable about."

Help your daughter (and your son) construct statements that are honest, assertive, direct, and sensitive.

Let a child know that decision-making is an ongoing process. Sexual activity is a sequence of decisions. Your child can say yes (or no) anywhere along the way from kissing, to hugging, French kissing, petting, oral sex, and intercourse. A yes in one situation does not mean she can't change her mind and say no next time. Each sexual situation is a new opportunity for decision-making. All decisions are personal and should be respected.

7. *Boys don't need as much sexual coaching as girls.* Boys are hungry for, and in dire need of, sexual guidance, according to the sex education gurus. Men, either fathers, stepfathers, uncles, or guardians, are indispensible teachers. Here are a few questions best answered by men.

• *"Is provocative clothing on a girl an open invitation?"* Girls sometimes dress to show off their bodies—tight sweaters, miniskirts, bustiers. What does that mean? That they want sex? No. Sexy clothes just mean a girl is getting accustomed to her womanly charms, getting a bit adventurous about showing herself off. It doesn't follow that she is advertising for a lover.

• *"If she doesn't stop me, can I go all the way with her?"* Consent is a topic in desperate need of father-son exploration. Boys must be taught that they need to hear an absolute, affirmative, out loud yes from a girl before they proceed sexually. The Mike Tyson tale is a helpful lesson. Yes, Desiree went up to the hotel room alone with him, maybe flirting shamelessly all the way. Perhaps she was a tease and a gold digger. But being a flirt, a tease, or a gold digger is not against the law. Getting into a compromising position is foolish, but not illegal, either. Overriding a girl's objections to sexual advances is. Sexual assault is a crime. Consent should never be assumed. Silence does not mean yes. It could mean she is scared. No should never be ignored.

• *"How should I handle a younger girl?"* Middler girls often find older boys attractive. Middler boys delight in younger girls because their exact peers rarely give them a tumble. Younger innocent girl plus older more experienced boy, sexually speaking, can add up to trouble, namely the girl getting taken advantage of. Middler boys need to be advised that persuading, pressuring, or manipulating a sexually inexperienced girl is akin to child abuse. A man doesn't do that.

Just as girls need to be warned about being seduced by older adolescents, boys need to have it spelled out that such behavior is unethical. Studies show that many teenage pregnancies involve this older boy/younger girl combination. In a national survey of fifteen- to seventeen-year-old teenage moms, at least half of the babies were fathered by males twenty years of age or older.

The fact is adolescent boys are just as pressured to have sex as their female counterparts. In a culture that glorifies sex with music video Valentinos, beefcake soap opera hunks, and *Cosmopolitan* male buff centerfolds, boys are not immune from the media mandate to "do it!" They need equal instruction. And because they are often (not always) the aggressors in sexual matters, they need customized lessons. How to act like a man and behave like a gentleman simultaneously is an amalgam for fathers and other male mentors to demonstrate and teach middlers. Fathers and mothers need to focus on these truths and forget myths.

Sexual Orientation

The most egregious insult one middler can hurl at another is the taunt: "You're gay!" Boys as well as girls cast this devastating aspersion. When he's angry at his friend or when she's trying to get even, out it comes.

One reason that insults contain homosexual references is because these middler years house the emergence of sexual orientation. Young adolescent boys feel that magnetic pull toward female supermodel pinups and, closer to reality, the girls in their class. Young adolescent girls develop crushes on professional hockey players and real live boys. Because middlers are mesmerized by sexual attraction, they get stuck on the orientation question. In this way they are much like that toddler who, having succeeded in climbing for the first time, is now obsessed with the staircase.

Take this development fixation and combine it with our cultural reaction to homosexuals. We are a society with a bad case of homophobia—a fear of homosexuality. Our homophobia can be mere discomfort about gay men or lesbian women, or full-blown disdain, even hatred, with biblical justification. Middlers mirror our homophobia.

It is in our best interests to come to terms with our homophobia. That bias can hurt our middlers as they struggle with sexual orientation. Take same-sex crushes. When we were young, same-sex crushes were just a blip on the growth meter. No one gave them much thought. But in this new world of bisexual rock stars and gay divas from k.d.lang to Elton John, a child with a passing attraction toward someone of the same sex can begin to have doubts. "Am I gay?"

A parent has to explain the difference between same-sex crushes and being homosexual. It is absolutely normal for young boys and girls to feel some sexual stirrings when they look at an attractive pinup of the same sex. Or watch a sexy rock star gyrating onscreen. Boys may even get an erection. This does not mean the child is destined to become homosexual. There is a world of difference between admiring someone of the same gender and being gay.

Homosexuality must be dispassionately defined for our middlers as a consistent preference, attraction to, and *desire to have sexual experiences* with a member of the same sex. Without candid explanations a confused young adolescent will not understand what is happening and may wallow in a state of terror and depression. Frank talk will educate a befuddled middler, not to mention restore peace of mind.

A nonjudgmental attitude toward gay men and lesbian women is controversial and a challenge for parents. Sex education experts insist there is good reason to aspire to this way of thinking. Your middler may grow up to be in this minority.

"Coming out of the closet," admitting one is a homosexual, usually occurs during later adolescence. Retrospective studies that asked homosexuals about their identity concluded that many gays just felt *confused* about sexual identity as young adolescents. Not until reaching age seventeen, on average, did gay males begin to believe they were homosexual, although many acted on these feelings at age fifteen. For lesbians, eighteen, on average, was the age of realization, and they didn't become sexually active until the age of twenty.

No parent expects to have a gay son or daughter. But the fact is that 10 percent of the population will grow up to be homosexual, regardless of a parent's wishes, guidance, or religious beliefs.

"The biggest secret I've kept from my parents is that I'm gay," confessed a thirteen-year-old girl from Hawaii in our survey. This middler worried about "falling in love with a girl" and admitted to having had cybersex. Did she feel she could talk to her parents about sex? She said, "No." How does someone like this learn to feel good about herself, much less learn how to find acceptance and love?

None of us can divine the sexual future of our middlers. It's best not to push for discussion or decisions about orientation at this early age. Meantime, it's wise to teach your child that you are lovable regardless of whom you love. And that good people come in all sexual orientations. Need help? Read *Free Your Mind* by Ellen Bass and Kate Kaufman.

Good, nonbiased judgment, intimacy skills, and romantic radar are the groundwork young adolescents need to navigate the terrain of lust and love. Some of our suggestions are groundbreaking. Others difficult. It is not easy to face head-on your middler's sexual awakening, initiation, and the risk that lurks beneath every kiss.

Our middlers need our best, most progressive advice if they are to keep their feet on the ground while their hearts and heads soar into the clouds. Our wisdom, tolerance, experience, courage, and love must be distilled into lessons they can live and love by. The Tunnel of Love is ready, waiting for your child to hop in and fasten a seat belt. Strapped in, trapped in its heady momentum, your son may lose presence of mind momentarily and your daughter may give in to urges of abandon. With your guidance, though, a thrill here or a brush with danger there won't derail young lives. A seventh-grade Utah girl gets the last word on middlers and sexuality: "Sex is for marriage and teenage life is for fun, so don't lose your carefree life over sex."

Strategies: Are Your Sexual Attitudes Inhibiting Your Child?

"I can't talk to my parents about sex because they are from a different time," remarked a fifteen-year-old girl. How you feel about your child's sexuality helps or inhibits his or her sexual development. Our survey found 59 percent of parents felt hopeful about their middler finding love and happiness, and sex (after marriage). The rest felt dread, fear, anger, or sadness. Don't let negative emotions impact negatively on your middler. Here's how:

It's all right to DREAD sex instruction talks. Give yourself permission to be uncomfortable (everyone is) but demonstrate a willingness to communicate. "The best exchanges happen when parents conversationally open the door," says Suzanne Witzenberg, a Planned Parenthood sex educator. Otherwise you silence your child's questions.

Let your FEAR of STDs, HIV, and AIDS galvanize you. Let it propel you away from avoiding sexual subjects and toward talking because unsafe sex is romantic Russian roulette. Tell your child all the positive arguments for abstinence you have learned in this chapter.

Don't just HOPE, hope your child won't have sex. Take an active stance. Use sitcoms and music to start discussions when sexually explicit examples come up. Talk about consequences.

Vent your ANGER at society for X-rated or biased situations by becoming an activist in your community. Work to keep unsavory magazines out of plain sight in stores or to close porn shops. When you hear people make negative slurs about lesbians or gay men, speak up.

Put SADNESS into perspective. One mother cried because today's generation will not know what unprotected sex is. Were the 1950s with backstreet abortions and shotgun weddings really so much better? The pendulum of sexual freedom swings and there are always losses and gains.

Eleven

Cotton Candy Time

Handling the Sticky Questions About
Your Own Past

*"I don't want my girls to have my experience.
I did some things that I'm not proud of now.
I am afraid, though, because I don't want them
to think less of me."*

(Stepmother of two from Texas)

When our children were small, we were their universe, the sun, the moon, the stars. We could do no wrong. They cried when we went away and chortled with delight when they glimpsed our faces anew. It was sublime to experience unconditional love. Whatever our faults, our children could not see them. Any past mistakes could lie buried.

Until now.

"Mom, did you ever smoke marijuana?"

"Did you sleep with anyone before you were married?"

"Dad, have you ever tried cocaine?"

"Did you ever pass out from drinking too much?"

"Was Dad still married when you started dating him?"

"Were you ever arrested?"

Such queries make us long for the days when our children asked questions like, "Why is the sky blue?" and "Where do babies come from?" (Although, for parents whose offspring were conceived in petri dishes or borne by surrogate mothers, that latter question is loaded, too.) The more inquisitive middler will probably not rest until he has exposed any cover-ups.

Time for truth or dare. Do we tell the truth or dare to lie? Do we risk being labeled as hypocrites if we establish rules we never obeyed ourselves? If we are honest with our children, will they use the information against us? "I made a big mistake when I was young and I'm afraid if my children find out, it will give them the freedom to do it, too," said the mother of two from California.

When our children ask us the tough questions, we have a hard time answering. It's not easy admitting that we made blunders. But beyond that, looking back forces us to examine who we are today. Our parenting styles have evolved over time, affected by our own experiences as children, adolescents, and adults. How many of us, raised by overly strict parents, for example, vowed that we would do things differently? "It's funny," mused one woman. "I tried to 'fix' all the things I thought my mother did wrong, and my daughter's a lot worse than I ever dreamed of being." Confronting such truths is a painful experience. We wanted to improve on the performance our parents turned in. Now, many of us fear our efforts will fall short.

This self-examination also forces us to look at our relationship with our spouse or parenting partner. Many childless marriages are able to survive even though the husband and wife have different ways of doing things. If she enjoys camping but his idea of roughing it is the Holiday Inn, they can take separate vacations. Does his habit of leaving the cap off the toothpaste drive her nuts? His and her bathrooms can save the union. When the first child arrives, however, negotiating compromises becomes more complicated. Many a marriage has gone on the rocks when parents don't see eye to eye. Is it possible for a couple (whether married or divorced) to reconcile their differences so that the children can be guided in a consistent manner?

In this chapter we will focus the magnifying glass on ourselves, how we became the parents we are. Only when we are comfortable with our own past will we be able to deal with the present so that we can guide our children into the future.

The years from ten to fifteen are critical ones as children formulate value systems. In doing so, they are apt to scrutinize the adults around them, particularly their parents, to see how these adults measure up on the value meter. The Spanish Inquisition has nothing on our middlers. Over the next few years, their questions will be rigorous. How we answer could affect the course of their history. So the wise parent will be prepared.

Been There, Done That

Generations have always been united by their life experiences. The Depression and World War II were cataclysmic events that left an indelible stamp on those who came of age during those intervals. Children were taught to appreciate the value of a dollar. As adults, these individuals would place a high priority on education, steady employment, and a stable family. They fully expected that their children would follow in their footsteps—go to college, get a good job, marry, buy a house, and start a family. Imagine their confusion when these solid citizens spawned a generation of rebels.

These rebels were the baby boomers, that bulge in the python generation whose sheer size—the population of teens swelled to thirty million in 1970—set the stage for monumental change. Adolescents no longer took for granted that grown-ups knew best. All around them were examples of the fallibility of adult authority. Young people witnessed the assassinations of John F. Kennedy, Martin Luther King, and Robert Kennedy. The Tet Offensive, where the Vietcong nearly succeeded in taking over the American Embassy in Saigon, was proof that the Vietnam War would drag on, despite statements to the contrary made by the White House.

The war became a symbol of youthful rebellion. Soon, that defiance spilled over into other aspects of youthful life. The sexual revolution, sparked by the birth control pill, found many eager followers. So what if parents preached abstinence? These young people preached love and what better way to express those feelings than through the sexual act?

Sexual pleasure was only one pursuit of this narcissistic, youthful society. Pleasures of all sorts were sought after and the vehicle for achieving these physical highs often involved drugs. Marijuana and LSD were the substances of choice, prized for their abilities to expand the mind and increase sensual enjoyment. According to the Partnership For a Drug Free America, 60 percent of baby boomer parents have tried marijuana, 15 percent have tried cocaine, and 10 percent have tried LSD.

The 1960s generation didn't invent adolescent rebellion, but they raised it to new heights. Embracing the youth culture wasn't possible without rejecting adult values. Most times that refusal was not a polite, "No, thank you." Young people talked back and acted out. "I taught in the Vietnam era," said a sixth-grade teacher from New Jersey. "The children back then at this age were much more disrespectful to society in general."

Sooner or later, however, this magical mystery tour was destined to end. Even the baby boomers could not reverse the aging process. And growing older, for many, meant growing up. Peter Pan was forced to leave Neverland and take his place in the real world.

The generation that thought it would change the world, however, had left its mark. Adolescence would never be the same. Succeeding generations, those who grew up during the 1970s and beyond, would continue to question adult authority. Sexual freedom, experimentation with drugs, protest rallies, and demonstrations became as much a part of growing up as getting a driver's license. Each new group of adolescents added something to the mix. And while succeeding generations haven't had to deal with a full-scale depression or war, societal changes have indeed had an impact.

Since the 1970s, the skyrocketing divorce rate has meant that many children have been raised in single-parent households. Coupled with the increased number of working women, the family structure experienced radical change. Latchkey children, those returning to an empty home after school, stood in stark contrast to children during the 1950s whose mothers greeted them at the door with milk and cookies. Working mothers, particularly those who were raised by clones of June Cleaver, struggled with their decisions. Those who grew up during the 1970s and 1980s have been called Generation X. While these individuals will continue to evaluate the job their parents did (not until Generation Xers become parents of adolescents themselves will they truly be able to appreciate what their parents were up against), the first reviews are coming in. One Generation Xer blasted parents on a bulletin board in cyberspace: "You tried to raise us 'openly.' What in the hell does that mean? Most of my friends had parents absent from their households due to divorce, or they were trying to cope with their problems in twelve-step programs. Our generation has been raised on a steady diet of 'Brady Bunch' and cereal commercials with an absence of parents from the scene, either due to divorce, disinterest, or career climbing. So as for parenting, I'd have to say there's been a lack of it."

Already, the following generations of parents are reacting to such criticism. There is a return to the discipline and structure practiced during the 1950s. "A lot of people are changing their minds about discipline based on all the disorderly kids they see out there," said Kevin Ryan, director of the Center for the Advancement of Ethics and Character at Boston University, in an article in the *New York Times*. But, as many parents of middlers are discovering, it isn't so easy to turn back the clock. The culture has changed and is changing our children. They are not going to obey us automatically, not without a fight. And often what we are forced to face is the legacy of our own past which, for better or worse, has affected our individual parenting styles. If you are a permissive parent, now is the time to scrutinize your approach and make some changes. We must set rigorous standards for our children, even if those rules were ones that we ourselves disregarded when we were young.

Perhaps the reason so many parents are frightened is because they have lived through the experiences they now worry could harm their children. One mother noted: "I thought I knew much more about life than my mom. 'Mom, this is the sixties, you just don't understand how it is now!' So every time I hear, 'Mom, this is the nineties . . .' I duck!"

We do understand and that's the problem. In many cases we understand all too well. We have been there. We've lived through alcoholism, drug addiction, the sexual revolution, violent demonstrations, and count ourselves among the survivors. These experiences have left us wiser. (How many parents back in the 1960s had even heard of marijuana, much less smoked it?) Yet this legacy also creates a burden. How do we use our knowledge in a positive way to help our children? Do we level with them and confess our past sins? Or should we hope we can use what we know surreptitiously, finding ways to intervene quietly?

The number of teens has declined since reaching a peak of almost thirty-four million in 1976. But experts say that during the first decade of the twenty-first century, the levels may once again approach those of the mid-1970s as the children of the baby boomers reach adolescence. How will this new groundswell of youth affect society? Truly, what goes around comes around. We are on the outside looking in, older, wiser, and ready to help our children.

The Times, They Are a Changin'

For most of us, adolescence was the first time in our lives where we had meaningful experiences that we can remember, oftentimes in vivid detail. We can recall the thrill of our first teenage kiss. We know the girl's name and what she was wearing, maybe even the scent of her perfume. We can still feel the humiliation of flubbing the lines during the class play in front of the entire school and our parents. We may recall the excitement of catching that winning pass in the end zone.

What we may not realize is that we are selectively editing our memories. The good times were probably never as good as we remember them to be, nor were the bad times as dismal as we now feel they were. "Whatever your current assessment and memories of your adolescence, it is helpful to recognize that they are probably only partially true," according to Dr. Robert C. and Nancy J. Kolodny, Dr. Thomas Bratter, and Cheryl Deep, authors of *How to Survive Your Adolescent's Adolescence*. "This selective memory can create problems for parents who try to remember how they felt as teenagers in a particular situation, or try to recall how they solved a problem in their lives, or even how they attained a particular success."

Thus, when we tell our children, "I know just how you feel," we may only be telling a half-truth. At one point in our lives, we may have known how they felt. But with the passage of time, we have lost that ability to connect with our past feelings and, therefore, have only a limited chance of truly empathizing with them. That doesn't mean we shouldn't try to feel for them. We should. But we should focus on their situations without dwelling on our own experiences.

While many of us can relate to the challenges and problems our children face, we cannot truly comprehend what they are up against. Truly, the world is a different place for our children than it was for us. Perhaps the most striking change is that the age of experimentation has dropped. We as parents are worried about our middlers being exposed to things we experienced as college students. The dangers are obvious. While many of these children are mature physically, they are still young psychologically. They are unprepared to deal with the ramifications that may result from having sexual relations or using drugs.

Reviewing all the ways that times have changed for children, is it any wonder that they feel stressed and depressed? Middlers under such pressure are prime candidates for substance abuse. "Societal attitudes of the sixties and seventies were much different from the attitudes of today," agreed one mother. "Kids feel a hopelessness today that I certainly didn't feel then and my experimentation was based on fun, not on depression and lost hope for a future."

Understanding the differences is important if we are to help our children.

Honesty—Always the Best Policy?

In our questionnaire, we asked parents whether they would tell their children about past indiscretions. An overwhelming majority (98 percent) said yes. The reason most often given was a desire to be honest. "We are open and honest with our children," said a mother from Missouri. "That's what we expect from them." Yet, is total truthfulness always the best policy?

In order to answer that question, we have to examine why we feel it is necessary for us to be honest with our children all the time. Upon close scrutiny, some of these reasons don't hold up.

> *"I demand honesty from my children. It's only fair that I be totally honest with them."*
>
> (Father of two from Nevada)

Is honesty the key here? Perhaps what we are really talking about is disclosure of information. It is possible for two people to have an honest relationship without there being full disclosure. Even in a marriage (an arrangement where the two parties are on a more equal footing than in the parent-child relationship) a husband and wife may choose not to tell each other everything. The union, however, may still be strong and honest.

So it should be with your child. As your child matures, you should not expect her to share her most intimate thoughts with you. It follows, then, that there are some intimate details about your own life that you should be entitled to keep private.

"I would tell the truth because I hate lying."

(Mother of one from New Hampshire)

No one says you have to lie to your child. Refusing to discuss every detail about your past is not lying. Declining to answer a direct "yes" or "no" when your son asks, "Did you ever smoke marijuana?" is not lying.

Aren't there other times when you decline to answer one of your children's direct questions? Do you tell your child how much money you make, for example? Or whether you dye your hair? Or whether you had two pieces of chocolate cake, not one? One mother said, "When I asked one of my friends what she'll do when her kids ask about her past, she laughed and said, 'I'll lie.' I don't know if I'll necessarily lie, but I'll sure as hell give them the edited version."

Let's propose that you decline to answer one of your daughter's questions. Will she naturally assume the worst? Not necessarily. When you decline to answer directly, you leave room for doubt. As long as you haven't confirmed her suspicions, she can still believe that you didn't do whatever it was she was asking you about.

Of course, this strategy isn't one you have to follow forever. Keep in mind that we are talking about your child from ages ten to fifteen, the years when you hope to hold off experimentation. "I will not tell my child the truth about certain things until I feel they are ready to handle it," said a father from Missouri. At some point in the future, perhaps when your child is in high school or college, you may feel more comfortable being honest. But there's such a thing as giving out too much information too soon.

Do you recall the story about the young child who asked, "Dad, where did I come from?" The father quickly broke out into a cold sweat and went through a detailed explanation of conception and birth. "Do you understand?" he hesitantly asked the child upon finishing his lecture. The confused child gave a tentative nod and said, "I think so. But, Dad, where did I come from? Bobby said he comes from New Jersey. Where did I come from?"

Listen to your child when you enter into a discussion about smoking, drugs, or sex. Suppose your daughter asks you: "Did you smoke when you were my age?" Whether you answer yes or no, the discussion will focus on you rather than on your daughter. A better response is to pose your own question:

"Why do you ask? Do you know of others your age who are smoking?"

"Yeah, Jennifer."

"Jennifer's one of your best friends. How do you feel about her smoking?"

In this case, your daughter's question is a cue that something is bothering her. She may be looking for strategies to say no while saving face with her peer group. You can role-play with her and give her the methods she needs to deal with her friends. What you did in the past, is less important to your daughter than how she is going to deal with her immediate problem. If you had gone off on a discussion of how you started smoking, why you quit, and ended up lecturing her about the health hazards in cigarette smoke, you would have lost a golden opportunity to really help your child.

If you suspect that your child is merely looking to trap you in order to receive tacit approval for his behavior, then the last thing you want to do is provide him with such ammunition. Denying to answer his queries may frustrate him, but it will also improve your chances of discouraging behavior of which you disapprove.

"I have had conversations with my children about things that I did in high school. I think it's important that they see you as 'human' and not this figure that did nothing wrong."

(Mother of two, New Jersey)

Our children know we are human. Without digging up our past, we make enough mistakes in our present day-to-day life to point up that fact. We burn the hamburgers on the barbecue grill. We smash up the car. We lose our tempers when someone takes our parking space at the mall. We scream at the dog when he messes in the house. We are grumpy in the morning and crabby in the evening. We sometimes look like something even the cat wouldn't want to drag in. We are going gray, bald, getting out of shape, and nearsighted. What other evidence do they need?

Most children want to believe that their parents are better than the parents next door. Your daughter may no longer believe in Santa Claus, but she still wants to hold onto her belief that her mom and dad can do things no other parents can do. At this stage of development, introducing the idea that Mom and Dad made mistakes (perhaps serious mistakes) may shake your daughter's sense of self and stability.

Be careful that you don't confess your sins for the wrong reasons. Many people have bought into the idea that confessing is good for the soul. We turn on TV and watch talk shows where people admit to every crime under the sun. Tell all and you'll feel better. It's possible you do have a need to talk with someone about your past. But that someone should probably be a trained therapist, doctor, spouse, or good friend. Not your child. While middlers often look and act like adults, they are still children. We need to shelter them, not inundate them with our problems.

"I would be honest with my child in the hope that she would learn from my mistakes."
(Mother of two from Maine)

In an ideal world, we would all learn from one another's mistakes. No one would drive after drinking. No one would smoke. No one would try drugs. The fact is that this approach often fails. Human nature still dictates, "It won't happen to me." And middlers, who view themselves as invincible, feel this sentiment more deeply than other age groups.

Then again, we have to deal with the fact that the person talking about the experience is Mom or Dad. Children this age have a hard time envisioning their parents being young, let alone engaging in the type of miscreant behavior that they are considering. Without that ability to empathize, they are unlikely to be dissuaded.

Of course, if a parent had a particular experience that was very dramatic, and she can tell about that event in such a way as to discourage imitation, then it might be worthwhile to share. "I've told my kids that at the age of sixteen, I was 'invited' to inhale a vegetable oil spray (inhalant) and I did it," said the mother of four from Vermont. "It was a terrifying experience for me, a terrible reaction. I related this to my kids as well as my decision never to try drugs."

This story will have more impact on a child than having a parent merely intone, "Don't sniff inhalants."

One caution: Be careful that you don't allow your own problems or opinions to interfere with your ability to parent. If you are battling substance abuse, for example, you will have difficulty dissuading your child from using. If you don't enjoy sex, you may allow your negative feelings to surface when discussing it with your middler. The best advice is to seek help yourself before you attempt to help your child.

"I know my kids talk to their friends and I sure don't want their friends (and their friends' parents) to know what I did as a youth. This is a very conservative community."

(Concerned mother)

What you confess to your children may not stop with them. Remember the old parlor game, Gossip? With every telling the tale gets taller:

"Mom, did you ever try LSD?"

"Only once, before a Rolling Stones concert."

Young people belong to a family of peers and it's perfectly possible that they will confide in their friends:

"My mom used to take LSD before she went to Rolling Stones concerts."

Where will the telling stop?

"Did you know that Ryan's mother used to take LSD before going to rock concerts?"

You may find that your secrets will soon be known—and exaggerated—by everyone in town.

"Ryan's mother and LSD were practically roommates all through college."

If you live in a progressive community where other parents will be understanding, you probably will not be risking much. However, if your hometown is conservative, you may find that you have isolated yourself and your children.

"No wonder Ryan has such problems in school. His mother's past drug use has probably affected him."

Be judicious in what you tell your children. Always assume that whatever you say will somehow end up in the public domain. Be particularly careful if your story involves someone else whose reputation could be harmed by your disclosure. (Telling your children that you once smoked pot with the town's mayor, for example, won't help his standing or yours.)

There are certain instances where you may owe your child the truth. One woman told this story: "I saw a time bomb go off when I was in high school and a fellow student discovered that his mother had given birth to him before she was married. It had been a very tragic situation. When he found out the details, he went out of control for over a year. He said the hardest thing for him to deal with was the knowledge that the man he had thought was his father had lied to him. He felt it was hard to trust either parent who left him in ignorance when the majority of the town was aware of the facts."

Obviously, these parents had not handled the situation well. They should have told their son the truth early on. This mother who observed the situation said it convinced her that she would never lie to her children, although she does not give out information unless asked a specific question.

Truth and Consequences

Of course there may be times when you are not given a choice about whether to be honest or withhold information. Your child may already know the truth. "Little pitchers have big ears." Over the years you may have talked with friends, reliving past escapades. You may have casually mentioned your drug use in college. Did you admit that you were once arrested after a demonstration? Or that you once drove after drinking and got into an accident? When your child was younger, these issues did not have the relevance they have now. It's too late to go back and erase the tape. So now that the truth is out, how do you deal with it? How do you characterize these past misdemeanors in a way that they will instruct and discourage your child from making similar mistakes? Here are some guidelines.

Find out exactly what your child knows. You may recall your son overhearing the entire story of your drug use when he was younger. But years later he may have forgotten. Don't assume he knows more than he does.

Find out the source of her information. If your daughter tells you, "Aunt Jenny told me all about how the two of you used to smoke dope in college," you can point out that your memories are different. It's possible that Aunt Jenny has a tendency to exaggerate, and you can present your own version of events to place your experience in better perspective.

Just the facts. Nothing will be gained by going into a long explanation of why you committed past indiscretions. Middlers are often looking for any opening they can find to justify their own behavior. Telling your daughter that you smoked marijuana because your boyfriend broke up with you may just give her the excuse she needs to do drugs herself when she suffers such a trauma. A better approach is to state the basic truth without embellishment. "I did try drugs when I was in college. It wasn't a positive experience."

Don't lecture. Your middler will probably not respond to the "older but wiser" approach. These young people want to experience things for themselves. Parents who believe that they can discourage their children through the benefit of their own awareness will be disappointed. You will have more success using contemporary figures (rock stars who have died from drug overdoses, for example) to bolster your points.

Use outside sources. Sometimes it's easier for your child to obtain information from someone besides a parent. A grandparent, favorite aunt, or good friend, for example, can talk to your child honestly without sounding judgmental. Make sure, however, if you ask someone to speak with your child that you trust this person to say the right things.

Provide written material. You don't need to do all the talking. When you come upon a good article that uses all the right words to express your feelings, clip it and save it. Look for TV programs or movies with themes that hit close to home. At some future point, you may want to watch one of these with your middler. Follow up with your own comments.

Capture the time and place. Cable TV has brought with it a wealth of historical programs. Many of these capture the intensity and emotions of past decades. While you don't want to present excuses for your past indiscretions, your middler is old enough to understand how current events can affect youthful sensibilities. Watching a documentary on the Vietnam War, for example, may help your son understand the feelings of anger that propelled many youth into the streets to protest. There are also many good books written for this age group that provide food for thought.

Focus on the differences. Without sounding preachy, try to sketch for your child why circumstances are different for her. Science has advanced and we now know much more about the dangers of smoking and drugs, for example. If you had had that information when you were her age, your decisions would have been different.

When the Past Involves Your Child

There are times when it isn't so easy to dodge your child's questions. Those times are when your past directly affects your child. In these instances, you owe your child an explanation, the sooner the better. If these issues haven't been discussed since early childhood, you may need to get some professional advice on opening up the issue now and being prepared and supportive of your child's reaction.

What are some of these situations you might have to deal with?

Your child's birth. The middler years are ones when a child begins to think about how he came to be who he is. When this self-examination begins, he is apt to scrutinize his biological parents. That's easy enough if the biological parents are the ones the child lives with. The situation becomes more complex if that's not the case. Adoption, artificial insemination, surrogate parenting all are topics that need to be discussed.

Alcoholism. There is ample scientific data proving that alcoholism runs in families. If that family happens to be yours, you need to share that information with your child. Young people become alcoholics faster than adults and children of alcoholics are at even greater risk.

Absent parent. Many children are being raised by single parents or by stepparents. In these instances, there may be a biological parent who has never been in the picture. During the middler years, a child is guaranteed to ask questions about this missing parent seeking to fill in information about himself. If you are the custodial parent, don't be surprised when your child asks to spend more time with the other parent or even move in.

Every family situation is unique. You may have other issues to deal with. Here are some suggestions for handling the dissemination of information:

Tiny bites. The truth will be easier to digest if it is given out in small amounts over a long period of time. Sitting your child down when he is fourteen suddenly to inform him that he was adopted as a baby will surely create a life crisis for him. Those talks should have started years ago. However, if you have withheld information from him until the middler years, don't waste another moment. Start parceling out the details now.

Pick the time. Seize the initiative. Go on the assumption that whatever the subject involved, your middler will ask about it sooner rather than later. While you may not be able to prevent injury to her feelings, you may at least soften the blow by being the one to broach the subject first.

Collect information. Since you are already playing catch-up, you want to avoid a situation where you are unable to answer your son's questions. Let's say you are dealing with alcoholism. Have pamphlets and written material from organizations such as the Department of Health and Human Services that deal with the subject in a straightforward manner. Many organizations have literature specifically aimed at young people. These publications can be a valuable ally in helping you explain the situation to your son. Also, the information will be comforting because he will know he is not alone. Other children must confront similar situations. Often these organizations have support groups for children. At the appropriate time, your son may be receptive to joining such a group.

Be prepared to help. Your daughter may need your help to satisfy whatever emotional needs come out of the situation. If she was adopted, for example, she may express a desire to search for her birthparents or, at the least, to obtain more information about them.

Offering to do whatever you can to assist her will send the powerful message that you are indeed on her side.

Be prepared for anger. Whatever your disclosure might be, your child will probably be angry and that anger will be directed at the closest target—you. It's not your fault that alcoholism is a family disease (any more than it would be if diabetes was). But your son will no doubt feel that you, as the parent, are somehow to blame. The best strategy is to empathize with his feelings. Tell him you understand his anger. You are angry, too, that his father abandoned him and you after his birth. But both of you must now move beyond that anger and deal with the issues involved.

Point out the positives. Even if you must search for them, there are always positives. It's upsetting that you and your son must deal with alcoholism, for example. But the fact that we know so much more today about the disease and the support systems are so much stronger means that you and your son will have a better chance of beating it.

Keep the focus on your child. Whatever trauma has struck your family has injured both you and your child. However, you are the adult and, hopefully, you have come to terms with whatever crisis—infertility, divorce, alcoholism—precipitated the present situation. Now you need to help your child. Try to remain calm, confident, and in control. Remember you are a role model. Your daughter will be thinking, "Dad coped with this crisis. I can, too."

The Past Is Prologue

"Today is the first day of the rest of your life," was a popular wall slogan from the 1970s. No one knows its origin and in many ways that makes it all the more appealing. It could have been written by anyone. It expresses the hope that we have all felt at one time in our lives, the hope that things can change for the better. Certainly it is an optimism we would wish for our children as they live through their middle school years. It's the sentiment that the past truly can serve as a beginning, a starting point. No matter what went before, we can make improvements.

So it goes with your own past. You made mistakes. You made wrong turns, followed the unqualified leaders or, perhaps, failed to strike off on your own when the situation warranted. But that was then. This is now. It's time to come to terms with those miscalculations and move on.

Guilt has no place in parenting. One survey found that many parents who had used marijuana themselves would feel guilty lecturing their children about the drug. Why? If we've learned nothing else in our lives, we should have learned that it's possible to grow as the result of our experiences. It's your past, but it's your child's future. Your son or daughter needs your guidance, a sure and steady hand, unimpeded by obstacles from your past. So lead on, not forgetting your past but using what you know to make you a wiser and more self-assured parent.

Strategies: Earning Your Child's Respect

"I was always embarrassed by my mother and swore I would try to be the 'cool' mom in the neighborhood. This is where I've made my biggest mistake. My daughter now speaks to me like one of her friends, teasing me and 'busting' on me like her girlfriend."

(Mother of an eleven-year-old)

Many parents mistakenly believe that the best way to get close to their adolescents is by acting young. Sharing secrets about the past may forge a bond, but at what cost? You will lose your child's respect. Without that respect, you will have no control.

How can you go about reestablishing your authority? It may take time, but it can be done. Start by examining your own behavior. What have you done to create this image of being your child's friend? Is it the way you dress? Your language? Your choice of music or TV shows? No one says you have to give up what you truly like, but if you have been making choices based on what appeals to your child rather than to yourself, some changes are in order.

You aren't going to change your child's behavior overnight. Decide which issues should be your top priority. Perhaps, like the mother quoted above, it's the way your daughter addresses you. The next time she talks to you in a manner you find demeaning, state your objection and correct her behavior. Be consistent. Don't let even one remark slide by. Soon she will get the point.

Once you have made progress on one front, choose another battleground. Does she disregard your rules, viewing them as optional? For example, if you tell her to be home at ten p.m., and she comes in at eleven p.m., is her response, "I didn't think you were serious"? Make sure she knows you are serious. When one of your rules is broken, punishment should follow. Follow our discipline guidelines (CARES) outlined in Chapter Four.

Epilogue

Today is the first day of your new parenting sensibility. You are now more knowledgeable about the physical, intellectual, and psychological development of your middler. You are more compassionate because you have walked in your middler's shoes and experienced the pull of peers, the trauma of cliques, the lure of tobacco, alcohol, drugs, and sex, and understood the promises and perils presented by the electronic media. You are more informed about what your middle school is trying to achieve and how you, as a parent, can use this resource to benefit your child.

Ultimately, you, however, are the most critical resource to the flourishing of your middler. Let reading our book be the first step in your search to learn all you can about your child's hopes, dreams, secret fears, and unspoken insecurities. We have put together a recommended reading and resource list, tapping a wide range of experts, products, and organizations, to help you continue to accumulate insights, ideas, and support.

At every opportunity, start a conversation with other parents of young adolescents. Share with them what you have learned. Ask them what experiences they have had. Debate issues such as sex education and violence on TV. Be open so that you can ponder new opinions and ideas.

Don't leave us behind. We, the authors, are eager to hear your reactions to our book and your day-to-day thoughts and feelings on living with your middler. We especially want to listen to your experiences and tactics in heading off (or working through) the terrifying triad of temptations—drugs, alcohol, and sex—that shadow the life of each and every child during the middle years. Send your words of wisdom to us:

> c/o Broadway Books
> 1540 Broadway
> New York, NY 10036

Guiding your young adolescent toward adulthood is going to be the adventure of a lifetime. Don't miss any of it. Take in all the sights. Savor watching your daughter score on the soccer field, your son staying glued to his science project until it works. Laugh as well at the outlandish fashion faux pas.

Don't pass on the smells—the cologne your son seems to have bathed in to impress a secret crush. This may be difficult at times because some of the scents of youth—the stench of smelly sneakers or the perfume of endless Doritos—are hard to take.

Listen well for the sounds of young adolescence—the laughter and the squeals and the silences that beg for sensitive exploration. Keep earplugs on hand for the loud music (you'll know your offspring is in adolescence when you and your child have mutually exclusive musical tastes) and the louder squabbles among siblings.

Be open to experiment with the tastes, too. Be ready to indulge in eternal pizza fests and anything and everything that friends find trendy. Bubble-gum ice cream, anyone? Don't miss the salty taste of the tears you can kiss away from your daughter's cheek after a heart-break or a clique crisis.

Above all, pay close attention to touch. Giving a hug is risky business where middlers are concerned. They don't want to be caught in that act! Be on the alert for those times when you can slip one in, because your embraces are the sustenance that will get your son or daughter through the tough times.

And finally, there is that sixth sense, the mystical one all parents are trying to cultivate, the intuitive voice that tells you what to say, what to do, as well as what *not to say* and what *not to do* to make your child's growing up happier and healthier. We humbly hope we have found a few words or delivered a couple of suggestions that will help you develop that sixth sense. We trust you are now better equipped to handle your middler, but above all, to enjoy these magical roller-coaster years.

Recommended Reading and Resources

*An asterisk indicates the book is out of print as of this writing. Check your local library.

Introduction—View from the Ferris Wheel

Suggested Reading

The Best of Free Spirit—Five Years of Award-Winning Views on Growing Up
The Free Spirit Editors
1 (800) 735-7323
Free Spirit Publishing, 1995 (Based on a newsletter, contributed to by psychologists, specialists, teachers, and students, this roundup features pieces of interest to both parents and middlers. For example the selections, "Three Things Your Parents Wish They Could Tell You," "Ten Tips for Making and Keeping Friends," "What's Your Learning Style?" are entertaining, fun, and insightful.

Living with a Work in Progress: A Parents' Guide to Surviving Adolescence
Carol Goldberg Freeman
The National Middle School Association
1 (800) 528-NMSA

Saving Our Sons: Raising Black Children in a Turbulent World
Marita Golden
Doubleday, 1995

The Shelter of Each Other: Rebuilding Our Families
Mary Pipher, Ph.D.
Grosset Putnam, 1996

Teen Tips—A Practical Survival Guide for Parents with Kids 11 to 19
Tom McMahon
Pocket Books, 1996

Your Ten- to Fourteen-Year-Old
Louise Bates Ames, Frances L. Ilg, and Sidney M. Baker
Dell, 1989

Suggested Reading for Middlers
Letters to Judy: What Kids Wish They Could Tell You
Judy Blume
Pocket Books, 1987
Parents should read this, too, and use it for starting discussions.

Organizations
Great Transitions Preparing Adolescents for a New Century (October 1995)
Carnegie Council on Adolescent Development
The Carnegie Corporation of New York
437 Madison Avenue
New York, NY 10022
(212) 371-3200
Send $10.00 for a copy.
Excellent source for parents, teachers, and community leaders.

National Middle School Association
2600 Corporate Exchange Drive, Suite 370
Columbus, OH 43231-1672
(614) 848-8211
FAX (614) 848-4301
1 (800) 528-NMSA
Offers free catalogue of pamphlets and books for parents and educators.
Our choice—*H.E.L.P. How to Enjoy Living with a Preadolescent* by Judith
 Baenen

One—Developing Intellect

Suggested Reading
Keeping Kids Reading: How to Raise Avid Readers in the Video Age
Mary Leonhardt
Crown, 1996
Methods for stimulating the intellectual side of your child. One way is to iden-
 tify reading pathways as defined by your child's taste in books.

*Playing Smart: A Parent's Guide to Enriching, Offbeat Learning Activities for Ages 4
 to 14*
Susan K. Perry
Free Spirit Publishing, 1990
(800) 735-READ

A Portrait of Young Adolescents in the 1990s: Implications for Promoting Healthy Growth and Development
Peter C. Scales
Search Institute, 1992
Available through the National Middle School Association
(800) 528-NMSA
For parents, teachers, and all others who work and live with preadolescents, an evaluation of the profound physical, emotional, and cognitive changes these children experience.

Wonderful Ways to Love a Teen—Even When It Seems Impossible
Judy Ford
Conari Press, 1996
Strategies for relating and connecting with your teen. Includes hints like, "Do the best you can," and "Try the playful approach."

Young Adolescent Development and School Practices: Promoting Harmony
John Van Hoose and David B. Strahan
National Middle School Association, 1988
(800) 528-NMSA

Your Child's Growing Mind: A Guide to Learning and Brain Development from Birth to Adolescence
Jane M. Healy, Ph.D.
Doubleday, 1994

Suggested Reading for Middlers
Good Clean Jokes for Kids
Bob Phillips
Harvest House, 1991
Includes over 900 favorite riddles, tongue-twisters, and knock-knock jokes.

The Kid's Guide to Service Projects: Over 500 Service Ideas for Young People Who Want to Make a Difference
Barbara A. Lewis
Free Spirit Publishing, 1995
(612) 338-2068

New Moon—The Magazine for Girls and Their Dreams
New Moon Publishing
2127 Columbus Avenue
P.O. Box 3620
Duluth, MN 55803-3620

(218) 728-5507

A magazine by girls for girls that is free of advertising and aimed at bolstering self-esteem.

Two—Growing Bodies and Distorted Images

Suggested Reading

The Body Betrayed: A Deeper Understanding of Women, Eating Disorders, and Treatment
Kathryn J. Zerbe, M.D.
Gurze Books, 1995

Body Traps: Breaking the Binds That Keep You from Feeling Good About Your Body
Dr. Judith Rodin
William Morrow, 1993

Kid Fitness: A Complete Shape-Up Program from Birth Through High School*
Kenneth H. Cooper, M.D., M.P.H.
Bantam, 1991
Useful for parents with good discussion of the preadolescent years.

The Secrets Our Body Clocks Reveal*
Susan Perry and Jim Dawson
Rawson Associates, 1988

Surviving an Eating Disorder: Strategies for Families and Friends
Michele Siegel
HarperPerennial, 1989

You and Your Adolescent—A Parent's Guide for Ages 10–20
Laurence Steinberg, Ph.D.
HarperCollins, 1991

Suggested Reading for Middlers

Girltalk: All the Stuff Your Sister Never Told You, third edition.
Carol Weston
HarperCollins, 1997

Finding Our Way—The Teen Girls' Survival Guide
Allison Abner and Linda Villarosa
HarperPerennial, 1995
Excellent multicultural resource listings for parents and children.

It's Perfectly Normal—A Book About Our Changing Bodies, Growing Up, Sex and Health
Robie S. Harris
Candlewick, 1996
Well written for middlers and humorously illustrated.

The Period Book: Everything You Don't Want to Ask (But Need to Know)
Karen and Jennifer Gravelle
Walker and Company, 1996
Written with her fifteen-year-old niece, the Gravelles talk to the young girls themselves.

Straight Talk About Eating Disorders
Michael Maloney, M.D. and Rachel Kranz
Facts on File, 1991

A Teen's Guide to Going Vegetarian
Judy Krizmanic
Puffin Books, 1994

Product Information
Girls Inc.
30 East 33rd Street
New York, NY 10016-5394
(212) 689-3700
An advocacy national youth organization that provides a variety of programs for girls, especially for high-risk girls. Also has educational offerings such as *The Girls Re-Cast TV Action Kit,* which was distributed to girls, polling them about self-image and media literacy. Good resource for teachers.

Vegetarian Times
4 High Ridge Park
Stamford, CT 06905
(203) 322-2900
Monthly magazine devoted to vegetarian cooking, nutrition, health, and fitness. Twelve issues for $29.99.

Organizations and Hotlines

American Academy of Orthopedic Surgeons
P.O. Box 1998
Des Plaines, IL 60017
(800) 824-BONE
Offers a free brochure, *Play It Safe*, for parents on sports and safety. Send a self-addressed stamped envelope.

American Anorexia/Bulimia Association (AA/BA)
293 Central Park West
Suite 1R
New York, NY 10024
(212) 501-8351
East coast referrals. For information, send a self-addressed, stamped 9-by-12 inch envelope, with $3.00 for postage and handling.

National Association of Anorexia Nervosa and Associated Disorders (ANAD)
Box 7
Highland Park, IL 60035
Hotline (708) 831-3438
Offers information, counseling, referrals, and support groups.

Women's Sports Foundation
Eisenhower Park
East Meadow, NY 11554
(516) 542-4700 or (800) 227-3988
Provides information on eating disorders, physical fitness, the female athlete, exercise, and drugs.

Three—Emotions and Tensions

Suggested Reading

The Complete Single Mother: Reassuring Answers to Your Most Challenging Concerns
Andrea Engber and Leah Klungness
Adams Publishing, 1995
Engber is founder of National Organization of Single Mothers.

Family Man: Fatherhood, Housework, and Gender Equity
Scott Coltrane
Oxford University Press, 1996
Takes a sociological look at the changing face of fatherhood. Good for single fathers.

The Good Divorce: Keeping Your Family Together When Your Marriage Comes Apart
Dr. Constance Ahrons
HarperCollins, 1995
Effective strategies for divorcing couples.

Growing Up with a Single Parent: What Hurts, What Helps
Sara McLanahan
Harvard University Press, 1996

How to Help Your Child Overcome Your Divorce
Elissa P. Benedek and Catherine F. Brown
American Psychiatric Press, 1996
Resource list includes addresses of support groups.

Learned Optimism
Martin E. P. Seligman, Ph.D.
Pocket Books, 1992

The Optimistic Child: A Proven Program to Safeguard Children Against Depression and Build Lifelong Resilience
Martin E. P. Seligman, Ph.D.
HarperCollins, 1996
For parents, teachers, and counselors.

Positive Self-Talk for Children: Teaching Self-Esteem Through Affirmations—A Guide for Parents, Teachers and Counselors
Bantam, 1993

The Quicksilver Years—The Hopes and Fears of Early Adolescence *
Peter Benson, Dorothy Williams, and Arthur Johnson
Harper and Row, 1987

The Resilient Self: How Survivors of Troubled Families Rise Above Adversity
Steven J. Wolin, M.D. and Sybil Wolin, Ph.D.
Villard Books

Reviving Ophelia: Saving the Selves of Adolescent Girls
Mary Pipher, Ph.D.
Ballantine Books, 1994

Single Fatherhood: The Complete Guide
Chuck Greeg
Sulzberger and Graham, 1995

Taming Monsters, Slaying Dragons *
Joel Feiner, M.D. and Graham Yost
Arbor House, William Morrow, 1988

Understanding Your Teenager's Depression: Issues and Insights for Every Parent
Kathleen McCoy
Berkley, 1994

Suggested Reading for Middlers
After a Suicide: Young People Speak Out *
Susan Kuklin
G. P. Putnam's Sons, 1994

It's Not the End of the World
Judy Blume
Dell, 1982
A book about divorce written for preadolescents.

Perfectionism: What's Bad About Being Too Good
Miriam Adderholdt-Elliot, Ph.D.
Free Spirit Publishing, 1987
1 (800) 735-7323
A how-to book geared to help children recognize unhealthy, perfectionist behavior, and how such behavior differs from ambition.

Stepkids: A Survival Guide for Teenagers in Stepfamilies
Ann Getzoff and Carolyn McClenahan
Walker and Company, 1984

Product Information

Changes: Short Stories Designed for Grades 6 through 9
Harry Vincenzi, Ed.D.
Future Press
P.O. Box 2569
Bala Cynwyd, PA 19004
A curriculum for self-esteem which would be helpful for teachers.

Organizations and Hotlines

American Academy of Child and Adolescent Psychiatry
3615 Wisconsin Avenue, NW
Washington, DC 20016
(202) 966-7300
Will give nationwide referrals.

Big Brothers/Big Sisters of America
230 North 13th Street
Philadelphia, PA 19107
(215) 567-2748
Can be a resource for single parents who have children in need of same sex role
    models. Trains and screens role models beforehand.

Big Brothers/Big Sisters of Canada
5230 South Service Road
Burlington, Ontario L7L 5K2
Provides adult volunteers for children.

Fathers' Rights of America
P.O. Box 7596
Van Nuys, CA 91409
(818) 789-4435
Provides seminars and reference services for fathers' rights issues, which include
    child custody, visitation, child support, and divorce.

National Adolescent Suicide Hotline
1 (800) 621-4000
Twenty-four hour service for youths contemplating suicide and for parents who
    need information or assistance.

National Runaway Switchboard
1 (800) 621-4000
For parents and runaways.

Stepfamily Association of America, Inc.
215 Centennial Mall South, Suite 212
Lincoln, NE 68508
(402) 477-STEP
Listings for local chapters offering support for stepparents and young people discussion groups. Catalogue of books and tapes for stepfamilies.

Youth Crisis Hotline
(800) 448-4663
Twenty-four hour service for young people contemplating suicide.

Four—Battle for Independence

Suggested Reading
The Difficult Child
Stanley Turecki, M.D.
Bantam, 1985

The Emotional Problems of Normal Children
Stanley Turecki, M.D.
Bantam, 1994
Both of Turecki's books are geared to parents of younger children, but the insights will help parents deal with middlers.

Grounded for Life! Stop Blowing Your Fuse and Start Communicating with Your Teenager
Louise Felton Tracy
Parenting Press, 1994

I Swore I'd Never Do That—Recognizing Family Patterns and Making Wise Parenting Choices
Elizabeth Fishel
Conari Press, 1991
Asks and helps you discover "What kind (style) of parent are you?"

P.E.T Parent Effectiveness Training—The Tested New Way to Raise Responsible Children
Dr. Thomas Gordon
Plume Penguin, 1970
A classic that is the basis for many parenting classes.

Learning How to Kiss a Frog: Advice for Those Who Work with Pre- and Early-Adolescents
James P. Garvin, Ph.D.
New England League of Middle Schools, Inc.
460 Boston Street, Suite 4
Topsfield, MA 01983-1223
(508) 887-6263 FAX (508) 887-6504
Written for teachers, but parents will benefit, too.

Raising Your Spirited Child: A Guide for Parents Whose Child Is More Intense, Sensitive, Perceptive, Persistent, Energetic
Mary Kurcinka
HarperCollins, 1992
Aimed at younger children, but the insights are helpful for handling young adolescents, too.

What Kids Need to Succeed: Proven, Practical Ways to Raise Good Kids
Peter L. Benson, Ph.D., Judy Galbraith, M.A., and Pamela Espeland
Free Spirit Publishing, 1995
1 (800) 735-7323

When Good Kids Do Bad Things—A Survival Guide for Parents of Teenagers
Katherine Gordy Levine
Pocket Books, 1993

Suggested Reading for Middlers
Bringing Up Parents: The Teenager's Handbook
Alex J. Packer
Free Spirit Publishing, 1993
1 (800) 735-7323

Product Information
The Family Forum Library
1 (800) 99-YOUTH
Offers a free catalogue of titles for parents, educators, and counselors. We recommend *Positive Parental Discipline,* which offers strategies and a discussion of parenting styles. Order by FAX (516) 349-5521 for a price of $1.95.

Five—Distracted, Disorganized, Disinterested

Suggested Reading

ADHD and Teens: A Parent's Guide to Making It Through the Tough Years
Colleen Alexander-Roberts
Taylor, 1995
Includes sections on positive discipline, sexuality and dating, and medical management.

The Homework Plan: A Parent's Guide to Helping Kids Excel
Linda Sonna, Ph.D.
Berkley, 1994
Ways to help your child be more responsible, resist peer pressure, and put an end to homework arguments.

How to Help Your Child with Homework: Every Caring Parent's Guide to Encouraging Good Study Habits and Ending the Homework Wars
Marguerite C. Radencich, Ph.D. and Jeanne Shay Schumm, Ph.D.
Free Spirit Publishing, 1996

How to Talk So Kids Will Listen and Listen So Kids Will Talk
Adele Faber and Elaine Mazlish
Avon, 1982

In Their Own Way: Discovering and Encouraging Your Child's Personal Learning Style
Thomas Armstrong, Ph.D.
J. P. Tarcher, 1988
Talks about the many different ways that children learn.

It's Nobody's Fault—New Hope and Help for Difficult Children and Their Parents
Dr. Harold S. Koplewicz
Times Books, 1996

The Myth of the A.D.D. Child
50 Ways to Improve Your Child's Behavior and Attention Span Without Drugs, Labels, or Coercion
Thomas Armstrong, Ph.D.
NAL-Dutton, 1995

Shyness: What It Is, What To Do About It
Philip Zimbardo
Addison-Wesley, 1990
Aimed at the adult, but a parent could pick up much good information on helping a middler who is withdrawn.

Your Hyperactive Child: A Parent's Guide to Coping with Attention Deficit Disorder
Barbara Ingersoll
Doubleday, 1988

Suggested Reading for Middlers
An American Hero—The True Story of Charles A. Lindbergh
Barry Denenberg
Scholastic, 1996
The inspirational story of the young flyer who made the first transatlantic flight in 1927.

The Baseball Hall of Shame: Young Fan's Edition
Bruce Nash and Allan Zullo
Archway, 1993
An antidote for any middler who has ever struck out with bases loaded, this book recounts the escapades of major league losers and blunders, including three Dodgers who somehow all ended up on third base at the same time, and Billy Herman, who was knocked out by his own foul ball in his first major league game.

Extraordinary Young People
Marlene Targ Brill
Children's Press, 1996
More than sixty stories of struggle, achievement, victory, and sometimes loss that may help to stimulate a disinterested middler.

The First Woman Doctor
Rachel Baker
Scholastic, 1987
The story of Elizabeth Blackwell's quest to become the first woman doctor in 1840, against formidable odds, will inspire middlers who also may be struggling.

How to Improve Your Study Skills
Marcia J. Coman and Kathy L. Heavers
VGM Career Horizons, 1994

Shows students how to take notes, take tests, increase reading speed, use the dictionary, and more.

I Would If I Could: A Teenager's Guide to ADHD/Hyperactivity
Michael Gordon
GSI Publications, 1992

My Own Two Feet, a Memoir
Beverly Cleary
Avon Camelot, 1995
This memoir by the popular children's author will inspire any young person acquainted with her books.

School Power: Strategies for Succeeding in School
Jeanne Shay Schumm, Ph.D. and Marguerite Radencich, Ph.D.
Free Spirit Publishing, 1992
Includes sections on organization, keeping track of daily assignments, and mapping out long-range assignments.

Organizations and Hotlines

C.H.A.D.D. (Children with Attention Deficit Disorder)
499 Northwest 70th Avenue, Suite 101
Plantation, FL 33317
(954) 587-3700

Learning Disabilities Association of America (LDA)
4156 Library Road
Pittsburgh, PA 15243
(412) 341-1515

National Center for Learning Disabilities
381 Park Avenue South, Suite 1420
New York, NY 10016
An organization to promote public awareness of learning disabilities. Publishes *Their World,* which includes up-to-the date information.
(212) 545-7510

National Information Center for Children and Youth with Disabilities (NICHCY)
1233 20th Street, NW, Suite 504
Washington, DC 20036
(800) 695-0285

Parent Training and Information Centers (PTIs)
These federally funded centers provide training and information to parents. There is at least one PTI in each state. Organizations such as NCLD, LDA, and NICHCY can provide information on listings for your individual state.

Six—Success in School

Suggested Reading

Beyond the Classroom: Why School Reform Has Failed, What Parents Need to Do
Laurence Steinberg, Ph.D.
Simon & Schuster, 1996
For parents and teachers. Among other issues, it addresses ethnicity and its role in education.

Education Today Parent Involvement Handbook
Susan Otterbourg and the Education Publishing Group, Inc.
20 Park Plaza, Suite 1215
Boston, MA 02116
(800) 248-EDUC
Filled with practical strategies for parents. Excellent resource list, too.

Emotional Intelligence
Daniel Goleman, Ph.D.
Bantam, 1995

Failing at Fairness: How America's Schools Cheat Girls
Myra and David Sadker
Charles Scribner's Sons, 1994

fish, stick, knife, gun—A Personal History of Violence in America
Geoffrey Canada
Beacon Press, 1995
Resonant and relevant African-American voice and perspective.

Frames of Mind: The Theory of Multiple Intelligences
Howard Gardner, Ph.D.
Basic Books, 1993
The classic that started the theory of different kinds of intelligence, from musical and athletic to linguistic and interpersonal. For parents, so they appreciate what is unique and special in their child.

How to Raise a Child with a High EQ—A Parent's Guide to Emotional Intelligence
Lawrence E. Shapiro, Ph.D.
HarperCollins, 1996

In Their Own Way: Discovering and Encouraging Your Child's Personal Learning Style
Thomas Armstrong
J. P. Tarcher, 1988
A book for parents who want to understand learning styles.

Involving Families
John Meyers and Luetta Monson
National Middle School Association, 1992
1 (800) 528-NMSA
For parents and educators as well.

Middle Level Teachers: Portraits of Excellence
Alfred E. Arth, John H. Lounsbury, C. Kenneth McEwin, John H. Swaim and Eighty-three Successful Middle Level Educators
National Middle School Association and National Association of Secondary School Principals
1 (800) 528-NMSA
Resource for teachers.

Peer Harassment in Schools
Charol Shakeshaft, Ellen Barber, Mary Ann Hergenrother, Yolanda M. Johnson, Laurie S. Mandel, and Janice Sawyer, Hofstra University, *Journal for a Just and Caring Education*, Vol. 1, No. 1, January, 1995
Informative description of peer harassment study, written in a style suitable for parents as well as teachers, counselors, and administrators.

SchoolGirls: Young Women, Self-Esteem, and the Confidence Gap
Peggy Orenstein
Anchor, 1995
For parents and educators.

Things Will Be Different for My Daughter: A Practical Guide to Building Her Self-Esteem
Mindy Bingham and Sandy Stryker
Penguin, 1996
Good selection to help parents show daughters how gender bias affects them.

This We Believe
National Middle School Association
1 (800) 528-NMSA
(Order # 0202) $6.00 for parent and educators.
Outlines how to create good middle schools.

Why Bright Kids Get Poor Grades and What You Can Do About It
Dr. Sylvia Rimm
Crown, 1995
For parents and teachers.

Suggested Reading for Middlers
Books on the Move—A Read-About-It Go-There Guide to America's Best Family Destinations
Susan M. Knorr and Margaret Knorr
Free Spirit Publishing, 1995
1 (800) 735-7323

The Gifted Kids Survival Guide
Judy Galbraith, M.A. and Jim Delisle, Ph.D.
Free Spirit Publishing, 1996 (updated and revised edition)
1 (800) 735-7323
For parents, counselors, and teachers as well.

Learning Power—Strategies for Student Success and *The Learning Power Workbook*
National Middle School Association
1 (800) 528-NMSA
$28.00
For eighth- and ninth-graders to assist with study skills, critical thinking, and relationship building. (*A Learning Power Teacher's Guide* is also available.)

Psychology for Kids
Jonni Kincher
Free Spirit Publishing, 1990
1 (800) 735-7323

Psychology for Kids II
Jonni Kincher
Free Spirit Publishing, 1995
1 (800) 735-7323

Product Information

Aristoplay, Ltd.
P.O. Box 7529
Ann Arbor, MI 48107
1 (800) 634-7738
FAX 1 (313) 995-4611
Free catalogue of games for fun and learning. Many good choices for young
adolescents.

Free Spirit Publishing, Inc.
400 First Avenue North, Suite 616
Minneapolis, MN 55401-1724
1 (800) 735-7323
FAX (612) 337-5050
Free catalogue. Offers many books, workbooks, and posters for parents, teachers,
and students themselves on a wide range of topics.

Handgun Safety Guidelines
Free brochure.
Send a self-addressed stamped envelope to:
Center to Prevent Handgun Violence
1225 Eye Street, NW, Suite 1100
Washington, DC 20005

The Middle School Companion
Totally for Teachers
Box 698
Pittsford, NY 14534
(716) 387-9438
(800) 330-9674
online:Mscompan@aol.com
Newsletter edited by Carla Clark designed for middle school teachers, grades 5
through 9. Contains many strategies and insights into young adolescent learning.

National Middle School Association
2600 Corporate Exchange Drive
Columbus, OH 43231-1672
1 (800) 528-NMSA
Free catalogue filled with books for parents, teachers, administrators, and counselors covering a wide range of topics, including instructional planning, cur-

riculum revision, teacher education, and family and community issues. Also available are the *Middle School Journal,* which reports on current research, trends, and professional ideas for middle school educators (comes with membership but some back issues are available), and *High Strides,* which is a national publication for the urban middle school.

Sexual Harassment: It's Hurting People Video
International Film and Video Festival Award-winning seventeen-minute video and sixty-page instructional guide designed to educate students, teachers, and administrators on peer-to-peer harassment. $176.00
Order #V102 NMSA catalogue

Organizations and Hotlines

American Association of University Women
P.O. Box 96974
Washington, DC 20077-7022
(800) 225-9998
Has a catalogue of briefs on gender bias. Report, *Hostile Hallways,* examines sexual harassment. Important report for parents and educators.

National Association of Social Workers
750 1st Street, NE, Suite 700
Washington, DC 20002-4241
Several free brochures available to help children and adults understand the root causes of violence. We recommend *100 Ways You Can Stop Violence.*

The National Congress of Parents and Teachers
330 N. Wabash Avenue
Chicago, IL 60611
(312) 670-6782
Publishes a magazine, *Our Children,* and has guides designed for parents to assist their children with specific academic subjects and issues.

The National Crime Prevention Crime Council
(800) WE PREVENT
Offers catalogue of booklets for parents, including *Stop the Violence, Start Something.*

The National School Safety Center
4165 Thousand Oaks Boulevard, Suite 290
Westlake Village, CA 91362

Offers information to parents and educators. For example, will send your school board a model plan for handling a crime emergency.

Seven—Sibling Rivalry, Peer Pressure, Other Obstacles

Suggested Reading

Born to Rebel—Birth Order, Family Dynamics, and Creative Lives
Frank J. Sulloway
Pantheon, 1996
Explores the profound consequences of sibling competition, not only on the individual but also on the family and society.

Bullies and Victims: Helping Your Child Through the Schoolyard Battlefield
Suellen Fried and Paula Fried
M. Evans & Co. Inc., 1996

Fifty Ways to Raise a Nonracist Child
Barbara Mathias and Mary Ann French
Harper Reference, 1996

Siblings Without Rivalry: How to Help Your Children Live Together So You Can Live Too
Adele Faber and Elaine Mazlish
Avon, 1988

Teaching Tolerance—Raising Open-Minded Empathetic Children
Sara Bullard
Doubleday, 1996

Teaching Your Children Values
Linda Eyre and Richard Eyre
Fireside, 1993

Virtues Guide: A Family Handbook
Linda K. Popov, et al.
Virtues Communications, 1993
(604) 537-4647

Suggested Reading for Middlers

*The Best Friends Book: True Stories About Real Best Friends, Fun Things to Do with
    Your Best Friend, Solving Best Friends Problems, Long-Distance Best Friends,
    Finding New Friends, and More!*
Arlene Erlbach
Free Spirit Publishing, 1996
(800) 735-7323

Between Sisters: Secret Rivals, Intimate Friends*
Barbara Mathias
Delacorte, 1992

But Everyone Else Looks So Sure of Themselves: A Guide to Surviving the Teen Years
Denise V. Lang
Betterway Books, 1991

City Kids Speak on Prejudice
Random House Books for Young Readers, 1995
Through interviews and photos, kids talk honestly about what prejudice is and
    how it affects them.

Coping with Cliques
Lee A. Peck
Rosen Publishing Group, 1992

Coping with Peer Pressure
Leslie S. Kaplan, Ed.D.
Rosen Publishing Group, 1996

Coping with Sibling Rivalry
Shari Cohen, Ruth Rosen, eds.
Rosen Publishing Group, 1989

Everything You Need to Know About Peer Pressure
Robyn M. Feller
Rosen Publishing Group, 1995

Extraordinary Black Americans from Colonial Times to Contemporary Times
Susan Altman
Children's Press, 1993

Famous Hispanic Americans
Janet Nomura Morey and Wendy Dunn
Dutton, 1996
Profiles of successful Hispanic Americans, from actor Andy Garcia to designer
   Carolina Herrera.

Funny Insults and Snappy Put Downs
Joseph Rosenbloom
Sterling Publishing, 1982
Great comebacks to arm your child with including, "Are you a man or a
   mouse?" "Squeak up!" or "I hope you never feel the way you look."

My Feelings, My Self: Lynn Madaras' Growing-Up Guide for Girls
Lynda Madaras
Newmarket Press, 1993
Recommended for teenage girls, this book deals with popularity, peer pressure,
   and crushes.

Respecting Our Differences: A Guide to Getting Along in a Changing World
Lynn Duvall
Free Spirit Publishing, 1994
(800) 735-7323

Stick Up for Yourself! Every Kid's Guide to Personal Power and Positive Self-Esteem
Gershen Kaufman
Free Spirit Publishing, 1990

This Same Sky: A Collection of Poems from Around the World
Naomi Shihab Nye, ed.
Simon & Schuster, 1996
A beautiful collection of poems that will help middlers realize that the "same sky
   connects us all."

When Kids Drive Kids Crazy: How to Get Along with Your Friends and Enemies
Eda LeShan
Dial Books, 1990

Organizations and Hotlines
Association of Multiethnic Americans
P.O. Box 191726
San Francisco, CA 94119-1726
(510) 523-AMEA
A clearinghouse for information on inter and multiracial relationships.

Be Your Own Best Friend Program (BYBF)/Organizacion Nacional de la Salud de la Mujer Latina
National Latina Health Organization
P.O. Box 7567
Oakland, CA 94601
(510) 534-1362
Organizes support groups for young adolescent Latinas to help them build self-esteem by learning about their culture.

Friends Forever PenPals
P.O. Box 20103
Park West Post Office
New York, NY 10025
Provides each member with five or more pen pals of the same age and interests.

Products
Hate Hurts Everyone
An educational video program to help students understand the primary causes of hate. An NMSA product
(800) 528-NMSA

Teaching Tolerance Magazine
Southern Poverty Law Center
400 Washington Avenue
Montgomery, AL 36104
Available to educators.

Eight—Electronic Media

Suggested Reading
Being Digital
Nicholas Negroponte
Thoughts on living in the electronic age.
McKay, 1996

Beyond TV: Activities for Using Video with Children
Martha Dewing
ABC-CLIO, 1991
(718) 935-0600

The Complete Guide to Special-Interest Videos: More Than 9,000 Videos You've Never Seen Before
James R. Spencer
Robert Publishing, 1994

The Connected Family: Bridging the Digital Generation Gap
Seymour Papert
Longstreet Press, 1996
Addresses parents' questions about the changes around us and how the electronic media can be transformed into a positive learning experience.

Life on the Screen: Identity in the Age of the Internet
Sherry Turkle
Simon & Schuster, 1995

Mind & Media: The Effects of Television, Video Games, and Computers
Patricia Marks Greenfield
Harvard University Press, 1984

Parents Who Love Reading, Kids Who Don't
Mary Leonhardt
Crown, 1995

Raising Media-Savvy Kids in the Age of Channel-Surfing Couch Potatoes
The Kidvidz Family Viewing Guide
Jane Murphy and Karen Tucker
Main Street Books, Doubleday, 1996
Methods for raising media-literate children.

*Raising PG Kids in an X-Rated Society**
Advice on how to cope with the electronic media.
Tipper Gore
Bantam, 1987

Sex, Laws, and Cyberspace: Freedom and Regulation on the Frontiers of the Online Revolution
Jonathan Wallace and Mark Mangan
M&T Books/Holt, 1996

The Smart Parent's Guide to Kids' TV
Milton Chen
KQED Books, 1994

That's Edutainment! A Parent's Guide to Educational Software
Eric Brown
Osborne McGraw-Hill, 1996

Video Movie Guide (updated annually)
Mick Martin and Marsha Porter
Ballantine Books, 1996

Viewing Violence: How Media Violence Affects Your Child and Adolescent
Madeline Levine
Doubleday, 1996
Summarizes four decades of research on the harmful effects of media violence on
children.

Suggested Reading for Middlers

*Read All About It—Great Read-Aloud Stories, Poems, and Newspaper Pieces for
Reading Aloud for Preteens and Teens*
Jim Trelease
Penguin, 1993
Tear them away from the TV by reading to them. This collection includes
classics like "Casey at the Bat," and "To Kill a Mockingbird."

YO-TV Production Handbook
Educational Video Center, 1994

Organizations and Hotlines

Action for Children's Television (ACT)
20 University Road
Cambridge, MA 02138
(617) 876-6620
Aims to eliminate commercialism and encourage diversity. Publishes numerous
books for all age groups, including teens.

Catholic Communication Campaign
Movie Review Hotline
(800) 311-4CCC
Provides callers with brief reviews of current movies evaluated for plot, entertainment, and moral content.

Center for Media Literacy
1962 South Shenandoah
Los Angeles, CA 90034
1 (800) 226-9494
This center produces books, videos, and lesson plans to help parents teach their
    children about the media.

Entertainment Software Rating Board
845 Third Avenue
New York, NY 10022
1 (800) 771-ERSB (help line for product information)

Mothers on Media
2848 East 194th Street
Bronx, NY
(718) 892-0692
In the New York metropolitan area, Lillian Diaz-Imbelli conducts (in English or
    Spanish) seminars for Media Aware Kids.

Motion Picture Association of America
15503 Ventura Boulevard
Encino, CA 91436
(818) 995-6600
also
1600 Eye Street, NW
Washington, DC 20006
(202) 293-1966

National Coalition on Television Violence (NCTV)
P.O. Box 2157
Champaign, IL 61825
(217) 384-1920
Seeks to lessen the amount of violence on TV and in the movies. Conducts
    seminars and also rates music, movies, television programs, and toys.

Recording Industry Association of America
1020 19th Street, NW, Suite 200
Washington, DC 20036
(202) 775-0101

Strategies for Media Literacy
1095 Market Street #410
San Francisco, CA 94103
(415) 621-2911
Services include a newsletter, resource lists, workshops, and educational resources.

Products
Children's Review Newsletter
(916) 273-7471

Children's Video Report
370 Court Street, Suite 76
Brooklyn, NY 11231
(718) 935-0640

Kids First! Directory
Coalition for Quality Children's Media
535 Cordova Road, Suite 456
Santa Fe, NM 87501
(505) 989-8076

Nine—Tobacco, Alcohol, Drugs

Suggested Reading
*Teen Addiction: A Book of Hope for the Parents, Teachers, and Counselors of Chemically Dependent Adolescents**
Marti Heuer
Ballantine Books, 1994

Suggested Reading for Middlers
Alcoholism: The Facts
Donald Goodwin
Oxford University Press, 1994

Drinking, Driving and Drugs: An Encyclopedia of Psychoactive Drugs
Jean M. Knox
Chelsea House, 1991

Living With a Parent Who Drinks Too Much
Judith S. Seixas
William Morrow, 1991

Living With a Parent Who Takes Drugs
Judith S. Seixas
Greenwillow, 1989

No If's, And's, or Butts: The Smoker's Guide to Quitting
Harlan M. Krumholz and Robert H. Phillips
Avery Publishing Group, Inc., 1993

Quit for Teens
Charles Wetherall
Andrews and McMeel, 1995
Deals with the effects of cigarette smoking in a straightforward yet humorous
  way.

What You Can Believe About Drugs: An Honest and Unhysterical Guide for Teens
Susan Cohen and Daniel Cohen
Dell, 1993

Organizations and Hotlines
Adult Children of Alcoholics (ACA/ACoA)
P.O. Box 3216
Torrance, CA 90510
(310) 534-1815

Al-Anon/Alateen Family Groups
P.O. Box 862, Midtown Station
New York, NY 10018-0862
1 (800) 344-2666 (US)
1 (800) 443-4525 (Canada)

Alcohol/Drug Abuse Referral Hotline
(800) 821-4357

Alcoholics Anonymous
P.O. Box 459
Grand Central Station
New York, NY 10163
(212) 686-1100

American Council on Alcoholism
(800) 527-5344

Center for Substance Abuse Prevention
National Clearinghouse for Alcohol and Drug Information (NCADI)
P.O. Box 2345
Rockville, MD 20847-2345
1 (800) 729-6686
This organization puts out many publications and pamphlets on alcohol and
    drugs.

Children of Alcoholics Foundation
P.O. Box 4185
Grand Central Station
New York, NY 10163-4185
(212) 754-0656

Families Anonymous, Inc.
P.O. Box 528
Van Nuys, CA 91408
(818) 989-7841
This organization was formed primarily for persons concerned about alcohol and
    other drug problems of a family member, especially children.

"Just Say No" International
2101 Webster Street, Suite 1300
Oakland, CA 94612
(800) 258-2766
This organization has a youth program that encourages young people to make
    use of their strengths in order to avoid substance abuse.

National Association for Children of Alcoholics (NACoA)
11426 Rockville Pike, Suite 100
Rockville, MD 20852
(301) 468-0985

National Association for Native American Children of Alcoholics (NANACoA)
611 12th Avenue South, Suite 200
Seattle, WA 98144
1 (800) 322-5601

National Black Alcoholism Council (NBAC)
1629 K Street, NW, Suite 802
Washington, DC 20006
(202) 296-2696

National Cocaine Hotline
(800) COCAINE

National Council on Alcoholism and Drug Dependence (NCADD)
12 West 21st Street, 7th Floor
New York, NY 10017
1 (800) NCA-CALL

Partnership For a Drug-Free America
405 Lexington Avenue
New York, NY 10174
(212) 922-1560

PRIDE (Parents' Resource Institute for Drug Education)
1240 Johnson Ferry Place, Suite F-10
Marietta, GA 30068
1 (800) 487-PRIDE

Regional Alcohol and Drug Awareness Resource (RADAR) Network
Located in every state and U.S. territory to provide local support.
Contact NCADI (1-800-729-6686) for location of nearest center.

SADD (Students Against Drunk Driving)
P.O. Box 800
Marlboro, MA 01752
(508) 481-3568
A student-based activist organization aimed at preventing deaths on the highway
   due to substance abuse.

Youth Crisis Hotline
(800) HIT-HOME

Ten—Sexuality

Suggested Reading

Between Mothers and Sons—The Making of Vital and Loving Men
Evelyn Bassoff, Ph.D.
NAL-Dutton, 1995

Free Your Mind: The Book for Gay, Lesbian, and Bisexual Youth and Their Allies
Ellen Bass and Kate Kaufman
HarperCollins, 1996
For middlers as well.

Going All The Way—Teenage Girls' Tales of Sex, Romance, & Pregnancy
Sharon Thompson
Hill and Wang, 1995 (division of Farrar, Straus, and Giroux)
Fascinating reading for parents and older adolescent girls.

Growing Up Gay: A Mother and Son Look Back
Marlene and Christopher Shyer
Houghton Mifflin, 1996

Raising Sexually Healthy Children
Lynn Leight
Avon, 1990

Suggested Reading for Middlers

Growing Up Gay: From Left Out to Coming Out
Jaffe Cohen
Hyperion, 1995

Heartbreak and Roses—Real Life Stories of Troubled Love
Janet Bode and Stan Mack
BDD Books for Young Readers, 1996
Examines, for ages twelve and up, dramatic romantic situations. For example, one teen grapples with a jealous boyfriend; another teen copes with the awkwardness of her disability. Based on interviews with a *crosscultural* section of adolescents.

*Lynn Madaras Talks to Teens About AIDS**
Lynn Madaras
Newmarket Press, 1988

*One Teenager in 10: Writings by Gay and Lesbian Youth**
Ann Heron, ed.
Alyson Press, 1983
Young adolescents tell their own stories, painful and inspiring.

*Reflections of a Rock Lobster: A Story About Growing Up Gay**
Aaron Fricke
Alyson Press, 1981
Recommended by sexuality educators.

Product Information

The Center For Family Life Education, Planned Parenthood of Greater Northern
    New Jersey, Inc.
575 Main Street
Hackensack, NJ 07601
(201) 489-1265
Offers resources for sexuality education programs. Good for teachers, counselors.
    We recommend *New Methods for Puberty Education Grades 4–9* by Carolyn
    Cooperman and Chuck Rhoades.

Organizations and Hotlines

Advocates for Youth
1025 Vermont Avenue, NW, Suite 210
Washington, DC 20005
(202) 347-5700
Offers resources for teachers on how to develop educational programs wherein
    young people counsel one another on HIV. Ask for: *Peer to Peer Youth
    Preventing HIV Infection Together.* Has a quarterly newsletter, *Transitions,*
    designed to keep teachers, counselors, and other professionals up to date on
    adolescent health and sexuality issues.

Gay and Lesbian Youth Hotline
(800) 347-TEEN (Thursday to Sunday 7–11:45 P.M.)

National AIDS Hotline
1 (800) 342-AIDS
Seven days a week, twenty-four hours a day. Offers information, counseling, and
    referrals. Counselors explain transmission, prevention, testing, and treatment.

National AIDS Hotline for Teenagers
1 (800) 234-8336
Offers young people exclusively, information, counseling, and support.

National STD Hotline
1 (800) 277-8922
Provides free information about prevention, testing, and provides clinic referrals.

Parents, Families, and Friends of Lesbians and Gays (PFLAG)
1101 14th Street, NW, Suite 1030
Washington, DC 20005
(202) 638-4200
Offers information, support, and local chapter listings for parents.

Planned Parenthood Federation of America
810 Seventh Avenue
New York, NY 10019
(212) 541-7800
(800) 829-7732
Offers a wide range of services, including birth control, pregnancy testing and
    abortion counseling. Call for information on programs and materials in your
    area.

SEICUS—Sexuality Information and Education Council of the United States
130 West 42nd Street, Suite 35
New York, NY 10036
(212) 819-9770
FAX: (212) 819-9776
Provides information on sexuality for educators and parents. We recommend
    Facing Facts: Sexual Health for America's Adolescents (The Report of the Na-
    tional Commission on Adolescent Sexual Health), written in plain language.
    This is an excellent resource for parents, sex education teachers, and counsel-
    ors.

Eleven—Your Own Past

Suggested Reading
Do You Believe in Magic? The Second Coming of the '60's Generation*
Annie Gottlieb
Times Books, 1987
A nostalgic look at the 1960s and how the baby boomers came to be the adults
    they are. If you fall in this age group, this book is a good way for you to begin
    exploring the roots of your parenting style.

*Getting Your Kids to Say No in the '90s When You Said Yes in the '60s**
Victor C. Strasburger
Simon & Schuster, 1993

*How to Survive Your Adolescent's Adolescence**
Dr. Robert C. Kolodny, Nancy J. Kolodny, Dr. Thomas Bratter, and Cheryl
    Deep
Little Brown, 1984

Making Sense of Adoption: A Parent's Guide
Lois Ruskai Melina
HarperPerennial, 1989
Sound advice for explaining adoption to a child and others. Includes a section
    that talks specifically about dealing with adoption during adolescence.

Suggested Reading for Middlers
How It Feels to Be Adopted
Jill Krementz
Knopf, revised, 1996
Children eight to sixteen talk about the frustrations and joys of adoption.

Organizations
Adoptive Families of America
3333 Highway 100 N.
Minneapolis, MN 55422
(612) 535-4829

Adoptive Parents Committee, Inc. (APC)
210 Fifth Avenue
New York, NY 10010
(212) 683-9221
Publishes a newsletter and pamphlets, including *How Parents Tell Their Children
    They Are Adopted.*

RESOLVE
(organization that deals with infertility issues)
(617) 623 0744 (help line)

National Middle School Association

Established in 1973, the National Middle School Association (NMSA) is the nation's only education association devoted exclusively to improving the educational experiences of young adolescents, ages ten to fifteen. NMSA supports those who live and work with young adolescents, recognizing these children's future as members of an increasingly diverse population. NMSA's membership includes principals, teachers, administrators, and parents who share the organization's goals.

The association sponsors an annual convention and numerous publications providing the most current information on learning for young adolescents. Its flagship publications, *Middle School Journal* and *High Strides,* serve as forums for ideas and opinions and have been solid sources of trends, current research, and innovative ideas for over twenty-five years. NMSA also publishes many books, monographs, and position papers.

In addition to its annual convention, which attracts more than 10,000 educators and parents, NMSA conducts an urban education conference, distance learning programs, overseas study tours, and a series of weekend workshops.

Membership information is available through NMSA, 2600 Corporate Exchange Drive, Suite 370, Columbus, OH 43231-1672, or by calling the information line, 800-528-NMSA.

Index